Genius, Creativity, and Leadership

GENIUS, CREATIVITY, AND LEADERSHIP

HISTORIOMETRIC INQUIRIES

Dean Keith Simonton

Harvard University Press
Cambridge, Massachusetts
and London, England
1984

#9896497

Copyright © 1984 by the President and Fellows of Harvard College
All rights reserved
Printed in the United States of America
10   9   8   7   6   5   4   3   2   1

This book is printed on acid-free paper, and its binding materials have
been chosen for strength and durability.

Library of Congress Cataloging in Publication Data

Simonton, Dean Keith.
   Genius, creativity, and leadership.

   Bibliography: p.
   Includes index.
   1. Genius—Mathematical models.   2. Leadership—
Mathematical models.   3. Creativity ability—Mathematical
models.   4. Personality and history.   I. Title
BF416.A1S55   1984   901′.9   83-12995
ISBN 0-674-34680-7 (alk. paper)

An die ferne Geliebte

Preface

FOR NEARLY TWO DECADES I have been fascinated by the idea of applying scientific research techniques to historical and biographical records in order to discover how certain creators and leaders came to exert such a big impact on history. In the last ten years this interest has taken the explicit form of research on the laws of genius using historiometric methods. I have also made myself aware of similar efforts by many predecessors and contemporaries. These enterprises have been sufficiently fruitful that it now seems appropriate to consolidate all the discoveries into a single book. Scientific studies of historical genius are widely dispersed in the technical journals of a half-dozen disciplines, and the publication dates extend over a century. If we are to fully appreciate what we have come to know about historical genius, this research must be brought together and interpreted.

Such a progress report on the historiometric laws of creativity and leadership presents something of a writing challenge: readers' technical proficiency may vary tremendously. Many of the empirical results reported here are based on elaborate mathematical procedures that may not be at the fingertips of everyone who shares my curiosity about genius-level creativity and leadership. Therefore, I have chosen to keep the discussion relatively nontechnical, with a few technical issues dealt with in the appendixes.

Acknowledgments are due to many who have provided me with assistance or encouragement over the years. Eric Wanner encouraged me to undertake the project and helped me solve some problems of organization. Susan Jan Koletsky gave the manuscript a careful and helpful reading. David A. Kenny was largely responsible for my being able to make my doctoral dissertation an exemplar of the way I wished to spend my research time. Others offered positive reinforcement that led me to believe I was on the right track. While they are too numerous to mention, Robert Albert, David Heise, Ravenna Helson, Colin Martindale, David C. McClelland, William McGuire, Derek de Solla Price, Morris Stein, and Peter Suedfeld stand out. On the more personal side, Susan Youel provided me with emotional support during the early stages of my career when prospects for success were still very much in doubt. Finally, and in all seriousness, I wish to thank all those historical figures who served as constant sources of inspiration. Of these, Ludwig van Beethoven was the most reliable source of solemn adagios when failure loomed on the horizon and of triumphal fanfares when success knocked at the door.

Contents

Genius, Creativity, and Leadership

1

THE SCIENTIFIC STUDY
OF HISTORICAL GENIUS

THOMAS CARLYLE WROTE in his essay *On Heroes, Hero-Worship, and the Heroic in History* (1841), "The history of the World is but the Biography of great men." Ralph Waldo Emerson echoed Carlyle in his own essay "History": "There is properly no history; only biography." The idea of history as biography is reflected in the work of modern popular historians as well. In the massive *The Story of Civilization* by Will and Ariel Durant, four consecutive volumes are entitled *The Age of Louis XIV, The Age of Voltaire, Rousseau and Revolution,* and *The Age of Napoleon.* History, according to this long-cherished belief, is molded by the personalities and accomplishments of certain exceptional individuals. These outstanding historical figures make history in one of two major ways. On the one hand there are the creators, who make lasting contributions to human culture, whether as scientists, philosophers, writers, composers, or artists. Creators of the stature of Einstein, Sartre, Joyce, Stravinsky, and Picasso have left a durable impression on the thoughts and sensitivities of innumerable men and women. On the other hand there are the leaders, who transform the world by their deeds rather than by their ideas or emotional expressions. Leaders of the caliber of Hitler, Stalin, Franklin D. Roosevelt, and Mao Tse-tung have made a permanent mark upon the course that history has taken. It is these creators and leaders whose biographies become tantamount to histories.

Another traditional belief, held both by the general public and by many social scientists, is that these outstanding individuals, creators and leaders alike, have in common a quality of "genius." This belief goes back at least as far as Francis Galton's classic book *Hereditary Genius* (1869), in which Galton tried to establish a genetic basis of distinguished achievement. His examples of genius included such leaders as the Duke of Wellington, William Pitt and his father the Earl of Chatham, along with such creators as the Bachs and the Schlegels.

More than a half a century later Catherine Cox followed suit in an influential volume entitled *Early Mental Traits of Three Hundred Geniuses* (1926). Her sample of historical geniuses, on which I will draw heavily in this book, included Napoleon, Cromwell, and Bolívar alongside Voltaire, Newton, and Cervantes. Both Galton and Cox believed that certain types of creators and leaders can be grouped under the single generic designation of genius. The way to recognize genius in a historical personage is to look for achievements that exert a rare influence over contemporary and succeeding generations (Albert, 1975). For the most part, to be identified as a genius an individual must become famous, and the fame must be attained for making durable contributions to cultural or political endeavors. Thus genius is defined by accomplishment.

Yet to earn the genius label a candidate does not have to be "right" or "good." Genghis Khan and Adolf Hitler can be styled geniuses of a kind: an "evil genius" remains a genius, however ethically repulsive. Likewise, it does not matter how wrong Plato or Aristotle may have been concerning certain philosophical or scientific issues; it is sufficient that even their biggest blunders succeeded in earning them adherents for millennia. Genius is gauged by the magnitude of the effect upon contemporaries and posterity, not by the morality or veracity of that effect. To count as a genius one can be either celebrated or cursed so long as one is not utterly ignored.

Defining genius by fame or eminence does not make any profound distinction between creativity and leadership. Eminent creators and eminent leaders merely represent the two main manifestations of genius in history. In a sense, when the most famous creators and leaders are under scrutiny the distinction between creativity and leadership vanishes, because creativity becomes a variety of leadership. Social psychologists who study leadership in laboratory and field settings often define a leader as that group member who exerts more influence on group performance and decisionmaking than do other members. The application of this definition to well-known leaders of the past is obvious. No individual held more sway over the history of the German people between 1933 and 1945 than did Hitler. Creativity, by this definition, can be considered a special form of leadership: creators are cultural leaders. Albert Einstein's theoretical ideas had an impressive effect upon his fellow physicists, the scientific community in general, and even the public at large. Beethoven's impact upon music, Michelangelo's upon sculpture, and Shakespeare's upon drama all were unequaled in their own time, and dominated generations to come. Shakespeare's rival for the applause of theater audiences, Ben Jonson, said that Shakespeare "was not of an age, but for all time!" Michelangelo was so idolized by his contemporaries and successors that he became known as the "divine Michelangelo." And Brahms explained why he put off writing a symphony for more than a dozen years with the remark, "You will never know how the likes of us feel when we hear the tramp of a giant like Beethoven behind us." Famous creators are leaders in artistic and scientific matters.

Many of the factors that help us understand notable creators are often of no less service to our comprehension of noteworthy leaders. To offer but a handful of examples, studying such factors as birth order, intelligence, education, age, zeitgeist, and political violence (all of which are discussed in later chapters) will advance our scientific appreciation of geniuses of whatever kind. Hence, there are both definitional and etiological grounds for discussing the two main types of exemplars of historical genius more or less simultaneously.

In this book I will examine genius using the techniques of historiometry. Frederick A. Woods coined this term in 1911 "for that class of researches in which the facts of history have been subjected to statistical treatment according to some method of measurement more or less objective or impersonal in nature" (p. 568). To avoid confusion with the method known as cliometrics, which has some current favor among some historians, this definition must undergo a little refinement. I define historiometry as the method of testing nomothetic hypotheses concerning human behavior by applying quantitative analyses to data abstracted from historical populations. To provide an understanding of this methodology I will discuss the significance of the key terms "nomothetic hypotheses," "quantitative analyses," and "historical populations."

NOMOTHETIC HYPOTHESES

The distinction between nomothetic and ideographic explanation is absolutely essential to the definition of historiometry. A nomothetic account is one that stresses universals of human behavior and ignores peculiarities of person, place, and time. An ideographic account, by contrast, concentrates on the particular. A nomothetic approach is an obvious prerequisite of science: a scientific explanation of creativity and leadership, for example, should not be contingent on the geographical location, transhistorical period, or personal idiosyncrasies of an individual creator or leader. This nomothetic emphasis ties historiometry to other behavioral science methodologies, such as psychometrics. A psychologist who wants to test the hypothesis that intelligence is related to creativity, for instance, first administers the appropriate psychometric instruments to a sample of subjects and then calculates the correlation between the two variables. Neither the psychometrician nor any reader of the resulting report has any interest in the names of the subjects who participated. Nor do they care whether any particular anonymous subject had scores inconsistent with the overall relationship and hence constitutes an exception to the rule. Since each individual provides an independent test of the hypothesis, the sole issue at stake is whether the number of supporting instances outweighs the number of disconfirmations. In the same way, a historiometrician will not generally care whether a specific creator or leader fits a discovered nomothetic relationship. The identity of the exceptions who make up the minority is no more pertinent to scientific knowledge than is the identity of the exemplars who constitute the majority.

This nomothetic use of historical data distinguishes historiometry from other endeavors that also rely extensively on the historical record. Historiography, certainly, is not dedicated to the discovery of behavioral laws that transcend the idiosyncrasies of a given period, location, and person. A historiographical monograph may go into minute detail about the precedents or ramifications of a particular political decision or creative product. Historiography is engaged in interconnecting specific instances rather than in testing, demonstrating, or even illustrating the laws of history.

Historiometry also is distinguished from psychohistory or psychobiography by this criterion of nomothetic design. From Sigmund Freud's psychobiographical studies of Leonardo da Vinci, Dostoyevski, and Woodrow Wilson to Erik Erikson's psychohistorical analyses of Mahatma Gandhi and Martin Luther, the enterprise of psychobiographers and psychohistorians is clearly ideographic. Freud, for instance, focused on explicating the peculiarities in the life and work of Leonardo. Freud's hypotheses, though derived from the supposedly nomothetic principles of psychoanalysis, were ideographic in essence. To show that Leonardo's omnivorous curiosity stems from an inadequately resolved Oedipal Complex gives us insight into the personality of one creative genius but does not lead to the discovery of general laws about human creativity.

Cliometrics, though like historiometry a quantitative discipline, is no more nomothetic than historiography, psychohistory, or psychobiography. Indeed, leaving the contrast in quantification aside, the main differences between cliometrics and psychohistory are that the cliometricians use economic rather than psychoanalytic theory and that they are more committed to explaining important events than important people. The much discussed book *Time on the Cross* by Robert Fogel and Stanley Engerman (1974) is a case in point. In this "new economic history," the institution of slavery in the antebellum South is analyzed to demonstrate the profitability of a slave economy. As important as this issue is to our comprehension of U.S. history, the question does not entail a scientific hypothesis in the sense that the analyses do not result in universal laws about slavery. Both cliometricians and psychohistorians intend to advance history through the application of science, not science through the analysis of history.

Of all the intellectual activities that bear any resemblance to historiometry, the only one that can be said to rival historiometry in its quest for nomothetic principles is the philosophy of history. From the time thinkers first became aware of the grand sweep of events, some have tried to fathom its inner workings, to reveal the universal lessons of history. The *Han Shu* by the first-century Chinese historian Pan Piao, the *Muqaddimah* by the fourteenth-century Moslem historian Ibn Khaldūn, and the *Decline and Fall of the Roman Empire* by the eighteenth-century English historian Edward Gibbon all contain attempts to explain the growth and collapse of political systems. More recently, Arnold Toynbee in his massive *A Study of History* (1946) unifies all human history under a single theory that he claims can account for the creative vigor and political vitality of every civilization. Founded upon the a priori superimposition of some overarching abstraction, philosophies of history stand or fall not by the weight of the evidence but rather by the power of subjective persuasion. And the grand theories are frequently motivated by a special advocacy: for example, Hegel's influential *Lectures on the Philosophy of History* (1831) sometimes seems to be a subtle propaganda piece for the Prussian state. Finally, even if Hegel's concept of a thesis-antithesis-synthesis sequence in the history of ideas and Toynbee's proposition that civilization is stimulated by a "moderate challenge" can both be interpreted as nomothetic hypotheses, Hegel and Toynbee fail to establish these propositions as scientific generalizations. The undisciplined citation of specific cases does not provide scientific proof but merely rhetorical flourish. The philosophy of history is nomothetic in intent but tends to be ideographic in execution. Of all these techniques of studying history, only historiometry is nomothetic in both intent and accomplishment.

This search for nomothetic conclusions does not require historiometricians to relinquish any attempt to explain particular historical phenomena. It does not mean, for example, that historiometry can yield no insight into the life of a genius such as Einstein. If cliometricians and psychobiographers can apply knowledge acquired from outside historical phenomena, whether from economics or from psychoanalysis, certainly historiometricians can apply knowledge derived directly from history. Any universal law must have some applicability to particular cases. If a rule of history did not at least apply to the vast majority of specific instances, historiometrics would have disconfirmed it as a valid generalization from the facts.

The interpretation of historical genius using historiometric laws has two facets. On the one hand, the interpretive efforts can be directed at showing how a particular creator or leader typifies a given generalization. If we note that Einstein's prolific publication record is typical of great scientists, Einstein becomes an "exemplar" illustrating a general rule. Since citation of a single case can never prove a rule, these exemplars serve only as instructional devices: a good exemplar, by rendering the abstract principle more concrete, makes the generalization easier to grasp. On the other hand, the attempt to use a general law to explain a particular historical personage may end in failure. Certain figures in history may not fit in well with a general principle. Although the existence of such negative instances does not threaten the nomothetic enterprise, the exceptions do pose a challenge to historian and historiometrician alike. The historian, perhaps allied with a psychobiographer, may decide to subject these atypical cases to a detailed ideographic analysis. Should it turn out that Hitler is not an exemplary dictator from a nomothetic standpoint, perhaps some peculiarity of his childhood or early adulthood might provide the missing clue overlooked by the scientist. The historiometrician, too, may find these nonexemplars stimulating, but will ask a different question: What does Hitler have in common with *other* atypical dictators that might explain the fact that these particular tyrants, Hitler included, depart from the general pattern? If a new commonality is found that stands up to further historiometric examination, our nomothetic understanding of dictatorship will be expanded and more historical figures will be moved from the ever dwindling list of atypicals to the ever growing list of exemplars. This ability to separate exemplars from nonexemplars of universal and invariant laws may one day add a new dimension to our appreciation of the notable names of the past. Along with such measures as intelligence, productivity, and influence, we may eventually be able to determine a "nomothetic probability score" for each of the world's historical figures: that is, a measure of how exceptional that person is. Consequently, although historiometry must be evaluated by its nomothetic achievements, it may contribute to ideographic understanding as well.

QUANTITATIVE ANALYSES

The contrast between quantitative and qualitative analysis is of primary importance in separating historiometry from several related disciplines. Traditional historiography is qualitative to its core: a page of Gibbon can never be mistaken for a page of Newton. Qualitative analysis is just as much a feature of the work of the grand philosophers of history, such as Hegel, Spengler, or Toynbee, and of the psychoanalysts who write psychobiographical interpretations of eminent creators and leaders. Freud's psychoanalytic study of Leonardo contains no quantifications of any kind. Of the diverse methodologies I have mentioned, only psychometrics and cliometrics are strictly quantitative. In a sense, historiometrics can be viewed as the merger of psychometrics and cliometrics: to discover the relationship between war and creativity, for example, we might use cliometrics to gauge the intensity of warfare and psychometrics to assess the amount of creativity. It is more elegant and accurate to say that we employ historiometrics to measure both variables. We may count the number of battles fought and the number of masterpieces created each year, and then calculate the statistical association between these two variables.

There are those who argue that, because "history never repeats itself," it is impossible to use quantitative methods in studying historical events. As with snowflakes, no two battles are alike, no two masterpieces identical. This argument would hardly convince a psychometrician. No two persons ever take the same intelligence test the same way, even when they both get exactly the same score. Generally speaking, science must always deal with abstractions that ignore some of the unique aspects of any event. No two chemical samples, no two biological specimens are ever the same. It does not require an unacceptable level of abstraction to postulate that more battles mean more war and that more masterworks signify more creativity. And if by counting battles and masterpieces we discovered that, say, whenever the battle count was highest the number of masterpieces was lowest, it would be absurd to assert dogmatically that war bears absolutely no relation to creativity—the abstraction intrinsic to the quantification notwithstanding.

Quantitative analysis in a historiometric inquiry typically consists of four distinct steps: defining and sampling the units of statistical analysis, operationalizing the crucial variables under investigation, calculating the relationships among these variables, and using more advanced statistical analyses to tease out the most probable causal connections in the data set. I shall discuss each of these four steps in turn.

UNIT DEFINITION AND SAMPLING

Psychological research does not ordinarily concern itself with defining the unit of analysis. That analytical unit is, almost without exception, taken to be the individual. In a study of creativity and leadership, the subjects would presumably be individual creators and leaders. When it comes to historiometric research, however, the definition of an analytical unit cannot be taken for granted. Sometimes we need to employ some alternative analytical unit in order to test certain nomothetic hypotheses.

Historiometricians sometimes use cross-sectional units and sometimes use time-series units. A good example of a cross-sectional unit is the individual, a unit that dominates traditional research on creativity and leadership. For example, in later chapters I will review studies of the differential fame of 2,012 philosophers, 696 classical composers, 38 American presidents, and 301 geniuses. Yet the cross-sectional unit is not always the individual human being. Some studies take the individual creative product or historical event as the analytical unit: I will discuss an investigation of more than fifteen thousand melodies drawn from the classical repertoire, and another of 326 land battles in world history. Alternatively, groups of individuals, such as nations or civilizations, may be taken as the cross-sectional unit of analysis.

In an investigation based on time-series units, the events under study are arranged in a temporal sequence. The unit may be only one year long, or it may be as long as a century. For example, in studies I will discuss in later chapters I have examined fluctuations in Napoleon's victory rate across one-year units and investigated general creativity in Western civilization over more than a hundred 20-year units. Whatever the unit of time, looking at a single individual over time, as in the case of Napoleon, means working with a biographical time series, whereas examination of a nation or a civilization over time entails a transhistorical time series.

A second distinction is between individual and aggregate units. Individual units, which may be either cross-sectional or time-series, consist of single entities such as creative products or creative persons. Aggregate units are composed of summary tabulations of individual attributes into some larger cross-sectional or time-series unit of analysis. A good example is the frequent use I will make in later chapters of generational time series, where history is divided into 20-year periods and the number of eminent creators per generation is tallied.

Any given historiometric study may combine cross-sectional, time-series, individual, and aggregate units into a single complex methodological design. A case in point is the study of two thousand famous philosophers that will figure prominently in Chapter 8, in which I utilize an individual-generational analysis, comparing the philosophical beliefs of a cross-section of individual thinkers with the prevailing philosophical zeitgeist of an aggregate generational time series. Such a comparison makes it possible to determine whether the fame of a thinker is dependent upon the thinker's compatibility with the zeitgeist. Another approach goes one step further by analyzing several individual careers into timewise units, yielding a *cross-sectional time-series design.* For instance, in an examination of the lives of the 10 most eminent classical composers, I subdivided each composer's career into 5-year age periods—producing 100 simultaneously cross-sectional and time-series units (Simonton, 1977a). Moreover, since I tabulated both individual events (such as the number of melodies composed in each period) and aggregate events (such as the number of battles fought in each period by the nation in which the composer lived), this design combined individual and aggregate levels of analysis as well. This mixed analytical design, a sort of unified biographical-transhistorical time series, is valuable in determining the relation between personal development and sociocultural change.

Once the analytical unit has been defined, the next step is sampling: deciding which cross-sectional or time-series units to scrutinize. If the units represent a cross-section of eminent personalities, then ordinarily eminence itself will be the sampling criterion. For instance, when Catherine Cox (1926) wished to study the IQs of creators and leaders, she took the 301 most eminent personalities on Cattell's (1903) rank-ordered list of a thousand historical figures. The rationale for the eminence criterion is simple: not only are the most eminent creators and leaders the ones we are most intrigued by, but the best biographical and historical information is usually available for them as well. The sample to be investigated must invariably be restricted to those analytical units for which data are readily accessible.

SCALES, VARIABLES, AND VARIANCE

How are biographical or historical materials quantified? It is customary in psychometric theory to distinguish four different levels of measurement, each representing an informational advance over the previous level. These levels are called nominal, ordinal, interval, and ratio scales.

A nominal scale does not properly involve a quantitative dimension, since its numbers serve only to identify qualitatively distinct entities. If in some statistical analysis we code all males with a zero and all females with a one, this does not mean that females have more than males of some mysterious quantity. Nominal scales are useful for recording discrete qualitative attributes such as field of achievement, nationality, or sex.

In contrast, the numbers in an ordinal scale tell us how the analytical units can be ranked along some attribute. For example, Farnsworth (1969) ranked the 99 most eminent classical composers (from Bach to Tartini) and the 50 most eminent modern composers (from Stravinsky to Kirchner). The main drawback of ordinal scales is that only the rank of the successive numbers, not the size of the interval between them, has any quantitative significance. To give Bach a rank of 1, Beethoven 2, and Mozart 3 is not to claim that Bach is as much more famous than Beethoven as Beethoven is more famous than Mozart.

When the intervals between the numbers themselves signify quantities, we have an interval scale. A prime example is ratings, that is, measures based on judges' assessments of units along some dimension, where something more than mere ranking is requested. For instance, Maranell (1970) had several hundred American historians rate 33 presidents of the United States on such interval dimensions as general prestige, strength of action, idealism, flexibility, and administration accomplishments. Knowing that President Kennedy's flexibility score is 1.61, Lincoln's 1.50, Andrew Johnson's −2.18, and Wilson's −2.23 tells us much more than the ordinal fact that Kennedy and Lincoln were more flexible than Johnson and Wilson. These scores also indicate that the difference in flexibility between Johnson and Wilson is only about half as large as that between Kennedy and Lincoln.

Statistical methods require nothing better than interval scales, but ratio scales do have certain interpretive advantages over interval scales. In a ratio scale, not only do the intervals between numbers mean something, but additionally the ratios of any two numbers have significance. A true ratio scale has a nonarbitrary zero point as well. For example, if we hypothesize that war inhibits technological invention, we might count the number of battle casualties per year and the number of patent applications over the same years. Each of these time-series tabulations would constitute a ratio scale: it certainly makes sense to say that in one year there were zero war casualties or zero patent applications, and that, say, 1000 casualties is 10 times as many as 100 casualties. Ratio scales are quite common in historiometric research.

In tabulations where all events cannot be counted equally, it is often preferable to employ weighted rather than unweighted scales. An example is my investigation of whether stressful events in the lives of composers influence the type of melodies they compose (Simonton, 1980c). I searched the biographies of famous composers for sources of stress. Rather than simply counting stressful events, I weighted the events according to a modified version of a "life-change" scale devised by Holmes and Rahe (1967). Death of a spouse was worth 100 points, a change in national residence 40, and litigations or lawsuits 30, to give just a few instances. Though one might quibble with the specific magnitudes assigned, such weighting schemes, however approximate, are often far more useful than merely treating all events equally.

The purpose of such quantifications, whatever the type of scale used, is to provide each unit of analysis with a value on some dimension or variable. A variable is some attribute on which the analytical units may differ or fluctuate. Thus the variable "battle casualties" may vary from zero to millions, the flexibility scores for the presidents from -2.23 to $+1.61$, the rankings of the 99 most famous classical composers from 1 through 99. And historical geniuses may be classed as either leaders or creators. For a variable to be a useful indicator of some trait, it must vary, and the more variation the better. Ranking the fame of 1000 men and women from 1 to 1000 offers more information about individual differences in historical greatness than does merely classifying everyone as either famous or obscure. To take the extreme case, a variable that does not vary at all is useless. If we want to know

11

whether female heads of state are less likely than male heads of state to involve their nations in military conflicts, it will not do to have a sample consisting solely of American presidents, all of whom have been men. The connection between sex and aggressiveness cannot be determined from a sample in which the variable "sex" has zero variability. Statisticians have defined a measure called the "variance," that tells how much the measurements vary about the mean or average value of a variable. The more widely casualty figures fluctuate from year to year, the greater the variance in the battle casualties variable. The more extensive the individual differences in assessed intelligence, the larger the variance in an IQ measure.

COVARIATION AND THE CORRELATION COEFFICIENT

Occasionally the variance belonging to a variable is of interest in itself, but the question more often asked by historiometricians is a more complex one: Given that we have two variables, to what extent is variation in one variable related to variation in the other?

Many early historiometric investigations never went beyond the quantification of data. After the data were quantified, the analysis would consist of the mere "eyeballing" of tabulations, charts, and graphs. Yet even experienced statisticians are incapable of looking over a complex array of numbers and spotting patterns that are really there. Human beings are unable to discern when a sequence of numbers is random or not, and will frequently see associations or cycles that are demonstrably absent—much as we find pictures in the randomness of clouds and inkblots. Seldom does a regularity of history stare us in the face. If historiometry is to succeed in isolating nomothetic principles, our procedures of data analysis must be as sophisticated as our techniques of quantification.

An important question is how to assess the degree of "covariation" between two variables across a sample of analytical units. The most frequently used statistic, devised by Karl Pearson, is the product-moment correlation coefficient, or Pearsonian r. This coefficient ranges from -1 to $+1$, where a minus sign means a negative relationship between two variables and a plus sign a positive relationship (a negative relationship means that as the value of one variable increases the value of the other decreases; a positive relationship means that as one variable increases the other also increases). When $r = 0$, the association between two variables is totally random and thus nonexistent (when one variable increases, the other is just as likely to increase as it is to decrease). Thus the absolute value of a correlation coefficient normally is a decimal fraction somewhere between 0 and 1. A correlation as high as .90 is rather rare; most correlations of substantive interest fall between around .20 and .50.

Ordinarily researchers are interested in the influence of one variable on another. The causal variable is called the independent variable, and the variable it affects is the dependent variable. For example, if the question under investigation were the effect of war on women's fashions, some measure of the amount or intensity of war would be the independent variable, and various characteristics of fashion, such as skirt length, might be chosen as dependent variables. The usual way of gauging the importance of a given causal variable is to square its correlation coefficient with the effect variable. That is, r^2 is the proportion of the variance in the dependent variable that is explained or predicted by the independent variable. An r^2 of 1 signifies perfect predictability, and an r^2 of 0 the lack of any explanatory value whatsoever. For example, the correlation between international war and skirt length is $-.30$ (the minus sign indicating that as warfare increases skirts become shorter), allowing us to conclude that 9 percent (the square of $-.30$) of the variance in skirt length is predicted or explained by international war (Simonton, 1977c).

Bivariate correlations—correlations between two variables—are useful tools in historiometric research. Even more useful, however, are multivariate statistical techniques. A multivariate analysis takes into consideration more than two variables, perhaps even hundreds. When the subject under study is as complex as creativity or leadership, for any given dependent variable there are a host of potential independent variables. Multivariate analysis allows us to treat this multitude of predictors simultaneously, thereby consolidating an array of bivariate correlations into a single comprehensive multivariate statement.

An illustration of this simplifying capacity of multivariate statistics can be taken from a study of 696 famous classical composers (Simonton, 1977b). The individual fame of these creators has a bivariate correlation of .56 with length of creative career, .71 with creative productivity, and $-.19$ with year of birth. That is, the most famous composers of Western classical music tend to have the longest productive careers, to be the most prolific, and to have been born long ago rather than more recently. But to determine the proportion of variance in the dependent variable that can be explained by these three independent variables as a group, it is not enough to square the three separate bivariate correlations and sum the three squares. These three variables correlate with one another as well. For instance, the correlation between creative productivity and length of career is .51, meaning that about 26 percent of their respective variance is held in common. In order to be productive it helps to have a long career: Mozart and Schubert would probably have produced more than a thousand works each had they not died young. Multivariate analysis makes it possible to obtain an estimate of the total predictability of fame that rejects the superfluous information due to the overlap among the independent variables. As it turns out, the multiple correlation, R, between fame on the one hand and productivity, length of career, and year of birth on the other is .78. The multiple correlation can be interpreted much the same way as a bivariate correlation, for it represents the correlation between the dependent variable and *all* the independent variables taken in a predictively optimal combination. The square of the multiple correlation is the proportion of the variance that can be explained using all three predictors: if $R = .78$, then $R^2 = .60$; 60 percent of the variation in fame among the 696 composers is attributable to the three given explanatory factors. The multiple correlation squared thus essentially measures how much we know about the phenomenon under investigation.

CAUSAL INFERENCE

One of the first things a student of the behavioral sciences learns is that "correlation does not prove causation." Yet I have been discussing cause and effect variables, prediction and explanation, just as if to correlate automatically means to cause. In fact the correlation between two variables may actually be spurious. Suppose two events A and B are each caused by a third event C, so that whenever C occurs, then A and B will occur together—not because A causes B (or vice versa) but rather because A and B have a common cause. The correlation coefficient between tabulations of events A and B will thus be the spurious repercussion of the third variable C. My inquiry into the differential fame of 301 eminent creators and leaders illustrates how a spurious relationship may intrude into the analysis (Simonton, 1976a). The correlation between the ranked eminence of these historical figures and their estimated IQ scores is .23, a result consistent with the causal inference that intelligence is a prerequisite of historical acclaim. However, a third variable, namely year of birth, correlates $-.14$ with IQ score and $-.23$ with ranked eminence: that is, there is a distinct tendency for more recent individuals to be less famous and to be assigned lower intelligence scores than their predecessors. It is possible, therefore, that the observed correlation between intelligence and eminence is a spurious consequence of the biasing effect of birth year.

What is needed is a method for calculating the relationship between two variables while "controlling for," "partialing out," or "holding constant" the third variable that may be a source of bias. One such technique is to determine the "partial correlation" between two variables while controlling for the third. Looking at the 301 geniuses again, the partial correlation between intelligence and eminence, controlling for birth year, is .20, a reduced but nevertheless significant relationship. In lieu of computing the partial correlation, historiometricians often use a related technique, multiple regression analysis. Multiple regression makes it possible to determine the impact of two or more independent variables upon a single dependent variable, where the causal effect of each predictor variable is estimated while controlling for all other predictor variables simultaneously. Thus multiple regression permits us to deal with more than one source of spuriousness. In the case of the 301 geniuses, it turns out that birth year is not the sole source of potential spuriousness in the correlation between intelligence and eminence. The reliability of the biographical data may also contaminate the relationship. When we control for birth year, data reliability, and several other variables, the relationship between intelligence and eminence becomes nonsignificant. The standardized partial regression coefficient, β (beta), for predicting eminence from intelligence, all other variables held constant, is only .14 (Simonton, 1976a). Like the correlation coefficient, the beta coefficient tends to range from -1 to $+1$, where 0 indicates the absence of a relationship. Its use, in statements of the form "$\beta = q$," where q is a positive or negative decimal fraction, indicates that the effect of the corresponding independent variable upon the dependent variable in the multiple regression has been estimated controlling for all other independent variables in the equation.

The inference that one event causes another requires more than the mere demonstration that the two events are associated. The demonstration of nonspurious association does not show which event is cause and which is effect. To infer that A causes B we must not only prove that no third event C constitutes a common cause responsible for the observed correlation, but additionally that A precedes B in time.

One way to introduce a time dimension into the research design is to employ some type of time-series analysis. By measuring the cause and effect variables over time, we can discern whether the fluctuations in the causal events tend to precede fluctuations in the effect events. Suppose we measure the territorial area of a particular political system, such as the Roman state, across successive 20-year periods or generations. Say that we also measure the achievement motive revealed in the national literature. We hypothesize that achievement motivation in the national character leads to military conquests after a one-generation lag. If this hypothesis is correct, then the bivariate correlation between achievement imagery and territorial extent should be largest when calculated between the achievement motive in one generation and territorial extent in the next. This particular lagged correlation should be larger in absolute value than the synchronous correlation between the two variables measured for the same generation, and larger still than the lagged correlation going in the reverse direction (that is, between achievement motivation in one generation and territorial expanse in the *previous* generation). Effect follows cause and not the reverse.

The analysis I have just outlined, called cross-lagged correlation technique, is one of several quasi-experimental designs. It is generally used in conjunction with some multivariate statistic, such as partial correlation or multiple regression analysis. For example, in Chapter 9 I will examine the relationship between creativity and political instability in the history of Western civilization (Simonton, 1975c). For this investigation I created a creativity index consisting of a count of the eminent creators who were active in each 20-year period, and a political instability index consisting of a tabulation of coups d'etat, military revolts, dynastic conflicts, and political assassinations. The correlation between these two measures was then calculated after controlling for several potential variables. The resulting partial correlation departed from zero only if creativity was lagged one generation after political instability. This result gives us considerable reason to infer that political instability has a causal influence on creativity after a one-generation delay. The partial correlation is negative, indicating that political instability in one generation inhibits creativity in the next generation. This example shows how meaningful even if tentative causal inferences can be drawn from historiometric data through the determination of temporal priority.

By combining multivariate controls for sources of spuriousness with quasi-experimental ascertainment of temporal priority, we in effect assume a minimal definition of causality: variable A is said to be a direct cause of variable B if (1) the correlation between these two variables is highest in absolute value when B is lagged some optimal temporal distance and (2) the correlation remains nonzero even after holding all other relevant influences constant. To be sure, the power of causal inference in correlational data can never equal that obtainable in a laboratory experiment. But the issues historiometricians study cannot be subjected to laboratory techniques. If we hypothesize that warfare tends to stifle technological creativity, we cannot test that hypothesis by randomly distributing declarations of war across a sample of nations to see what happens to patent applications. Practical and ethical considerations preclude the use of anything more powerful than correlational techniques.

HISTORICAL POPULATIONS

Historiometricians concentrate on historical rather than contemporary subjects. One rationale for this focus is that exploitation of historical populations may maximize our ability to discover any transhistorically invariant laws of creativity and leadership. Hypotheses about the nature of genius should be tested on samples with the maximum amount of cultural and historical variety. If a behavioral law holds across such diversity, then it has the highest probability of universal validity. For example, to discover whether the peak age of literary creativity tends to be just such an invariant, I studied more than four hundred literary creators from 25 centuries of history and from the Japanese, Chinese, Indian, Persian, Arabic, Greek, Latin, and numerous modern European literatures (see Chapter 6). A rule or relation that holds for such a multifarious group of writers is likely to continue to hold into the future.

Another advantage of concentrating on historical samples is that it is easier with famous people of the past than with contemporary figures to decide precisely who should be considered a creator or a leader. The judgment of contemporaries is notoriously far from being error free; reputations that have stood the test of time are more reliable. Among their contemporaries in the middle of the eighteenth century, Telemann was more highly regarded than Handel or Bach. Similar mistakes have been made in science; the classic case is the long-neglected Gregor Mendel, who discovered the principles of genetic inheritance. The scientist John Tyndall put it well in 1897: "To look at his picture as a whole, a painter requires distance; and to judge of the total scientific achievement of any age, the standpoint of a succeeding age is desirable."

Another reason historiometricians study historical populations is that certain nomothetic questions cannot be addressed without going back vast distances in time. In this respect historiometry resembles astronomy: its processes may take more than a human lifetime to work through their normal course. Edmund Halley discovered his comet in 1704 by reviewing observations made in 1531, 1607, and 1682. If he had confined himself to observations he could make personally, the recurrent nature of comets would have remained a mystery. Similarly, many laws of history may take several generations to unfold. These laws could not be discovered if creativity and leadership were studied only in contemporary populations.

Even when the processes under consideration take place entirely within the confines of the normal human life span, certain questions about genius can be answered reliably only for deceased creators and leaders. An example is the question of the relationship between age and achievement. Richard M. Nixon's political career seemed finished when he lost the California gubernatorial election in 1962, just two years after his narrow defeat by John F. Kennedy. Who imagined then that a decade later Nixon would be reelected president with almost 97 percent of the electoral vote? A productive career can never be said to be completed until an obituary has appeared. Thus, it often behooves the researcher to restrict the sample to those who have died.

Historiometricians do not always study just dead people: as the hypotheses permit, the subjects can be very much alive. Creators and leaders can make history in their own lifetimes. A person who has been honored with an entry in *Who's Who,* an encyclopedia, a historical treatise, or even a biography can be treated like any eminent figure of the past.

RELIABILITY AND VALIDITY

Sir Robert Walpole is said to have replied, when his son offered to read something to him: "Anything but history, for history must be false." Why should the discoveries of historiometry be any less false? Is the historical record really adequate as the basis of scientific inquiry? The answers to these questions lie in a distinction that figures prominently in psychometrics. According to psychometric theory, measures of any psychological trait may vary on the two evaluative dimensions of reliability and validity. To be reliable a measure must be precise, whereas to be valid the measure must measure what it purports to measure. Historiometric measures must be carefully formulated to fulfill both of these requirements.

The reliability of historical data. To determine the precision of measures, psychometricians calculate a "reliability coefficient." This coefficient is a decimal fraction that ranges from 0 to 1, where 0 means no reliability whatsoever and 1 signifies the unattainable goal of perfect measurement. Ideally, the reliabilities should be above .90 or at least .80, though it is not uncommon for even established psychological measures to have reliabilities around .70, .60, or sometimes lower still.

One way of estimating reliability is the retest method, which entails giving the same test twice to the same group of subjects and then calculating the correlation between the two sets of scores. For example, an IQ test might be given twice, a year apart, to the same elementary school students; the estimated reliability is the correlation between the IQ scores on the two administrations of the test. Needless to say, if the subjects remember the questions from the first time around, this method will tend to inflate the estimated reliability. By contrast, if the psychological traits being measured change rapidly over time, the retest method will underestimate reliability.

This second consideration has some implications for historiometric measures of eminence. As the posthumous appreciation accorded to Bach and Mendel suggests, fame can be fickle, fluctuating from generation to generation. In fact, however, the retest approach can be used to demonstrate convincingly that eminence is surprisingly stable over time. Farnsworth (1969) has adequately shown, for example, that musical taste possesses appreciable transhistorical stability. Looking at the works performed by the Boston Symphony Orchestra, Farnsworth found that the frequency of a composer's appearance on the program in the decade 1915–1924 correlates .98 with the frequency in 1925–1934, .90 with the frequencies in 1935–1944 and 1945–1954, and .89 with the frequency in 1955–1964. The interdecade reliabilities do decline as the separation between the two decades increases, but a fair portion of this modest drop may be due to the addition of modern composers to the program. Moreover, this stable musical consensus is not confined to the concert hall. Farnsworth obtained very similar results by looking at the amount of space devoted to various composers in music histories, music encyclopedias, and general encyclopedias published more than fifty years apart. Thus the retest reliability of eminence measures tends to be very high (also see Over, 1982). Sometimes fashion places Bach on top, other times Beethoven, and yet other times Mozart, but never have their contemporaries Gebel, Reicha, and Türk been propelled to the top of the list.

A second approach to estimating reliability involves alternative forms; rather than administer the same test to the same subjects at two separate times, this method administers two different tests to the same subjects at roughly the same time. For example, two alternative forms of an IQ test might be given to a set of students and then the correlation calculated between the two sets of scores. Historiometric studies can often obtain at least two measures of the same variable, calculate the correlation between them, and use that correlation for the reliability coefficient. I have made several studies, for example, of the reliability of separate counts of the number of scientific discoveries and inventions per unit of time and for a particular cross-sectional unit, either defined for science as a whole or broken down by discipline. The separate counts of events often came from different types of sources, such as histories versus biographical dictionaries. The estimated reliability coefficients are uniformly high, with an average of .90.

Many historiometric studies take into consideration more than just a pair of alternative measures. In an investigation of the fame of 2,012 philosophers I employed 10 distinct measures, and in an inquiry into the eminence of 696 classical composers I used 6 different measures. In cases of multiple measures, the common procedure is to run a "factor analysis" to determine whether there exists a single dimension called "eminence" underlying the various measures. Factor analysis reveals that about half of the total variance in the 10 measures in the philosopher study and about 60 percent of the total variance in the six indicators in the composer study could be attributed to the single factor of fame. These factor analyses can also reveal if there are other dimensions to greatness, such as ethnocentric or epochcentric biases in the sources. It is most comforting to report that the vast majority of analyses find only single-factor solutions, signifying that such biases have only a minor impact, if any, on ratings of eminence.

Factor analysis does not give us all the information we need. The next step is to calculate an "internal consistency" reliability coefficient. This coefficient indicates how much the several measures band together for the same measurement purpose. Normally the "Kuder-Richardson" or "coefficient alpha" formula is used. The result is a coefficient that can be compared with reliabilities calculated by the retest and alternative form methods. For instance, in a study of American presidents I factor analyzed seven ratings of performance and found that a single presidential "greatness" factor accounted for 71 percent of the variance (Simonton, 1981c). Accordingly, I generated a composite measure of greatness by summing the separate ratings and then calculated coefficient alpha, yielding a very respectable reliability of .98. There exists a firm consensus on who were the great, the medio- cre, and the bad chief executives in United States history (also see Kynerd, 1971). The coefficient alpha reliability of philosophical emi- nence is .94, indicating a comparable agreement on the greatness of thinkers.

Many investigators have evaluated the reliabilities of numerous his- toriometric measures and have found them to be consistently depend- able. The reliability holds up whether we are looking at creativity or leadership, biographical or historical data. If reliability is the criterion of whether the historiometric enterprise is considered scientifically le- gitimate, then the criterion has been met.

Nevertheless, historiometricians must be ever aware of the factors that may affect the reliability of data. One such factor is sample selec- tivity. A group of eminent creators and leaders is a very selective sam- ple indeed. Because nonentities are seldom subjects of historiometric research, the variation in such measures as intelligence is severely truncated, and this truncation means that reliability coefficients are lower than would be expected in more diverse samples. For example, in the highly select group of 301 historical geniuses collected by Cox (1926), the reliability coefficients for her IQ estimates are around .50 (Simonton, 1976a). This reliability, though low, is respectable once al- lowance is made for the fact that these subjects form an extreme elite. The reliability coefficients of creativity and intelligence test scores when calculated for gifted children are even lower: around .30 (Wal- lach and Kogan, 1965; Hudson, 1966).

A second factor historiometricians must keep in mind has to do with historical proximity. Historiography has always been dominated by battles, wars, revolutions, and conspiracies—by what William Cullen Bryant called "The horrid tale of perjury and strife, / Murder and spoil." Thus we can be reasonably secure about historiometric mea- sures as long as they are restricted to these readily accessible political events. The reliability of biographical data, in contrast, becomes ever more fragile as we consider the geniuses of antiquity. As an example, the reliability of the IQ scores estimated by Cox for her 301 geniuses has a high positive correlation ($r = .43$) with how recently each genius was born (Simonton, 1976a). If we wish to study creators and leaders from the more remote past, we can protect the reliability of our mea- sures by concentrating on the most famous creators and leaders of history—the ones for whom the most information exists. For the Cox geniuses, data reliability and eminence exhibit a modest correlation ($r = .14$).

Even when reliability estimates are impossible to obtain, our confidence in historiometric methodology can often be buttressed by the replication of one investigator's results by other investigators. To offer a clear-cut case, numerous researchers spread over a century and utilizing varied archival sources have all converged on the same life expectancy for famous creators (see, for example, Beard, 1874; Sorokin, 1925; Simonton, 1974, 1976a, 1977b; Eisenstadt, 1978). The mean is around 66 years of age (with a standard deviation of 14). This example may seem trivial; yet life span will be a crucial parameter when I discuss productivity in Chapters 5 and 6. More important, the idea of replication is basic to science, including the science of historiometry.

The validity of measures of eminence. Besides proving that historiometric measures are reliably measuring something, we also must show that they are measuring the right thing. One solution to the problem of validity is "operationalization": to operationalize an abstract concept is to ground it in specific concrete operations. Thus intelligence is operationalized by defining it as a score that a subject receives on an intelligence test. Then we can maintain that "intelligence is what an intelligence test measures." Needless to say, this way of asserting validity is more glib than illuminating. Fortunately, most historiometric measures enjoy a conspicuous degree of face validity; that is, there exists a prima facie case for the assumption that the measure lives up to what it advertises. If we are interested in assessing the intensity of a war, for example, it makes good sense to take the duration of the war, the number of nations in conflict, and the frequency of battles as elements making up an index of warfare. Some composite of these quantities would possess clear face validity.

The question of validity becomes especially urgent when we enthrone fame as an indicator of creativity, leadership, or genius. This practice has a long history, going back as far as Francis Galton's *Hereditary Genius* (1869). When we think of the highest-grade creativity or leadership it is natural to consider lists of eminent names from history. Thus the definition of genius in terms of citation counts, space allocations, performance frequency, and similar archival measures has some face validity. Yet not everyone might consent to this operationalization. As Lord Byron said in *Don Juan* (III, 90):

> And glory long has made the sages smile,
>> 'Tis something, nothing, words, illusion, wind—
> Depending more upon the historian's style
>> Than on the name a person leaves behind.

The distinguished men and women of the past sometimes appear as mere legends created by the myth-makers we call historians. A favorable pen may make giants out of the undeserving, while a disapproving neglect can cast the mighty into a historical dungeon of obscurity. This is a story as old as the Bible. By oppressing his people with tax levies and forced labor to build the Temple in Jerusalem, King Solomon managed to stay in the good graces of the priestly chroniclers, and thus went down in history as the wisest and best of all monarchs. Jeroboam II, by contrast, despite a reign filled with spectacular reconquests and the resurgence of economic prosperity, was opposed by the reformist prophet Amos, and thus received but a passing note in the Hebrew chronicles. Hence, any consensus among historians may be meaningless.

I do not see this problem as a serious objection to the historiometric enterprise. My position is in basic concordance with Carlyle's: "Fame, we may understand, is no sure test of merit, but only a probability of such." For every mediocrity who receives unwarranted acclaim from posterity there are probably thousands of outstanding minds buried forever in historical namelessness. But the contrast between the eminent and the noneminent is largely between a modest number of exceptional geniuses (with a small contingent of famous unworthies) and a great many unexceptional individuals (with a larger absolute number but a smaller relative proportion of overlooked geniuses). Thus, there should remain some systematic differences between the eminent and the noneminent, differences due to contrasting developmental experiences, personality characteristics, and sociocultural milieu. I believe that eminence is the best indicator we have of historical genius.

The vast amount of scholarly and popular literature devoted to the great geniuses of the past—the notable creators and leaders of history—leaves no reason to doubt that such figures are of immense intrinsic interest. These personalities have shaped the past, influence the present, and will probably continue to affect the future. Their lives, when subjected to more scientific analysis, may reveal some general laws of history, broad principles of the creation and transformation of human civilization. It is here that historiometry comes to the fore. Dedicated to the discovery of nomothetic generalizations through the application of quantitative techniques to historical populations, historiometry is specifically designed to abstract any regularities from the confusing richness of names, dates, and places. The key aim of historiometry is objective generalization, to reduce the bewildering array of historical facts into a much smaller set of abstract statements about how a special class of individuals come to reorder the direction of human history.

2

PROGENITORS, GENES, AND GENERATIONS

A LONG-STANDING debate in psychology is the so-called nature-nurture controversy. At one extreme are the nativists, who believe that human behavior is mostly guided by the dictates of certain biological givens, or nature. They hold that there is something that can be labeled "human nature," something that constitutes an instinctive basis for thought and action. Individual differences among human beings do not confound the nativists, since such variation can be neatly ascribed to heredity, a strictly biological process that inadvertently produces genetic variability. At the other extreme are the environmentalists, who assign the primary role in shaping human personality to the events that make up life from the moment of birth, events that nurture the development of the human individual. Because some experiences are universal across cultures and history, certain cognitions and actions are universal and hence on the surface *appear* to be innate. Variation among individuals is easily ascribed to the obvious diversity of physical, personal, and social environments. Needless to say, the nature-nurture or heredity-environment controversy is very old, as old as philosophy itself. Plato and Descartes both believed that certain ideas are innate, while such British Empiricists as Locke and Hume maintained that the mind begins as a blank slate on which environmental experiences are inscribed.

Most psychologists today would not defend either of these extremes. Human behavior is now seen as a function of both nature and nurture. The legitimate question is not whether nature *or* nurture determines our behavior, but how nature and nurture interact and what is their relative importance in forming human character. This question is pertinent to an understanding of creativity and leadership: some people think that genius is "born," others that genius is "made." Presumably the truth lies in some combination of the two. A way to throw light on this issue is to examine factors that affect the early development of geniuses.

Family Influences

Much of what we know about the childhoods of eminent persons comes from the work of Victor and Mildred Goertzel (1962). The Goertzels studied biographies of more than four hundred twentieth-century leaders and creators, probing into the early lives of their subjects to discern whether specific family and school settings support the development of genius. They scrutinized such things as handicaps, early traumas, troubled homes, dominating mothers, opinionative fathers, attitudes toward learning in the home, and reactions to school and teachers. In a later work, the Goertzels examined more than three hundred more recent personalities, added items to their biographical inventory, and ran statistical tests (Goertzel, Goertzel, and Goertzel, 1978). I shall concentrate here on the three characteristics that have been most thoroughly studied, namely, birth order, orphanhood, and family heritage.

Birth Order

There is a strong theoretical reason for looking into birth order as a variable that may explain the emergence of genius. If a certain type of family background promotes creativity or leadership, this background is in all likelihood shared by all children in a family. If, say, high socioeconomic status, a stimulating home environment, and bright parents all contribute to genius, then every child in a given family should have the same shot at success. But how many people have heard of the siblings of Bach, Rembrandt, Cervantes, Descartes, Darwin, Gandhi, or Sun Yat-sen? None of these were only children. To be sure, instances can be given of famous siblings. Jacques and Jean Bernoulli developed the calculus, August and Louis Lumière pioneered cinematography, Orville and Wilbur Wright invented the airplane. All of these pairs consist of collaborators; it is even more rare for two siblings to strike out on separate paths to glory. Beyond the James brothers (William the philosopher-psychologist and Henry the writer of fiction) and the Weber brothers (Ernst Heinrich the physiologist and Wilhelm Eduard the physicist) it is quite difficult to find such cases.

Birth order goes a long way toward explaining why siblings do not achieve the same level of eminence. Research on the eminent has demonstrated that first-born children—and especially first-born sons—tend to achieve more than later-born children do. Francis Galton

(1874) found far more first-born and only sons among famous scientists than could ever be expected by chance. Havelock Ellis (1904), in *A Study of British Genius,* replicated Galton's conclusions, this time showing that the preponderance of first-borns held for women as well as men and for endeavors besides science. Ellis added one refinement: the youngest child was also favored over the intermediate child, though not to the degree enjoyed by the eldest. The Goertzels found that in their sample of 314 eminent personalities of the twentieth century, 30 percent were first-borns, 16 percent only children, 27 percent youngest children, and only 26 percent middle children (Goertzel, Goertzel, and Goertzel, 1978). First-borns are disproportionately represented in comparison to the population at large, youngest children having the next best advantage.

The first-borns do not come out on top in every field of endeavor. In the Goertzels' sample, first-borns who are only children tend to be underrepresented in the political arena, while middle children tend to be overrepresented among modern political figures. In addition, two studies using different samples indicate that revolutionaries are much less often first-born children (Stewart, 1977; Walberg, Rasher, and Parkerson, 1980).

What are the specific developmental mechanisms through which ordinal position in the family affects achievement? This question has never really been satisfactorily answered. Research on contemporary populations has shown that birth order is associated with both intelligence and educational attainment (Adams, 1972). In the next two chapters I will show that both of these factors may be responsible for achieved eminence, but this explanation begs the issue. Why are first-borns smarter or better educated? It has often been suggested that a family might funnel limited resources to the first-born as a modern type of primogeniture. Only the oldest child would go to college. Yet the birth-order effect may have less to do with intellectual development than with interpersonal experiences within the family (Stewart, 1977; Albert, 1980). The finding that politicians are more likely to be middle children and less likely to be only children fits in nicely with this idea. Only children probably lack the social expertise that can be acquired from day-to-day interactions with siblings. Intermediate children, especially, may get plenty of practice in negotiating, compromising, and mediating between older and younger siblings.

The tendency for revolutionaries to be later-born children may have less to do with birth order than with family size. Obviously later borns tend to come from larger families. Matossian and Schaefer (1977) have proposed an intriguing theory about the origins of revolution, which I will consider more fully in Chapter 9. According to their view, large families are characterized by high interpersonal conflict and tension both among siblings and between parents and offspring. This intrafamily tension, particularly between father and son, leads to a rebellious attitude in the son. The outcome may be his recruitment for revolution should the appropriate political situation arise. This theory predicts, though Matossian and Schaefer do not specify as much, that revolutionaries will tend to be later-born children, especially males. In addition, because family size rather than birth order is the decisive factor, more than one sibling from a large family has a high probability of becoming a revolutionary. Fidel Castro, the fifth of his father's seven children, was joined by his younger brother Raúl in the revolution that overthrew Batista. All the male and female siblings in the Ulyanov family joined the revolutionary movement in Russia; the eldest son was executed for plotting the assassination of the tsar, and the third-born child led the Bolsheviks to victory under the pseudonym Lenin.

Loss of Parents

Lenin's father died while Lenin was a teenager. Beethoven lost his mother when he was 16 years old, and when he was 18 his father was expelled from Bonn for alcoholism, making Beethoven the head of the family. Napoleon became head of his family at 15 when his father died, and Julius Caesar lost his father at about the same age. Newton's father died before Newton was born. Cases such as these have stimulated several investigators to wonder whether orphanhood deserves any credit for the growth of genius. The evidence gathered to date seems confirmatory. Between 22 and 31 percent of the eminent persons in the Cox (1926) sample lost a parent before adulthood (Albert, 1971; also see Walberg, Rasher, and Parkerson, 1980). Martindale's (1972) sample of famous English and French poets included 30 percent from father-absent homes. In the Goertzels' sample of famous moderns, 18 percent lost their fathers and 10 percent lost their mothers before the age of 21 (Goertzel, Goertzel, and Goertzel, 1978). Roe's (1952) interviews of distinguished contemporary scientists revealed that 15 percent lost a parent by death before age 10.

By far the most systematic inquiry into orphanhood is J. Marvin Eisenstadt's essay "Parental Loss and Genius" (1978). Eisenstadt scrutinized 699 eminent individuals from various nationalities and walks of life. The frequency of orphanhood was quite large: fully one-quarter of the geniuses lost their first parent by the time they were 10, more than two-thirds by 15, almost half by 21, and more than 60 percent by age 30. About 10 percent lost both parents by age 21. Eisenstadt compared these percentages with information drawn from census data and from studies of juvenile delinquents and psychiatric patients. In the main, the proportion of orphanhood among his geniuses far exceeds those found in these comparison groups. The only groups that come close to having the same proportions are the delinquents and, especially, the severely depressed or suicidal patients. The latter result is consistent with the somewhat higher rates of suicidal depression among the eminent (see Chapter 3).

Eisenstadt ascribed the effect of parental loss to a bereavement trauma, but he failed to pursue all of the empirical ramifications of this interpretation with his own data. If eminence is a symptom of a bereavement syndrome, for instance, it should make a difference when and how the loss occurred. It is most improbable that Newton experienced a severe shock upon the death of his father. Another possible explanation has to do with the disruption of sexual identification caused by an absent parent of the same sex (see Martindale, 1972). (Most research on this topic has focused on fathers and sons, so I will restrict this discussion to males.) If the father dies or is often absent from home, the son may fail to identify fully as a male and instead become more intimate with the mother. The outcome could be an androgenous and even slightly feminine male, a type of personality that may be conducive to creativity (but see Harrington and Anderson, 1982). Alternatively, the absence of a strong male role model may produce a chip on the shoulder; the insecure child may overcompensate by assuming an exaggerated masculinity. Poets, dictators, and military heroes have one biographical datum in common: they exhibit a high percentage of dominating, possessive, or smothering mothers (Goertzel and Goertzel, 1962). More than half of famous male poets display some cross-sexual identification in the guise of traits traditionally considered female (Martindale, 1972). Perhaps the despots and conquerors have the same basic personality as poets but cover it with a veneer of machismo. One advantage of this hypothesis in comparison to that of bereavement is that it is more specific in its predictions and hence more verifiable. The loss of the same-sex parent, whether by death, divorce, exile, or alcoholism, is the critical event. If that parent is adequately replaced by another appropriate same-sex figure, such as an uncle or a grandfather, an aunt or a grandmother, the cross-sexual identification should be less likely. Further, the loss of a close brother or sister or other relative should have no general impact. Thus even though research has not yet done so, it is feasible to pin down the psychological processes behind the effect of orphanhood on eminence.

FAMOUS FAMILIES

The incidence of orphanhood among geniuses, though surpassing chance expectation, is far too small to be the principal contributor to fame. If we are looking to the family for sources of genius, some other factors must be found. Socioeconomic status has often been suggested as one possible variable. Most of the creators and leaders in the Cox (1926) sample were from the upper classes. The Goertzels found that some 80 percent of the eminent of modern times came from middle-class business or professional homes, whereas only 6 percent had suffered poverty in childhood. Blondel (1980) determined that 60 percent of the leaders in the modern world were from middle-class backgrounds. But in spite of these percentages, the evidence suggests that the social status of parents exerts no direct effect on achieved eminence. My reanalysis of Cox's leaders and creators disclosed that the father's socioeconomic status correlates with the rated IQ and educational level of his offspring but not with their achieved eminence once IQ and education are controlled (Simonton, 1976a). Thus the consequence of social class for eminence may be only indirect; its influence may be mediated by intelligence and education.

It is not implausible that intelligence, and hence eminence, might run in families. This possibility is the main point of discussion in the earliest historiometric investigation on record, Sir Francis Galton's *Hereditary Genius* (1869). As one might expect from the founder of eugenics, Galton wanted to show that intellectual genius was entirely responsible for all the achievements of human civilization. Environmental circumstances he considered irrelevant. He also wished to prove that genius was totally inherited by biological means from parent to child. These two generalizations converge on a single prediction: if genius runs in families, and if genius is a necessary and sufficient cause of eminence, then persons of distinction should cluster into families too. Much of Galton's treatise is devoted to demonstrating that eminent people have eminent relatives in proportions that could not be expected by chance.

On the face of it, the evidence looks convincing. Galton listed judges, politicians, English Peers, generals and admirals, literary authors, scientists, poets, musicians, painters, divines, and even prize-winning athletes. These lists reveal a striking number of renowned family lines. The musical Bachs epitomize this tendency. Johann Sebastian Bach came from a family that had been producing professional musicians for many generations. Bach himself had several composer sons, of whom Carl Philipp Emanuel, Wilhelm Friedmann, and Johann Christian became outstanding composers in their own right. Altogether Galton counted at least 20 eminent Bachs, 57 important enough to appear in dictionaries of musicians, and well over a hundred having some musical interest or talent. In some parts of Germany, so the story goes, the very name "Bach" became synonymous with "musician."

Less dramatic but nonetheless impressive family trees can be found for other fields. The Huxley family is an example from more recent times. Biologist and scientific administrator Sir Julian, Nobel laureate in physiology Andrew Fielding, and eminent author Aldous all were grandsons of the Thomas Henry Huxley who so vigorously defended the theory of evolution that he became known as Darwin's bulldog. Speaking of Charles Darwin, we can now add to Galton's own list—which is highlighted by grandfather Erasmus Darwin, the precursor evolutionist—two additional names. Charles Darwin's son, Sir George, became an eminent astronomer. And there is Darwin's first cousin, Sir Francis Galton himself. No wonder Darwin commented on Galton's *Hereditary Genius,* "I do not think I ever in all my life read anything more interesting and original."

Galton's thesis of hereditary genius encounters difficulty on two counts. To begin with, the data are not so secure as Galton first makes them appear. An attempted replication done three generations later showed only the eminent judges to cluster into family configurations (Bramwell, 1948). Almost half of the eminent judges have relatives who are famous judges, but in other endeavors the percentage drops to 20 percent or less. Galton himself was embarrassed by the fact that military commanders, scientists, and poets did not have long and distinguished pedigrees. To explain away such anomalies he cited the early death of commanders, the importance of the female line in the inheritance of scientific genius, or the bad luck of the draw. Needless to say, other explanations are plausible—and they constitute the second weakness in Galton's thesis. The clustering of historical celebrities along family lines may say more about social advantage and class privilege than about the genetics of genius. It is hardly amazing that those endeavors with the most family clustering of eminence tend to concern either social elites having special "connections" (as in law and politics) or a craft orientation in which skills are handed down from generation to generation (as in aesthetic activities). When music and art ceased to be considered crafts, extensive family lines vanished.

To get around these difficulties, I designed an investigation that took a different approach (Simonton, 1983d): I focused on a single endeavor, examined several successive generations, and measured both eminence and intelligence instead of using eminence as a proxy indicator of intelligence. The study included 342 hereditary monarchs from England, Scotland, France, Spain, Portugal, Netherlands, Austria, Prussia, Denmark, Sweden, Russia, and Turkey, from the end of the Middle Ages to the Napoleonic era. The eminence of each ruler was determined using a citation measure, while the intelligence scores were taken from Woods's (1906) ratings. These two scores were also determined for the father and paternal grandfather of each monarch. If eminence and intelligence really are equivalent, as Galton maintains, they should both be inherited in the same manner.

That is not the way it happens. On the one hand, intelligence does seem to be transferred across generations according to the laws of genetics. For example, a son's intellectual inheritance from his father is twice as great as that from his grandfather, a differential that makes sound genetic sense. In addition, the grandfather makes no contribution to the son's intelligence once the father's contribution is controlled. Finally, the inheritance of intelligence is the same no matter what the sex of the monarch may be: a queen owes just as much of her intellect to her father as a king does to his.

Eminence is inherited in an entirely different way. A monarch's fame is related to that of both his father and his grandfather. Not only does the influence of the grandfather operate independently of the father's influence, the grandfather's contribution actually exceeds that of the father. Furthermore, this transfer of eminence across generations works only for same-sex relationships. A king is guided by his father and grandfather in the attainment of greatness, but a queen is not; there is no relationship between a queen's fame and that of the previous two male generations. The way eminence transfers from generation to generation is best explained as an example of role modeling. Each king can imitate or identify with his male predecessors in the royal line of succession. Because both the father and the grandfather are often present during the childhood of the royal heir, both can be used as models of the role called kingship.

The restriction of this identification process to same-sex predecessors is consistent with what we know about role modeling in general (see, for example, Goldstein, 1979). Furthermore, this mechanism, unlike genetic inheritance, can account for the preference for the grandfather over the father. The royal prince may see his father as a rival, that is, as someone who, if he lives too long, may deny the heir the chance to wear the crown. This rivalry may make the son more willing to model himself after his grandfather than his father. This conjecture is supported by my finding that there is no relationship between the rated leadership of the son and that of the father, but a strong positive relation does exist for son and grandfather. Frederick the Great, who made Prussia a continental power to be reckoned with, is more likely to have modeled his leadership qualities after his grandfather, Frederick I, who boldly proclaimed himself the first King in Prussia, than after his far more cautious father.

These studies of royal families show that Galton was only partly correct. Intelligence is indeed genetically inherited, though not to the degree Galton envisioned. Yet eminence may be passed from one generation to the next largely by role modeling, a sociopsychological rather than biological process.

INTERGENERATIONAL INHERITANCE

Alfred Kroeber, one of America's pioneer cultural anthropologists, set out in *Configurations of Culture Growth* (1944) to prove that Galton was wrong—that individual genius has no explanatory value when discussing creativity. To make this case, Kroeber shows that so-called creative geniuses are not randomly scattered throughout history but rather are clustered together into configurations. These configurations represent the Golden or Silver Ages of a civilization, and are separated by wide gaps, or Dark Ages, in which cultural creativity stagnates. Thus we speak of the Golden Age of Greece or the Italian Renaissance with an implicit notion that the clustering of so many first-rate minds in such a small space of time is something special. If genius is totally inherited, as Galton maintains, then how can it possibly be so unevenly distributed throughout the course of history? The proportion of the population with genius-level intelligence must be fairly constant over time, and yet the populations of Greece and Italy have increased without any corresponding addition to the list of distinguished Greek philosophers or Italian artists. Galton put forward a racist (and therefore still genetic) explanation for this phenomenon: the brilliant Athenian "race" unfortunately interbred with "inferior" races to the point of destroying the intellectual foundation of the great Athenian civilization.

Kroeber discounted any influence of race upon the creativity of the human species, arguing that the cultural atmosphere in which an individual exists is the sole determinant. As the experiences of modern times amply prove, cultures can change far more rapidly than can the biological underpinnings of intelligence under even the most stringent and unconscionable program of eugenics. Creativity in a civilization waxes and wanes not in synchrony with human marriage practices, but with the growth, saturation, and exhaustion of the cultural pattern.

But why does creative genius cluster into these particular cultural configurations? Kroeber suggests the possible role of "emulation." He quotes the Roman historian Velleius Paterculus: "Genius is fostered by emulation, and it is now envy, now admiration, which enkindles imitation, and, in the nature of things, that which is cultivated with the highest zeal advances to the highest perfection; but it is difficult to continue at the point of perfection, and naturally that which cannot advance must recede" (quoted in Kroeber, 1944, p. 18). Velleius had also noticed that genius tends to congregate into generations of fecundity preceded and succeeded by generations of creative scarcity. His evoking of emulation as a possible explanation is not unreasonable. Each generation of creative geniuses may try to surpass the accomplishments of the generation before. Leonardo tries to outdo his predecessors only to be outdone by Michelangelo, a person more than 20 years his junior. A point is reached where no higher heights can be attained within the restrictions of a given cultural pattern, and creativity starts its downward plunge. Only when a new foundation is established will creativity resurge. Raphael culminates the High Renaissance style in painting, and in doing so condemns the remaining generations to creative oblivion. Subsequent painters either can continue the movement in imitations of increasingly academic blandness or else must strike out totally anew, and at great risk.

ROLE MODELS AND MENTORS

The notion of emulation is similar to that of role modeling, which I used as an explanation for the clustering of eminence within families. Role modeling may also explain the clustering of eminence into configurations. Because each generation is stimulated by, or reacts to, prior generations, a certain amount of continuity must be involved both in the Galton case of famous families and in the Kroeber case of cultural flourishing.

One recent inquiry into the biographical antecedents of fame found that about 82 percent of those studied were exposed to numerous adults very early in life, about 68 percent grew up in the presence of adults who were working in areas where eminence would be achieved as an adult, and 63 percent were exposed to eminent persons at a very early age (Walberg, Rasher, and Parkerson, 1980). These eminent individuals thus had many potential role models to identify with in the course of their early development. At another age level, it has been shown that over half of the Nobel laureates in science were apprentices to previous laureates (Zuckerman, 1977). These facts suggest that the availability of creative role models may be essential to the development of genius. This intergenerational influence may not always require personal contact between mature masters and young admirers; growing up in times of exceptional intellectual or aesthetic vitality may be conducive to creative development all by itself. Admiration is a strong force in personal development, and we can all admire from a distance if need be.

But what happens if such role models are utterly missing? One approach to answering this question is to employ a generational time-series analysis. The first step is to divide history into slices called generations; the usual length of a generation in recent research is 20 years. The next step is to make an extensive list of creators in a particular discipline. Each creator is then assigned to each generation according to his or her fortieth birthday. For example, a study of artistic creativity in Europe would assign Michelangelo to the generation 1500–1519 because he turned 40 in 1515. The fortieth year of life is adopted in this design as an all-purpose "center of mass" in a creator's productive career—the floruit or acme. The last step is to count the number of creators in each generation. The tabulation for each 20-year period directly measures the amount of creativity: the larger the number the more creative the generation.

We can also calculate the correlation between two consecutive generations to see how creators cluster together into Kroeberian configurations. A correlation of a variable with itself at two different times is called an autocorrelation. The autocorrelations for various types of creativity are usually very large and positive (Simonton, 1974, 1975b, 1976e): For example, the average autocorrelation across 15 creative disciplines for 130 generations of Western civilization was .39 (Simonton, 1974). Generations with very few creators are followed by similarly deficient generations, whereas generations with many first-rate creators tend to be followed by similarly flourishing generations. These cultural configurations account for between 10 and 80 percent of the variance in historical changes in creativity, depending on the discipline studied and the time span surveyed.

These autocorrelations can throw light on the role-modeling hypothesis. If creators are assigned to a generation according to their fortieth birthday, that means that the average age of creators in that generation is 40 years. Since the generations are only 20 years long, creators who are 40 years old, on the average, in one generation were 20 years old in the previous generation. Stated more formally, assigning creators to generation g according to a 40-year floruit is equivalent to assigning the same creators to generation $g - 1$ according to their twentieth year of life. The index g is merely a count of the generations from the first ($g = 1$) to the last ($g = N$, where N is the number of generations studied). What are these creators doing at age 20? Probably they are not fully productive yet, but are still susceptible to various developmental influences, including role models. That is, they probably identify with, or model themselves after, the creators who are flourishing in the generation just before theirs. Thus the autocorrelation, or the correlation between generation g and generation $g - 1$, can be taken as a measure of the role-modeling effect, especially if various extrinsic variables have been controlled. The autocorrelation suggests that the number of creators in generation g is a positive function of the number in generation $g - 1$, as predicted by a role-modeling hypothesis.

I pointed out earlier that the eminence of a king is a positive function of his father's and his grandfather's separate eminences. If fame clusters in royal families with a three-generation continuity, might not creativity cluster in the same way? In fact it does (Simonton, 1975c). The number of creators in generation g is a positive function of the number of creators in both generation $g - 1$ and generation $g - 2$, the previous *two* generations. This means that potential creators in their late teens or early twenties are influenced not only by contemporary creators in their late thirties and early forties but also by the patriarchs in their late fifties and early sixties. This effect, however, does not go any further than the parental and grandparental generations. The number of creators at generation $g - 3$ has no impact upon the number at generation g beyond that contributed by generations $g - 1$ and $g - 2$.

If the creativity of a generation is a function of the creativity in the previous two generations, the fluctuation of creativity across historical time is under considerable restraint. Creativity in the history of a civilization can move up and down only gradually. Dark Ages do not convert into Golden Ages overnight. Indeed, this three-generation linkage implies that it may require a century or so for creativity to recover from the depths of cultural stagnation. At the same time, this inertia assures us that it would be difficult to destroy a Golden Age instantaneously. Even if one whole generation were wiped out in some devastating war, the preceding generation might survive as efficacious models. Thus, although a whole generation of creators in the People's Republic of China was lost in the disruption of the Cultural Revolution, the elders might still inspire the young across the generational hiatus. Europe managed to recover much the same way though it lost so many promising creators in the trenches during World War I. Role modeling is a psychological mechanism that can explain Kroeber's cultural configurations. The idea of emulation is not far off the mark.

Generational analysis, with its emphasis on 20-year intervals, may seem arbitrary or artificial: not only are the generations 20 years long, but potential creators are assumed to seek role models at about age 20, and the role models they select are assumed to be about 20 years older than the developing creators. In fact, there is empirical evidence that this scheme is not so arbitrary after all. As I mentioned earlier, many Nobel laureates have studied under previous laureates. Zuckerman (1977) calculated the typical age difference between mentor and disciple. Some 42 percent of these pairs are between 16 and 25 years apart, with an average age difference of just over 19 years. Since Nobel laureates tend to earn their doctorates at around 25 years old, their masters are just over 40 at the time their apprenticeship begins.

INFLUENCE AND IDEAS

Max Planck's greatest contribution to science was the formulation of quantum theory. Originally designed to handle some oddities in the relatively minor problem of black-body radiation, quantum theory has since expanded to become the basis for much of chemistry, physics, and even astronomy. Planck's constant is considered to be one of the fundamental constants of the universe. Yet Planck began publishing his papers on quantum theory in 1897; and he did not receive the Nobel Prize for Physics until 1918. It took 20 years for his revolutionary contribution to receive its due recognition. This is not the only time the Nobel Prize has been bestowed some time after the event.

Einstein had to wait 17 years for his own Nobel medal, and even then he received it, ironically enough, not for his relativity theory but for his application of Planck's quantum theory to the photoelectric effect. The reason Planck had to wait so long was that his theory was not immediately accepted by the scientific community. Quantum theory demanded that classical physics be restructured down to its very foundations. In Planck's own words, "a new scientific truth does not triumph by convincing its opponents and making them see the light, but rather because its opponents eventually die, and a new generation grows up that is familiar with it" (quoted in Cropper, 1970, p. 18). In fact, it was the paper by Einstein, 21 years younger than Planck, that helped convince the scientific world that quantum theory had been unjustly ignored by Planck's own generation. When Niels Bohr, 27 years Planck's junior, later used quantum theory to explain the features of the atom, the success of Planck's theory was assured.

Planck's interpretation for the long delay in recognition has been empirically confirmed in a paper entitled "Planck's principle: Do younger scientists accept new scientific ideas with greater alacrity than older scientists?" (Hull, Tessner, and Diamond, 1978). The authors focus on Darwin's theory of natural selection, and compare the average age of those biologists who accepted Darwin's position with the average age of those who rejected it. There is about a decade's difference in the mean ages. The amount of variance explained by the age effect is not large, but the younger scientists did have a higher probability of accepting new ideas than did the older ones.

Planck's principle raises the question of how the ideas of one generation affect the ideas of the next generation. What are the consequences of exposing young developing creators to the discoveries, inventions, or ideologies of the mature productive creators in the preceding generation? I have examined the way major achievements in one scientific discipline stimulate achievements one generation later in another discipline (Simonton, 1976e). It is easy to cite specific cases of such interdisciplinary influences across generations. Charles Lyell's revolutionary *Principles of Geology* (1830) was a major inspiration for Darwin's *Origin of Species* (1859). The question is whether such instances are exemplars of general tendencies in the history of scientific ideas. I sought the answer by applying cross-lagged correlation analysis to generational tabulations of the number of inventions and discoveries in nine scientific disciplines. Several interdisciplinary influences were found: chemistry has a stimulating effect on geology, a tendency that probably reflects the importance of chemical analysis in mineralogy. Biological advances tend to be stimulated by earlier advances in the disciplines of geology, chemistry, and medicine. The stimulating impact of medicine on biology is perhaps the most intriguing. This time-lagged effect suggests that the "applied" research of medicine may lead to the "pure" research of biology. Many fundamental findings in biology may have come in response to major advances in pathology, pharmaceuticals, and surgery.

Intergenerational influences operate in broader ways in the history of ideas. I have used generational time series, for example, to determine how the prevailing ideas of one generation affect the ideas advocated by the next generation (Simonton, 1978c). I divided the history of Western thought from 540 B.C. to A.D. 1900 into 122 20-year periods. The timewise fluctuations were determined for the basic philosophical beliefs concerning seven issues in philosophy using ratings done by professional philosophers (Sorokin, 1937–1941). (An example of a philosophical issue is experience versus faith; the beliefs that may be held concerning this issue include empiricism, which founds all human knowledge on sensory experience, rationalism, which founds knowledge on reason, skepticism, which holds that knowledge is unattainable, and fideism, which considers knowledge attainable only through an act of faith.) The intensity with which these beliefs were held was gauged from the number of philosophers in each generation who advocated each position, the tabulation being weighted by each philosopher's eminence. A cross-lagged correlation analysis was applied to the data after removing time trends.

The autocorrelations for the philosophical beliefs are uniformly large. For example, the intensity of empiricism at generation g has a correlation of .89 with the intensity of empiricism at generation $g - 1$. These large autocorrelations signify that the dominating philosophy of Western civilization does not change very rapidly from generation to generation. This inertia in the flow of ideas is not strong enough, however, to prevent change. In fact, the philosophical beliefs of one generation can affect what beliefs prevail in the next in a fashion not unlike the Hegelian notion of thesis and antithesis. For example, a generation characterized by extreme empiricism tends to be followed by a generation in which skepticism is preeminent. That is, once people start believing that the only source of knowledge is our senses, the next step is the growth of doubt about whether we can know anything at all about the world beyond our senses. Even more dramatically, the belief that abstract ideas are real (realism) is followed one generation later by the belief that abstract ideas are mere names (nominalism); the idea that only society exists (universalism) is succeeded 20 years later by a resurgence of individualism (singularism); the notion that nothing changes (eternalism) gives way to the notion that everything is in constant flux (temporalism); the belief in free will (indeterminism) tends to emerge as a reaction to the preceding generation's mechanistic fatalism (determinism). It is as if the young thinkers of generation g are rebelling against the ideological excesses of their predecessors in generation $g - 1$. By so reacting, these rebels push the philosophical pendulum in the opposite direction.

One curious aspect of the way ideas impinge on other ideas across generations is that some ideas appear to be entirely "active" and others "receptive." In more individualistic terms, some types of philosophers tend to exert a tremendous influence over the philosophical thinking of the next generation, whereas other types of philosophers are the result of influences coming from the preceding generation. An instance of an active idea is empiricism: once a large number of empiricist thinkers appears in a certain generation, the next generation features an increased number of thinkers who advocate that matter is the ultimate substance of reality (materialism), that only the individual and not society has real existence (singularism), and that abstractions are but psychological constructs existing within individual minds (conceptualism). In a sense, materialists, singularists, and conceptualists may be seen as working through the implications of the ideas espoused by the preceding generation's crop of empiricists. Yet empiricist thinkers themselves are not stimulated by any other antecedent philosophical ideas, and thus empiricists may be viewed as causal agents in the history of ideas. In contrast, those thinkers who put forward conceptualism seem to be reacting to the philosophical fascinations of the preceding generation of thinkers, but without having any impact on the following generation. Though no particular type of philosopher succeeds a generation of conceptualists, conceptualists themselves appear to be responding to the antecedent generation's involvement with empiricism, skepticism, materialism, temporalism, singularism, and the ethics of happiness. That is, when one generation of thinkers takes sensory experience as the source of truth or doubts the very capacity to know, holds reality to consist of matter in a constant state of change, and gives the individual such primacy over the community that morality becomes predicated upon the pleasure principle, the next generation will place the source of all ideas within the individual mind rather than in the consensus of the linguistic community or in the world of immutable, immaterial forms.

The thinkers of a given generation will not all respond in the same way, of course, to the ideas of their intellectual predecessors. Sometimes the response is polarized into quite contrary ideological reactions. If one generation is obsessed with empiricism, materialism, nominalism, determinism, temporalism, singularism, and the ethics of happiness, for example, the key thinkers of the following generation may turn to doubt or to faith. If reality consists of nothing but matter in unending flux, if knowledge can be gained only through the data that strike our sense organs, if ideas are nothing but linguistic conventions, if each individual is the pawn of mechanistic fate and yet at the same time is encouraged to follow the egocentric pleasure criterion of moral choice, one philosophical recourse is to doubt absolutely everything. Or this same cluster of ideas can just as well cause the appearance of fideism. A fideist is one who believes in God or some other spiritual reality—not out of a firm conviction based on reason and evidence but rather out of a need to believe. The fideist must act *as if* God exists, must take a "leap of faith." But no matter whether the thinker chooses skepticism or fideism, the fact that such an extreme bifurcation takes place may reveal a certain malaise with the antecedent set of beliefs.

On the whole, environment seems to play a much larger role than heredity in the emergence of genius. Though intelligence is to some measurable degree subject to genetic inheritance, environmental family and intergenerational influences appear far more important in the development of a potential creator or leader. The sociocultural availability of appropriate role models raises the odds that any given generation will contain eminent genius, and family circumstances help decide which particular members of a given generation will achieve fame. Each generation, building upon the accomplishments of the previous generation, propels human culture forward until civilization reaches a Golden Age, after which creativity can only decline into an aftermath of imitators. Yet the geniuses who are active during those uppermost ascents owe something to their less well-known precursors. Isaac Newton knew this, and said at the zenith of his own fame: "If I have seen farther than other men, it is by standing on the shoulders of Giants."

3

PERSONALITY
AND CHARACTER

BOTH CREATIVITY AND leadership were traditionally considered to be proper subjects for personality researchers. Creative persons were thought to possess distinguishable character traits; leaders were believed to have personalities that set them apart from their followers. This personological approach was popular partly because it complied so well with common stereotypes about greatness. Genius was conceived as a very broad quality of extraordinary mental and motivational powers. As Dr. Samuel Johnson put it in *Lives of the English Poets,* "The true genius is a mind of large general powers, accidentally determined to some particular direction." Geniuses in various endeavors, whether political or cultural, were thought to have more in common with each other than with their colleagues. According to this view, Michelangelo is more the intellectual and emotional brother of, say, Galileo, or even Julius Caesar, than of some third-rate artist messing up a chapel ceiling or mutilating a block of marble.

Personality researchers have attempted to test the hypothesis that creators and leaders have distinct and identifiable character traits. The usual procedure is to find groups of persons who vary in either creativity or leadership, as judged by tests or ratings, and then have them fill out personality inventories. Research on leadership in the first half of this century, and research on creativity at the beginning of the second half, consisted of myriad studies reporting correlations between creativity or leadership scores and hundreds of personality constructs. The results of these efforts were rather disappointing. Very few personality traits emerged as general predictors. Not only were creators a breed separate from leaders, but different types of creativity and leadership had to be differentiated as well. As the world of achievement became more and more compartmentalized in the quest of secure predictors, the romantic view looked less like an insight and more like a myth. Researchers began to discard the idea of a generalized "genius type" character, and then went on to reject the notion that achieved eminence might have a personological foundation.

Several reasons might be offered for this disillusionment. The ratings of leadership may be inadequate, the creativity tests invalid. The personality inventories may be contaminated by artifacts and artificialities. Or, in fact, there may be no generalized personality underlying greatness. My own view is that these investigations have not managed to divorce genius from talent, talent from mediocrity. Most of the subjects of this research have been college students taking introductory psychology courses; I doubt that many minds of the first caliber have filled out the questionnaires. I believe that if we are to discover the personality characteristics of genius-level creators and leaders we must make minds of unquestioned distinction the center of our scientific attention.

INTELLIGENCE AND COMPETENCE

When we think about creators and leaders of the highest rank, we tend to think of their intelligence. This reaction is not limited to historical hindsight or myth-making retrospection: contemporaries pass similar judgments. Newton's most distinguished colleagues were often amazed at his intellectual powers. In 1696 Europe's best scholars were challenged by a Swiss mathematician to solve two particularly difficult problems. Newton anonymously returned solutions to the challenger—one day after seeing the problems. The challenger figured out Newton's identity at once, and commented, "I recognized the claw of the lion." And it is not just creative geniuses who enjoy this kind of respect; Napoleon's mental gifts evidently impressed Goethe, himself one of history's last universal intellects.

Various studies have sought empirical evidence of whether eminent creators and leaders tower above others in intelligence. For example, White (1931) has shown that the eminent tend to display exceptional versatility—that is, to exhibit competence in a wide array of endeavors. And Walberg, Rasher, and Parkerson (1980) found 90 percent of the eminent personalities they studied extremely high in intelligence and questioning curiosity. Both of these investigations are essentially continuations of an earlier inquiry, which has become a classic of historiometric technique: Catherine Cox's *The Early Mental Traits of Three Hundred Geniuses* (1926).

Cox's book is the second volume of Lewis Terman's influential *Ge-*

netic Studies of Genius (1926). Terman was engaged in one of the most monumental longitudinal inquiries in the history of psychology; he took a sample of children who scored exceptionally high on standardized intelligence tests and then traced their lives into adulthood to see if they achieved distinction. Cox attempted to replicate Terman's longitudinal results, but in reverse. Beginning with a sample of eminent persons from history, she traced their biographies back into childhood in a quest for evidence of intellectual precociousness. This search entailed a massive collation of biographical data on the early mental traits and behaviors for 301 geniuses born since 1450. Cox had three independent raters use this information to calculate IQ scores. IQ was defined according to the traditional concept of a ratio of mental age to chronological age. The raters were to judge what mental age was required for a given precocious act, divide this estimate by the genius's chronological age at the time of the act, and then multiply by 100 to yield an IQ score. If a behavior falls within the range of expected behaviors for a certain age, this definition yields a score of 100, the average IQ.

As an example of this way of measuring IQ, take John Stuart Mill. Mill began to learn Greek at 3, read Plato at 7, studied geometry and algebra at 8 and calculus at 11. He wrote a history of Rome when he was 6 and could discuss the relative merits of Wellington and Marlborough at age 5. To determine his IQ, one must know the average age at which a person of normal intelligence could accomplish these same tasks. Thus the study of calculus usually commences, if at all, around age 18. Dividing the mental age required for calculus (18) by Mill's chronological age (11) and multiplying by 100 yields an IQ score of 164. Taking Mill's entire early biography into account, Cox and her collaborators arrived at an IQ estimate of 190.

Such estimates were calculated for all the geniuses in Cox's sample. She also went to the trouble of demonstrating that these IQ estimates featured respectable reliabilities. The range of IQ scores for Cox's 301 geniuses is large—from 115 to 210, with an average of about 165. Only a tiny proportion of the general population has IQs this high.

Cox wanted to demonstrate that intelligence was related to achieved eminence. To measure achieved eminence she modified rankings published by Cattell (1903). To give some idea of the variation in fame that can still be found in so elite a group, the most eminent leader was Napoleon and the most obscure was General P. H. Sheridan; the creators ranged from Voltaire to Harriet Martineau. Cox correlated these eminence rankings with her IQ scores and found a connection between achieved eminence and IQ. Unfortunately, she did not have available the sophisticated analytical equipment for avoiding spurious results. Consequently, the connection she claimed to have found may be a methodological artifact (as discussed in Chapter 1). Another drawback of Cox's work is that she did not treat leaders and creators separately. There is good reason to look at the link between intelligence and creativity apart from that between intelligence and leadership.

IQ AND CREATIVITY

Research on creativity in contemporary populations suggests that the functional relation between intelligence and creativity may be a bit more complicated than first meets the eye (Barron and Harrington, 1981). There is a positive relationship between intelligence and creativity (McNemar, 1964), but it tends to vanish in the upper reaches of intelligence. Beyond an IQ of around 120, further gains in IQ do not increase the likelihood of creative achievement. An IQ of 120 is not a very selective cut-off point; it marks the average intelligence of college graduates (Cronbach, 1960); and about 10 percent of the general population has an IQ of 120 or higher.

These empirical findings must be taken with some caution. Intellectual ability is assessed by IQ tests, psychometric instruments of questionable validity. This deficiency in validity dates back to the birth of the IQ test, which was the brainchild of the French psychologist Alfred Binet. Henri Poincaré's performance on the early Binet tests was so miserable that if he had been judged as a child instead of a famous mathematician, he would have been rated as an imbecile (Bell, 1937). We must look beyond psychometric IQ before drawing conclusions about the role of intelligence in creativity.

Although Cox's definition of IQ is founded on Binet's, the fact that she scrutinized concrete behaviors rather than abstract test items gives her scores superior validity. The IQs for the creators in her sample are impressive: Goethe had an IQ of 210, Pascal 195, Hume 180, Michelangelo 180, and Mozart 165. The average IQ for creators in various disciplines—science, philosophy, literature, music, and art—is nearly 170, a very striking figure indeed. Still, no significant association between intelligence and eminence appears when the calculations are run on the 192 eminent creators in Cox's sample using appropriate controls. This result is not surprising. Even if the sample does feature appreciable variation in both eminence and intelligence, the 301 belong to a highly elite club nonetheless. The musicians are a case in point.

What can be done with a privileged group of eleven composers who range in eminence from Beethoven, Bach, and Mozart down to no lower than Gluck and Palestrina? Almost seven hundred composers are responsible for the works performed in the classical repertoire. The IQs of this top 2 percent range from genius level to super-genius level. If we are to discern a positive relation between eminence and intelligence, we must study a much more heterogeneous sample. This can be accomplished for leaders.

IQ AND LEADERSHIP

Research on contemporary populations has indicated that intelligence may be no more an unequivocal determinant of leadership than it has been shown to be of creativity (Stogdill, 1948). Even though intelligence is one of the few personality traits that have been consistently associated with leadership, it is likely that a person can be too intelligent to attract the allegiance of followers (Hollingworth, 1926). A high-powered genius may talk over the heads of potential followers. In American presidential history, Adlai Stevenson lost two elections to the less brilliant Eisenhower; one of the few presidential candidates with a Ph.D., George McGovern, lost by a landslide in 1972; and Woodrow Wilson, the only president with a doctoral degree, was first elected to office with a mere plurality, not a majority, of votes.

Cox's IQ estimates seem to bolster the conclusion that excessive intelligence may be a handicap in a leader. The average IQ of the 109 leaders in her sample—politicians, soldiers, revolutionaries, and religious leaders—is four to six points below that of her 192 creators (Simonton, 1976a). Creative geniuses can sometimes afford to be misunderstood by contemporaries: when a violinist complained about Beethoven's Razoumovsky quartets, the composer could confidently retort, "Oh, they are not for you, but for a later age!" (Knight, 1973, p. 67). Leaders, by contrast, must achieve greatness in their own lifetimes or else fall into permanent oblivion. Unpublished or unperformed creative masterworks may be rediscovered after a creator's death—but it is unlikely that hitherto unrecognized yet notable political reforms, religious movements, or decisive battles will suddenly surface in an heir's attic and provoke a posthumous upsurge in a leader's reputation.

The area of leadership may determine just how important it is to be comprehensible. The least intelligent of Cox's 109 leaders are the 27 soldiers—mostly generals and admirals—with a mean IQ of 140; compared with the overall average of 164 for the 301 geniuses. Military leaders are often placed in the position of having to persuade and cajole their soldiers. Napoleon was particularly effective in such morale-boosting tasks, as in his famous 1798 address before the Battle of the Pyramids. Such compatibility with the masses is far less crucial in other domains of leadership. The IQs of the politicians and revolutionaries in the Cox sample average around 165, a full 25 points above those of the military figures. Prime ministers, legislators, and revolutionaries may have to pay more attention to the intricacies of power brokerage and coalition formation than to the summoning of support from the masses. Interestingly, the 8 most famous U.S. presidents have a mean IQ of only 152, 13 points lower than that for politicians in general. The American chief executive is far more dependent than many other politicians upon direct communication with the public for his political success.

It turns out that among the leaders in Cox's sample achieved eminence is uncorrelated with IQ. Perhaps intelligence does not in fact predict achievement—but there are other possible explanations for this finding. In the first place, there might be something wrong with the definition of intelligence. The concept of IQ assumed by Cox may be slanted toward intellectual abilities of a rather narrow kind. An alternative definition might do a little better. For example, a psychological trait closely related to intelligence is versatility: the number of separate fields in which an individual attains distinction. The classic case of such a versatile mind is Leonardo da Vinci, who was notable as a painter, sculptor, inventor, engineer, physicist, biologist, and even musician. Among leaders, one of the greatest factotums is the scientist, author, publisher, inventor, politician, and diplomat Benjamin Franklin. My reanalysis of Cox's data revealed that such versatility is significantly correlated with achieved eminence ($r = .23$) and that this relationship is particularly conspicuous for leaders (Simonton, 1976a). If intelligence is defined in terms of intellectual versatility, then intelligence does predict leadership.

Another possibility is that Cox's sample may have been too selective for the full impact of intelligence to manifest itself. As far as the phenomenon of creativity is concerned we have little choice but to confine attention to elite samples, but leadership can escape this limitation. It is feasible to have a stupid person assume the highest positions of leadership. In hereditary monarchies, for example, a royal heir can claim by birthright a throne that would be denied if mental capacity were required for succession. Cox deliberately left out of her sample all eminent persons who she believed had not achieved eminence by their own merits. This selection criterion meant the omission of some of the most eminent leaders of history—leaders like Louis XIV of France, Elizabeth I of England, and Peter the Great of Russia. To be sure, among monarchs even the obscure and incapable go down in the historical records along with their most famous and competent colleagues. For our purposes this inclusion of the unworthy is an asset: it provides a comparison group for estimating intelligence, fame, leadership, and other pertinent personality attributes. It extends the range of these variables and thus permits a more valid test of their interrelationships.

Frederick Woods (1906) rated several hundred members of royalty on a 10-point scale using biographical data (with reliabilities between .77 and .81). Woods made no attempt to assess either leadership or eminence, so all we can conclude from his data is that the proportion of geniuses is somewhat higher than we would expect in the population at large, a fact that was also true of Cox's leaders. Woods also found a large proportion of feeble-minded persons among the royalty. In a second investigation, Woods (1913) calculated leadership scores for several hundred rulers in hereditary monarchies from more than a dozen European nations. He never directly compared these leadership ratings with his earlier intelligence scores; I made such a quantitative comparison, however, in two studies of 342 kings, queens, and regents (Simonton, 1983d, 1984b). I also added a measure of the eminence of these rulers (with a reliability of .90). Rated leadership was significantly and positively correlated with intelligence ($r = .80$). Furthermore, I found monarchal eminence to be a positive function of intelligence, just as Cox had hoped to prove ($\beta = .16$). Interestingly, intellectual aptitude has comparable relevance for both length of reign and life span. The brighter monarchs live longer ($\beta = .22$), an effect perhaps due to the shrewdness required to deflect assassination plots and attempted coups. Intelligence is also related with length of tenure on the throne ($r = .26$), but much of this relation between intelligence and length of reign results from their mutual correlations with life span. If we control for longevity, the relationship between intelligence and length of reign becomes a curvilinear U-shaped function. That is, of monarchs with equal lifetimes, the ones who rule the longest are either very dim-witted or extremely brilliant. The power-preserving influence of genius requires no explanation, but that of feeble-mindedness does. Perhaps stupid rulers manage to stay in power longer because they serve as passive pawns in the hands of kingmakers.

To date, research has established a more definite and positive link between intelligence and leadership than between intelligence and creativity. Insofar as it is reasonable to extrapolate from hereditary monarchies to rulers generally, intelligence is associated with political success. Mental brilliance brings superior leadership, more conspicuous fame, and even a long life and therefore a long reign.

MOTIVATIONS

Intelligence is not enough to guarantee eminence. Although the proportion of genius-grade intellects is small, the absolute number is quite large. Even if only one out of ten thousand persons can compete with Cox's geniuses, in a population of two hundred million people or more there must be a group large enough to populate a small city bursting with intellects having the same power as Beethoven, Montaigne, Hegel, or Darwin. And yet most of them never achieve fame. Evidently some other personality attributes intervene in the determination of creativity and leadership.

THE NEED FOR ACHIEVEMENT

Cox (1926) noted that among her 301 geniuses the desire to excell was a primary factor in achieved eminence, often compensating for an intellect below the highest rank. A more recent investigation found that 90 percent of the eminent exhibit a strong need to achieve excellence (Walberg, Rasher, and Parkerson, 1980). The most influential study on this subject is McClelland's *The Achieving Society* (1961). McClelland does not directly investigate the relationship between achievement needs and attained eminence; his goal is to prove that the chief psychological agent responsible for economic growth and prosperity is this need to set standards of excellence and to strive to attain them. This study is of significance to us for two reasons. First, if we view entrepreneurs and businesspersons as a special subgroup of leaders, McClelland's study may help us understand the basis of leadership. In a capitalist society such as the United States where names like Rockefeller, Carnegie, Ford, and Morgan have been so influential, such an inquiry hardly requires justification. Second, the economic power of a nation or civilization may provide the ultimate foundation of its cultural and political achievements (Gray, 1961). The dependence of military might upon a nation's economic strength is obvious; as Rabelais put it, "Money is the sinews of battle." In the case of cultural achievements, as the economist H. T. Davis said, "Art and literature flourish in a rising economy, but they wither and perish in one that declines" (1941, p. 572). McClelland himself claims that the empirical study of the achievement motive will help us understand the rise and fall of civilizations.

McClelland and his colleagues ventured into the historical record in order to define and trace the key variables of a nation's achievement orientation and economic well-being. To measure achievement needs, they looked to the national literature as a repository of national values; for example, they analyzed the content of the classical literatures of Greece, Spain, and England to determine how the achievement motive fluctuated through history. They also examined the graphic artifacts of a civilization. Research has shown that the doodles and drawings of people with high achievement drives contrast sharply with those of people with low achievement drives (Aronson, 1958); in principle, then, the artistic productions of entire societies might reveal underlying achievement needs. The decorations on the vases of ancient Greece and the funerary urns of pre-Incan Peru have been coded for the use of diagonals, S-shapes, multiple waves, and other motifs. Economic conditions have also been measured creatively, using such indicators as the extent of the Athenian trade area (as betrayed by the distribution of pottery jars used for transporting wine and olive oil), the number of ships cleared from Spain for the New World, the rates of gain in London coal imports, and the volume of public building in the Virú valley of Peru.

Combining these two sets of measures leads to the conclusion that the achievement motive stimulates economic growth. This relation seems to hold for pre-Incan Peru, ancient Greece, medieval and early modern Spain, England up to the Industrial Revolution, and the United States (see Cortés, 1960; Bradburn and Berlew, 1961; DeCharms and Moeller, 1962). The work of DeCharms and Moeller illustrates how such an inference is arrived at. These investigators wanted to demonstrate that McClelland's achieving-society hypothesis would explain the economic history of the United States from 1800 to 1950. To obtain a measure of American achievement imagery over that period, they studied the children's readers that were most widely read in American schools. This choice is similar to the selection of literary works, but has the advantage that along with teaching reading, children's readers also attempt to inculcate fundamental values. DeCharms and Moeller found that the incidence of achievement imagery in these readers increased fairly smoothly until 1890, after which there appeared a sharp decline without even a small momentary recuperation. By 1950 the achievement motive had fallen to about the same strength as that seen a hundred years earlier.

To gauge the U.S. economy over the same interval, DeCharms and Moeller began with the number of patents issued by the United States Patent Office, and used census figures to transform this index into a per capita measure. This per capita index displayed a time trend very similar to that found for the achievement motive: the number of patents increased evenly up to around 1890, continued at a high level until the onset of the Depression in 1929, and declined dramatically immediately afterward. The correlation between the achievement imagery in children's readers and the number of patents per capita is .79, a respectable coefficient. Moreover, since the curve for the achievement images seems to anticipate the curve for the patent index, it is plausible that achievement motivation may exert some causal influence on technological growth. The economic downturn takes place about 40 years after the fall in achievement imagery. The young students fed on less achievement-oriented readers took some time to grow up and make their dearth of ambition evident on the economic scale.

The research of McClelland and his co-workers, though bold and important, is not without its deficiences (see Finison, 1976; Mazur and Rosa, 1977). From our present standpoint the greatest failure of this research may be its exclusion of the individual. It would be instructive to obtain scores for Andrew Carnegie, Henry Ford, J. P. Morgan, and other eminent entrepreneurs to see whether the need for achievement can be said to contribute directly to personal economic success.

THE NEED FOR POWER

Investigations of the power motive reverse the emphasis of the achievement studies by concentrating solely on the individual—and on a special type of individual at that. Most research to date on the need for power has focused on political leadership; in fact, such historiometric research has tended to concentrate on a very narrow subgroup of political leaders, namely, American presidents.

The earliest inquiry into presidential power needs is David Winter's *The Power Motive* (1973). Winter analyzes the content of the inaugural addresses of the dozen presidents from Theodore Roosevelt through Richard M. Nixon, tracing both power and achievement imagery. He finds Presidents Kennedy and Theodore Roosevelt to have the highest needs for power, while the highest achievement needs belong to Nixon and Johnson. Taft rates lowest on both dimensions. In the case of presidents, though not for people generally, there is a strong positive correlation between the need for achievement and the need for power. As Winter points out, this relationship probably reflects the bipolarity of the American political system. By philosophy Democratic presidents pursue an active policy calling for the expansion of control and the transformation of society, whereas Republican presidents prefer restraint. The presidents with strong needs for power and achievement tend to be the strong executives, the presidents without such needs the weak ones, though the latter may be acting out of a commitment to a philosophy rather than out of personality weakness. Calvin Coolidge, for instance, conscientiously made political passivity a fine art. Of the two motives, the need for power seems to be the most critical in determining how a president performs in office. The power motive is correlated with ratings given these presidents by 571 historians on general prestige, strength of action, presidential activeness versus passivity, and administration accomplishments (ratings from Maranell, 1970).

Winter finds that the presidents most governed by the need for power are those most likely to enter the United States into a war. With one exception the wartime presidents are all high on the power motive and the peacetime presidents are all low. The exception in fact proves the rule—it is the peacetime president Theodore Roosevelt, one of the most belligerent chief executives in American history. Power-driven chief executives also have higher rates of cabinet turnover, and are more likely to be the targets of assassination attempts. The four presidents with the highest scores on the need for power—the two Roosevelts, Truman, and Kennedy—are the only presidents in the study who had guns fired at them. Winter speculates that such powerful presidents may elicit stronger animosity from some people, or that perhaps power-driven presidents tend to expose themselves more to the public and thus make themselves more available as assassination targets.

Winter's results are founded upon only a dozen American presidents. A second investigation by Wendt and Light (1976) extended the sample to include all presidents since Hayes and replicated many of Winter's findings. Power images again were found to correlate with achievement images, attempted assassinations, and membership in the Democratic party, as well as with effective press relations. So it seems safe to surmise that the need for power has repercussions for political leadership, at least in the special case of the American presidency.

REASON AND EMOTION

Intelligence, and specifically IQ, connotes the ability to reason effectively. But inner drives such as the need for power and the need for achievement may undermine an individual's rationality. For a closer look at these contrasting elements of the human character, I will examine intellectual complexity and emotional instability.

INTELLECTUAL COMPLEXITY

Few revolutionaries ever manage to overthrow a hated government or ruler. Fewer still succeed in retaining the power so arduously acquired. The characteristics that make a successful revolutionary are not necessarily those of a competent head of state. What are the attributes that promote long-term and not just short-term success in a revolutionary? Suedfeld and Rank (1976) hypothesized that intellectual sophistication may provide a key. To overthrow a government, a revolutionary leader must be utterly dogmatic, must reduce the political world to a "good guys versus bad guys" dichotomy. There must be no doubts in the leader's mind as to which side represents truth and justice. But after the revolutionaries assume the reigns of power, they must master the enormous intricacy of running a nation. The party unity that propelled them to the top often turns out to be a temporary coalition of numerous special interests with conflicting goals. Retaining power under these circumstances requires an altered mind set. Dogmatism is out and flexibility is in. To achieve long-term success revolutionaries must be capable of switching from simple-minded ideology to sophisticated pragmatics.

To test this hypothesis, Suedfeld and Rank scrutinized 19 leaders of 5 successful revolutions—the American, Russian, Chinese, and Cuban revolutions plus the English Civil War. A revolutionary was classified as a success if he was a conspicuous participant in the pretakeover phase and additionally held some significant official position in the posttakeover regime until either voluntary retirement or death by natural causes. Revolutionaries who were forced to leave power against their will were branded as failures. The next step was to assess the intellectual complexity of the 19 revolutionaries before and after the takeover. Personal letters, published treatises, and public speeches were collected from the pre- and posttakeover periods of each revolutionary's career. Content analysis of these documentary materials yielded two separate measures of cognitive sophistication. The first, which Suedfeld and Rank styled "conceptual complexity" but which in more recent studies is called "integrative complexity," refers to the cognitive differentiation and integration of incoming information. A person who is high in conceptual complexity is one who perceives the world in a multidimensional and flexible manner, simultaneously considers diverse viewpoints, and yet manages to integrate all these inputs into a single perspective. A person who lacks conceptual complexity tends to reject information that does not fit within rigid preconceived schemes and tends to be submissive to authority. The second measure, "polar contrast," gauged the extent to which an individual treats two points of view as polar opposites. People who prefer simplistic polar contrasts are likely to score low in conceptual complexity.

The data analysis confirms Suedfeld and Rank's hypothesis. All revolutionaries tend to lack intellectual subtlety during the pretakeover phase of their careers. Their verbal pronouncements weigh very few points of view and those standpoints which are considered are conveyed in a polarized way. Once the revolutionaries take control, however, the successes rapidly shift to less polarized outlooks on national issues, whereas the failures persist in their dogmatic ways. The Russian revolution illustrates this contrast. Bukharin, Lenin, Stalin, and Trotsky were all single-minded ideologues uniformly dedicated to the cause. After the establishment of the Soviet State, however, these comrades-at-arms had a parting of ways. Lenin adopted a more pragmatic approach to governing a nation. In the interest of consolidating his power base, Lenin actually retreated toward capitalism in his New Economic Policy of 1921. Lenin's successor, Stalin, continued this pragmatic trend. The Russian Communist movement took on a more nationalistic cast, and the idealism of the October Revolution gave way to the opportunism behind Stalin's 1939 Nonaggression Pact with Hitler, the arch-anticommunist. Meanwhile, Bukharin and Trotsky failed to make the mental transformation and lost touch with the direction taken by the Soviet Union. Bukharin went through a purge trial and was executed in 1938; Trotsky was exiled from Russia and later was assassinated.

Suedfeld and Rank never really specify whether they are measuring abilities, preferences, or transient cognitive strategies. Are pretakeover revolutionaries truly that dogmatic or are they extremely sophisticated individuals who employ an apparent simplicity as a manipulative ruse? The answer might be mixed. Those revolutionaries who fail to make the intellectual switch requisite for political survival in the aftermath of revolution may indeed be simplistic to the core. These revolutionary failures may be incapable of adjusting their customary modus operandi to the changing times. In contrast, those revolutionaries who succeed in making the necessary shift may have always possessed complex—and manipulative—intellects.

MADNESS AND PATHOLOGY

The poet John Dryden expressed a widespread belief when he wrote: "Great wits are sure to madness near allied,/ And thin partitions do their bounds divide." This perception of genius has a very long history (Becker, 1978). Aristotle, for example, thought that a melancholic temperament was a sine qua non of extraordinary talent. And Seneca said "There is no great genius without some touch of madness." The list of eminent and unstable personalities is long and diverse, including such names as Newton, Nietzsche, Schumann, and van Gogh. The eminent suffer from a wide range of disorders. Some are plainly psychotic and end their lives in mental institutions. Others have personality or affective problems that do not totally incapacitate them. One sample of acclaimed twentieth-century leaders and creators contained 9 percent with serious mental illness, 2 percent suicides, and 3 percent attempted suicides (Goertzel, Goertzel, and Goertzel, 1978). Almost all of the suicidal personalities were seriously manic-depressive. Such difficulties are much more frequent among creators than among leaders, and within creators are more common among artists than among scientists (Goertzel, Goertzel, and Goertzel, 1978). In one study of famous poets, almost half exhibited some pathological symptoms, and 15 percent were downright psychotic (Martindale, 1972).

Though these statistics apparently endorse the mad genius stereotype, they cannot be taken at face value. The issue of finding a suitable comparison group is critical. Is the proportion of geniuses with pathological symptoms significantly larger than that characteristic of normal populations? One way to approach this question is to look at contemporary subjects, so that control groups are more readily available. Studies of contemporary populations have found that creative personalities are not necessarily pathological, but that there is a distinct tendency for artistic creators to display more emotional instability than scientific creators (see, for example, Barron, 1963). But such studies seldom compare geniuses with normal individuals but rather compare creative with noncreative subjects, where creativity is usually defined in terms of a creativity test. A way to get around this weakness is to compare measures of mental health calculated for distinguished historical personalities with measures calculated for contemporary subjects. In this cross-era comparison we can never be completely sure that the observed differences are not caused by historical changes rather than by personality contrasts, but the comparison can be instructive nonetheless. According to such studies, neither mental illness nor suicide seems conspicuously more evident among the eminent. Some professional groups, including psychiatrists, are more prone to self-destruction than geniuses are, and the frequency of psychological pathology in the general population is about the same as the frequency among the eminent: around 10 percent.

The important substantive issue is whether mental illness contributes to genius. Conceivably, pathological symptoms could be the consequence rather than the cause of achieved eminence. Many eminent creators encounter fierce opposition to their ideas, an opposition that might undermine their sanity. Ignaz Semmelweis died in a mental institution after a nervous breakdown precipitated by the controversy surrounding his discovery that the mortality rates from puerperal fever could be sharply reduced if obstetricians would only wash their hands before delivering babies. Julius Robert von Mayer attempted suicide and was treated in a mental institution after the scientific community repeatedly ignored his original ideas, such as the law of the conservation of energy.

Even if the adverse response from society does not cause a mental collapse, psychological problems may be more effect than cause. Creativity is associated with being a self-actualizing person, and self-actualization provides one basis for mental well-being (Maslow, 1962). Beethoven said the one thing that prevented him from committing suicide upon learning that he was going deaf was his art; too many masterworks still waited in his mind to be placed on paper. Perhaps creative geniuses suffer mental anguish only when they come to a dead end in the development of their intellectual or aesthetic potential. The last compositions of Schumann, noticeably inferior to his earlier works, may not be symptoms of his mental disintegration; rather, his emotional stability may have been upset by the waning of his creative powers.

More historiometric research is needed before these questions can be settled. What is specifically required is an investigation determining the relationship between mental health and achievement. Until this obvious question has been addressed, we will not know whether the instability of a Newton or a Michelangelo was integral, incidental, or detrimental to the magnitude of the accomplishment.

SOCIAL STYLE

People differ radically in the style they bring to their social lives. Some persons are extraverted, others introverted. Some seek to dominate their fellows, others find greater comfort in submissiveness. And people vary immensely in the importance they assign to morality in their interpersonal relations. Do differences in social style have any repercussions for creativity and leadership? This question is easier to address for leaders than for creators. Many creative individuals are extremely introverted, sometimes revealing a virtual disgust for the usual social exchange (Cattell, 1963; Roe, 1952). Henry Cavendish, for example, who discovered hydrogen and calculated the mass of the earth, never spoke at all to a woman and never said more than a handful of words to a man. He communicated with his female servants entirely by written notes, instantly fired any servant who crossed his path at home, and had a separate entrance to his house constructed so that he could come and go without human contact.

Leaders, in contrast, cannot be hermits. The very definition of leadership is rooted in social relations. Napoleon imprisoned on the island of St. Helena ceases to be a leader. This dependence of leadership upon society is a two-way street; the leader's social style affects the group's social patterns.

DOMINANCE AND EXTRAVERSION

The interactions among nations frequently seem to have the same pattern as the relationships among individual human beings. Nations, like people, can lose face, act tough, or pull a bluff. Some countries assume roles of mediators, just as some persons tend to be conciliatory or diplomatic. And some nations seem quite outgoing while others are virtual isolationist recluses. This analogy between individual and social systems makes sense; after all, individual people formulate and execute the policies of nations. Perhaps when policymakers contemplate foreign affairs they generalize their preferences in interpersonal relationships to the realm of international relations.

Etheredge (1978) has tested this "interpersonal generalization theory" in an objective and quantitative way. He examined American foreign policy between 1898 and 1968, focusing on disagreements among various members of a given presidential administration, such as the president himself, his secretary of state, and other miscellaneous advisers. Altogether he examined 62 foreign policy debates: 49 concerning the use of force, such as coercion or threat, in foreign affairs, and 13 concerning the desirability of a more conciliatory posture toward the Soviet Union. The 36 policymakers who participated in these debates were assessed on two crucial personality dimensions—extraversion and dominance over subordinates. Three independent raters based these assessments on biographical and historical records, achieving a substantial degree of interrater consensus (reliabilities around .90). The ratings were then used to predict the direction of disagreement in the policy debates. In more than 75 percent of the trials, the sides taken by these policymakers fell right into line with their known differences in interpersonal relations. Those who preferred to dominate in their social dealings with subordinates tended to advocate the employment of force, whether by threat or by actual intervention. They also opposed moves toward arbitration and disarmament agreements. Highly extraverted policymakers tended to advocate more cooperative relations toward the Soviet Union, including trade agreements, diplomatic recognition, negotiations to resolve conflict, and summit conferences. These results support the basic tenets of interpersonal generalization theory. The persons who make American foreign policy do indeed model international affairs after their favored patterns of social relations.

Etheredge consolidated his findings by offering a tentative typology of orientations toward international politics. First, policymakers can be classed as either high-dominance or low-dominance types, the former seeking to reshape the international political system through force, the latter striving merely to persevere. Second, policymakers can be classed as introverted types, who maintain exclusive positions respecting other nations, or extraverted types, who wish to expand interrelationships among nations. Combining these two dimensions yields a fourfold typology. High-dominance introverts, such as President Woodrow Wilson and Secretary of State John Foster Dulles, attempt to form rather exclusive blocs as a counterforce to other blocs. Low-dominance introverts, in contrast, seek only to maintain the status quo. Secretary of State Frank Kellogg, proponent of the Kellogg-Briand pact to outlaw war, is a good example of such a maintainer. Conciliators such as President Warren Harding and Secretary of State John Hay are low in dominance but high in extraversion and thus take a more active role in foreign affairs than do maintainers. Finally, Presidents Theodore and Franklin Roosevelt exemplify the high-dominance extraverts who take on the integrative role of world leaders. Etheredge's findings imply that policymakers may dangerously project their interpersonal dispositions into the world of international affairs. In only 25 percent of the debates did an individual support policies that went against the grain of his personality.

MORALITY

Ethical considerations are not normally deemed germane to the discussion of creativity. Seldom do we care about a creator's personal life in judging the aesthetic merit of a poem or melody or the scientific status of a theory. Our taste for Beethoven's music is unaffected by the unscrupulousness of his dealings with publishers.

Society is much less tolerant of improprieties when it comes to assessing leadership. Leadership, because it involves a social relationship, presumes some minimal trust in the leader's good intentions. A country's head of state is a conspicuous symbol of that country's values and aspirations. This symbolic function was one reason for the vehement public reaction to the Watergate tapes of President Nixon's private conversations with his advisers: many Americans were embarrassed by the discovery that a nation that claims to be ethical in world affairs was governed by someone of questionable ethical standards. In Hobbesian terms, the tarnishing of the head must presage the corruption of the body politic.

Even though people would rather have faith in the benevolence of their nation's leaders, they tend to be skeptical as well. Politicians are frequently viewed as opportunistic and power-hungry demagogues. Many people believe Lord Acton's famous assertion: "Power tends to corrupt, and absolute power corrupts absolutely. Great men are almost always bad men." Too many political leaders, perhaps, select Machiavelli's *The Prince* as their handbook for political success. Hitler kept a copy by his bedside and Mussolini praised it as his supreme guide on tactics and strategy. Machiavelli's treatise specifically asserts that political achievement must be founded upon the baser human passions. The ideal prince is one without ideals, except for barely concealed manipulatory, amoral, and self-interested opportunism.

What is the actual relationship between morality and leadership? There is surprisingly little research on this point. The Goertzels have indicated that twentieth-century politicians tend to be rather more conventional in sexual behavior than are creators of comparable eminence (Goertzel, Goertzel, and Goertzel, 1978). But to find any systematic attempt to gauge the virtuousness of rulers we have to go back to 1906, to *Mental and Moral Heredity in Royalty* by Frederick Woods. In this pioneer work, Woods rated more than six hundred members of royalty on both intelligence and morality. He found that intelligence and morality are moderately correlated ($r = .40$). So if intelligence is pertinent to political accomplishment, then morality may make a positive contribution too. The shrewd ruler may also be an ethical one. Woods's results, however, are open to doubt, because he based his measurements of both intelligence and morality on rather subjective and global ratings, leaving considerable latitude for the introjection of bias. Fortunately, Woods's work was replicated in 1936 by Edward L. Thorndike, one of the most eminent of early American psychologists. Thorndike had several raters assess intelligence and morality on the basis of extensive biographical materials. He also analyzed the various sources of error that might raise or lower this correlation. He concluded that the association between intelligence and morality may actually be stronger than Woods had maintained ($r = .60$). A good example of a ruler with both these qualities is King Gustavus Adolphus, the Swedish military genius of the Thirty Years War, who was among the top three rulers in both intelligence and morality.

I have also replicated Woods's research, this time restricting attention to the 342 ruling monarchs on his list of royalty (Simonton, 1983d). My study, like Thorndike's, demonstrated the basic reliability of Woods's ratings of intellect and virtue. The correlation between these two traits was also substantiated. But I assessed other attributes as well: I measured eminence according to the frequency of appearance in standard histories and reference works (with a reliability coefficient of .90); I adapted leadership scores from another work by Woods (1913); and I measured the length of time a monarch ruled along with the monarch's life span. Contradicting Machiavelli to some degree, the leadership ratings were found to correlate with morality in a positive direction ($r = .28$). Yet I found no relationship whatsoever between morality and a monarch's length of rule, length of life, or ultimate fame in the annals of history. If morality does favor political success, it does so through its connection with intelligence and leadership, character traits that are firmly related to reign span, life span, and eminence.

The absence of an association between morality and eminence requires qualification. In a subsequent study I did find a curvilinear U-shaped relationship between these two attributes (Simonton, 1984b). That is, the most eminent leaders are either those who are models of saintly virtue or those who go down in history as the devil incarnate. Thus the social moralists and the cynical opportunists are both vindicated if the final aim is to achieve historical immortality.

There is another implication of morality for leadership: good tends to nurture good while evil begets evil. I found evidence, for example, that in hereditary monarchies morality is subject to role modeling, as I discussed in Chapter 2. The heir to the throne tends to adopt the ethical standards of the governing parent. I also found modest empirical evidence that those rulers who attain power by violent means tend to fall from power by equally violent means (Simonton, 1984b). The correlation is not strong ($r = .13$), but it is neither zero nor negative. So we can conclude that those who usurp the throne are likely to suffer the same fate as their hapless predecessors.

SUMMARY

Personality is deeply ingrained in the phenomena of creativity and leadership. Intelligence, in particular, has predictive utility. Both an individual's choice of endeavor and the amount of achievement in that endeavor are determined by intellectual ability. Two variables intimately related to intelligence also have predictive value: versatility is generally associated with the achieved eminence of leaders, while intellectual sophistication, or at least the capacity for quick conversion from dogmatism to pragmatism according to circumstance, is linked with the long-term success of revolutionaries. These cognitive influences are supplemented by motivational ones. The passion for achievement is a significant feature of genius, and it may have special relevance for economic growth and prosperity. Furthermore, the need for power is linked with political success. The power motive also determines performance; power-hungry chief executives have a proclivity for interpersonal and also international fighting. Policymakers who prefer dominating rather than egalitarian roles vis-à-vis their subordinates tend to recommend similar roles for the United States vis-à-vis the community of nations. The policymaker's disposition toward extraversion or introversion has an impact as well. The effects of the power motive, dominance, and extraversion may or may not be moderated by ethical considerations. Though morality is correlated with the intellectual and leadership skills of a nation's ruler, a leader can achieve a permanent place in history just as easily by being evil as by being good.

4

EDUCATION

ALBERT EINSTEIN IS often quoted in support of the romantic view that genius is hampered, not nurtured, by traditional education. In Einstein's "Autobiographical Notes," for instance, the following condemnation of educational methods appears: "One had to cram all this stuff into one's mind for the examinations, whether one liked it or not. This coercion had such a deterring effect on me that, after I passed the final examination, I found the consideration of any scientific problems distasteful to me for an entire year" (quoted in Hoffman, 1972, p. 31). And speaking in broader terms, Einstein complained: "It is, in fact, nothing short of a miracle that the modern methods of instruction have not yet entirely strangled the holy curiosity of inquiry; for this delicate little plant, aside from stimulation, stands mostly in need of freedom; without this it goes to wreck and ruin without fail. It is a very grave mistake to think that the enjoyment of seeing and searching can be promoted by means of coercion and a sense of duty" (quoted in Schlipp, 1951, p. 17).

Research on the worth of education tends to be confined to creativity, excluding leadership. But the question of whether education has any role in the development of leadership deserves empirical attention as well. Certain school experiences and opportunities may, as the football coaches would have us believe, "build character"; as the Duke of Wellington asserted, "The battle of Waterloo was won on the playing fields of Eton." Wellington's remark suggests that the constructive aspects of education may be more extracurricular than scholastic. We are very much in the dark about the actual impact of education. It is as easy to cite favorable examples as it is unfavorable ones. In the realm of leadership, the fact that Theodore Roosevelt graduated Phi Beta Kappa from Harvard does not explain why he was such an effective leader in the White House; John Quincy Adams was both a Harvard Phi Beta Kappa and an ineffective chief executive. In contrast,

Franklin D. Roosevelt followed an undistinguished undergraduate career at Harvard with a presidency that revealed the highest capacities for leadership.

This chapter will be devoted to surveying the consequences of education for both creativity and leadership. I will begin with a detailed examination of the relationship between the level of educational attainment and the final amount of creativity or leadership. Then I will investigate the worth of academic honors in the development of genius.

FORMAL TRAINING

Some people proudly display their advanced degrees on their office walls. Others hide the fact that not even a high school diploma carries their name. The common assumption is that those with less formal schooling are less fortunate and less successful. And yet two of the most esteemed American presidents, George Washington and Abraham Lincoln, had less formal education than is usually the case for U.S. chief executives. The great scientist Sir Isaac Newton never went beyond the bachelor's degree. Perhaps the impact of formal education on achievement is neither positive nor negative but rather curvilinear. That is, perhaps the relation can be described by a curvilinear "inverted-U" function (and arch-shaped curve). Some formal education may nurture creative development, but excessive amounts of academic training may inculcate an overcommitment to traditional perspectives and thus stifle originality. If the functional relation is indeed curvilinear rather than linear, the crucial question concerns the location of the optimum point: How much formal education is required to maximize the development of creative potential?

As described in Chapter 3, Catherine Cox (1926) calculated IQ scores for 301 geniuses. In the process Cox gathered extensive data on the educational attainments of these notable personages. I used these data in an investigation of the links between education and achievement (Simonton, 1976a). For each of the 301 subjects I coded the level of formal education according to the following system: 0 points for no formal training of any kind, 1 for high school or its equivalent, 2 for a baccalaureate or equivalent degree, 3 for a master's, and 4 for a doctorate or other professional degree. If a person fell somewhere between two points on the scale, I added half a point to the lower of the two. Thus someone who did not finish college received 1.5 points. This scheme is admittedly crude, but it does capture the conspicuous variation in the formal education received by the 301 geniuses. Hans Christian Oersted, a Danish physicist who discovered electromagnetism, earned a Ph.D.; the great English physicist Michael Faraday, whose portrait was one of just three on the wall of Einstein's study, was obliged to leave school at 14 years of age. Thus in my coding system Faraday earned a mere 0.5 points in comparison to Oersted 4 points on the education scale.

I determined the relationship between formal education and achieved eminence separately for leaders and creators (while controlling for such variables as father's socioeconomic status, intelligence, versatility, life span, year of birth, and data reliability). Figure 1 depicts the outcome. For leaders, fame is a strictly linear and *negative* function of formal educational level. The highest-ranked politicians, generals, admirals, reformers, diplomats, revolutionaries, and religious innovators have the least formal education. Evidently higher education does not contribute much to the development of leadership potential.

The curve for creative eminence is the shape I predicted earlier: a curvilinear inverted-U function. Though a certain amount of formal

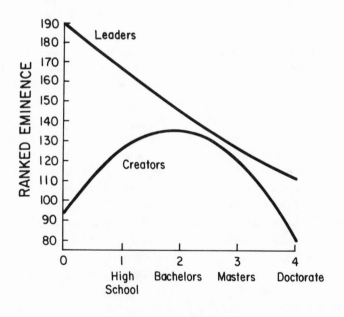

FORMAL EDUCATION

Figure 1. The relationship between formal education and ranked eminence for 109 leaders and 192 creators in the Cox sample (from Simonton, 1981a).

education may enhance the probability of creative achievement, beyond a certain point additional training seems to decrease the chances of attaining eminence. Curiously, creators with doctorates tend to be slightly less eminent than those with little formal education. The peak of the eminence curve falls at 1.85 on the education scale, a value which translates as a college education just shy of a bachelor's degree. That is, the most famous scientists, philosophers, writers, artists, and composers tend to complete their junior but not their senior year of college. Both Edwin Land and R. Buckminster Fuller left Harvard College without obtaining their degrees. Land evidently did not need a bachelor's degree to invent the Polaroid lens, and Fuller similarly managed without one to conceive the geodesic dome.

The details of the functional form, including the specific turn-around point of 1.85, must not be taken too seriously on the basis of one study. But corroboration from a different set of data does suggest that the inverted-U curve is accurate. Several hundred American historians have rated 33 presidents of the United States on seven distinct aspects of political leadership, including idealism and flexibility (Maranell, 1970). A president's idealism is negatively associated with his flexibility in dealing with political affairs. Indeed, a factor analysis reveals a clear-cut bipolar "dogmatism" dimension consisting of idealistic inflexibility at one end and pragmatic flexibility at the other (Wendt and Light, 1976; Simonton, 1981c). It is possible to register differences among the presidents along this dimension by subtracting each president's flexibility rating from his idealism rating. This measure is useful because there is ample evidence that dogmatism and creativity represent opposite ends of a bipolar dimension. In contemporary populations, scores on creativity tests have been shown to be negatively associated with psychometric indicators of authoritarianism (Grossman and Eisenman, 1971), cognitive rigidity (Leach, 1967), and dogmatism (Uhes and Shaver, 1970). Moreover, the general personality characteristics of creative individuals tend to be almost identical to those of persons who are low in dogmatism or authoritarianism (Adorno et al., 1950; Rokeach, 1960; Stein, 1969). Thus the observed relationship between formal education and eminence in creativity will be substantiated if the curve relating dogmatism and education is a mirror reflection of that seen in Figure 1. To verify this expectation I first coded the educational levels of the 33 presidents as follows: 0 points for high school or less, 1 for some college, 2 for a college degree, 3 for a master's degree, and 4 for a Ph.D. (Simonton, 1981c). I then calculated the relationship between this measure of formal education and the dogmatism variables (again controlling for other variables).

The resulting curve, shown in Figure 2, reveals a curvilinear U-shaped relation between formal education and assessed dogmatism. The most dogmatic presidents either have very little formal education or have advanced degrees. Andrew Johnson, who was illiterate until his wife taught him to read and write, and Woodrow Wilson, the only president with a doctorate, are the two most dogmatic chief executives in American history. Johnson's inability to compromise with the Radical Republicans on Reconstruction led to his impeachment; Wilson's comparable intransigence concerning the League of Nations brought him to physical ruin and his party to political defeat. The least dogmatic presidents tend to have a moderate amount of formal education. Thomas Jefferson, who attended college, and Franklin Roosevelt, who graduated, were two of the more flexible chief executives.

The low point on the curve occurs at 1.53. Before comparing this

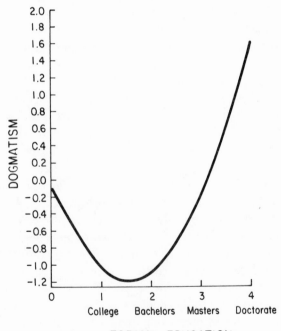

Figure 2. The relationship between formal education and dogmatism of 33 American presidents (from Simonton, 1981a).

figure with the 1.85 in Figure 1 we must adjust for the difference in the two scales. A value of 1.53 in Figure 2 translates into 1.76 in Figure 1, a number strikingly similar to the 1.85 maximum point. The curves for dogmatism and creative eminence as a function of education are mirror reflections of each other. Some college experience short of a bachelor's degree tends to diminish idealistic flexibility, the peak reduction taking place by the close of the junior year. At roughly that same point creative potential is at its height. The first years of college may widen the student's outlook and provide the intellectual tools and knowledge needed for reasoning in a practical, flexible, and creative manner. After the junior year, formal education may begin to reverse this trend in the process of training a more academic, ivory-tower intellect. In support of this interpretation I can cite one additional fact: when the effect of formal education is controlled, those presidents with prior experience as college professors tend to exhibit the most idealistic inflexibility (Simonton, 1981c). John Quincy Adams, once a professor of oratory and rhetoric at Harvard, was one of the more dogmatic presidents, as was Woodrow Wilson, a former professor of jurisprudence and political economy at Princeton.

The near equivalence of the results for the 192 creators and the 33 presidents is significant. The Cox sample is highly heterogenous; the geniuses come from a large assortment of nations, historical periods, and fields of achievement. This diversity has the asset of permitting the curve to be verified over a very broad sample and thus of demonstrating the generalizability of the discovery. Replication for the American chief executives—all born in the same nation within a comparatively short time span, and all engaged in the same ultimate occupation—shows that the effect has specificity as well as generality. Therefore, we should have all the more confidence in the curvilinear function.

The results of these two investigations cannot be taken as broad condemnation of advanced education. At least three critical issues must be addressed before these results can be interpreted with confidence. The first question is whether the effect of formal training is large or small. In the case of creative eminence, approximately 2 percent of the total variation can be specifically accounted for by educational attainment. Though this percentage may sound small, it actually represents a significant proportion of variance. This figure embodies only the unique impact of formal education, excluding any variance that this predictor may share with other variables in the regression equation. So 2 percent may be a lower-bound estimate. It is likely as well that achieved eminence in any creative endeavor is a very complex phenomenon characterized by multiple determinants, some physiological, others psychological, and yet others sociocultural. Say an equation that completely predicts the occurrence of genius has some four dozen predictors, a not unreasonable degree of causal richness. Then the unique contribution of each predictor can only average around 2 percent of the variance in any case. Given the extreme complexity of the phenomenon, moreover, it is unfair to just ask what proportion of the total variance in eminence is explained by education. Much of the variance may be left unaccounted for because of the high unpredictability of the dependent variable. Therefore, the question to ask is what share of the variance actually explained by the total predictive equation is attributable to education. It turns out that in this light formal education accounts for almost 9 percent of the variation. And for presidential dogmatism, about 13 percent of the total (and 23 percent of the predicted) variance can be uniquely attributed to formal educational level. When the sample is more homogeneous in time, place, and occupation, education becomes an even better predictor. The effect of education is not trivial.

A second consideration has to do with the applicability of the curvilinear relationship across various disciplines. It is not unlikely, for example, that artistic and scientific activity may require different amounts of formal education for optimal creative development. Hudson (1966) has indicated that "divergent" thought processes may be more necessary for artistic creativity, "convergent" processes more mandatory for scientific creativity—and traditional educational techniques favor convergent over divergent cognition (Haddon and Lytton, 1968). When we consider the severe complexity and sophistication of modern science, it seems probable that even if the function is curvilinear, the peak is shifted toward higher amounts of formal education. The Goertzels discovered that the scientists in their sample of 314 eminent twentieth-century personalities were much more likely to have graduate degrees (Goertzel, Goertzel, and Goertzel, 1978). But it may be that formal education is conducive to achievement in established areas of science, but not to becoming a truly revolutionary scientist. Einstein did not have good enough grades to go on to graduate school. He was obliged to procure his doctorate not through formal training but rather by submitting one of his (lesser) publications for consideration as a dissertation while he was working full time in a Swiss patent office. Thus truly revolutionary scientists may display curvilinear relationships not unlike those found for artists.

A third question is whether the observed relationship between formal education and creativity is transhistorically invariant. After all, Cox's 301 geniuses come from the fourteenth through nineteenth centuries, before the extensive democratization of higher education. But there are several reasons for accepting the transhistorical invariance of the discovered relationship. To begin with, trend analysis of the formal educational levels achieved by the 301 geniuses reveals no general tendency for the amount of such education to increase over time (Simonton, 1976a). Moreover, the study of presidential dogmatism revealed a mirror-image curve for the antithesis of creativity even though that sample consists of primarily nineteenth- and twentieth-century historical figures. Thus although the average birth dates of subjects in the Cox and president samples are over a century apart, the two studies agree almost perfectly that the turn-around point occurs just after the junior year of college. The function has been valid from Leonardo da Vinci through President Lyndon B. Johnson. In addition, empirical studies of contemporary populations have noted a decline in creativity scores during the college years, especially upon entrance into programs of augmented specialization (Eisenman, 1970; Bednar and Parker, 1965). Finally, the increased complexity and sophistication of a society may require more formal education on the part of its technocrats, but that requirement may nevertheless exert an adverse effect on creativity. In Byzantine society, for example, scholars needed an awesome erudition far surpassing that demanded of their predecessors in the Golden Age of Greece. But unlike ancient Greece, the Byzantine world exhibited very little creativity.

The best way to settle these issues is to conduct another investigation that will (a) sample an even more contemporary group of eminent persons and (b) separate the scientific creators from the other types of creators. Besides dealing with the questions of transhistorical and interdisciplinary invariance, a third study will provide yet another estimate of how much formal education really matters in the emergence of genius.

For this third study, I will use the 314 famous personalities examined by Goertzel, Goertzel, and Goertzel (1978). The average birth year of these persons is 1902, with a range from 1841 to 1948—about a century more contemporary than the presidents study, two centuries more recent than the Cox sample. The eminence of these individuals was defined in terms of the amount of space devoted to each in six reference works. The Goertzels coded educational level in the following fashion: 1 point for eighth grade or less (15 percent of the sample), 2 for some high school (11 percent), 3 for a high school degree (19 percent), 4 for some college (9 percent), 5 for a college degree (19 percent), 6 for some graduate work (4 percent), and 7 for a graduate degree (19 percent). Observe that only about half of the 314 famous persons even went to college; there are more primary and secondary school dropouts than higher degrees among them. The Goertzels grouped their subjects into 20 areas of achievement; I combined their categories into four general domains of achievement so that the effect of education upon eminence could be separately determined for each domain.

The first group consisted of 78 leaders, mostly politicians and government officials with a smattering of military men, reformers, labor leaders, and revolutionaries. Contrary to the negative linear relationships between education and eminence among the Cox sample of leaders, the fame reached by these more recent leaders is predicted by a curvilinear inverted-U function of formal education. The peak of this curve falls at 5.7, or some modest amount of graduate education. This optimum level may suggest only that the most eminent leaders in modern times tend to be lawyers. The discrepancy between this result and that of the Cox sample may imply one of two things. On the one hand, perhaps the transformation from rural to urban life in the last two centuries means that modern leaders need more formal training. On the other hand, it may be far too difficult to evaluate the fame of leaders who are so contemporary. Perhaps as time brings more objectivity into these assessments the functional relation will revert to a linear negative form.

The second group, which has no counterpart in the Cox sample, was made up of 91 miscellaneous people who were neither leaders nor creators in the restricted sense and yet enjoyed some contemporary fame. Many of these individuals are performers of some kind; the rest are athletes, adventurers, businesspersons, editors and publishers, mystics and psychics, and persons who have merely been associated with the eminent at some point in their lives. What all these diverse people have in common is that they are celebrities—a category Cox did not include in her sample because their fame is ephemeral. The eminence attained by these celebrities is a straight linear and positive function of formal education; that is, the more education they have the greater their fame is likely to be. This is the only group in this sample for which the effect of education on eminence is linear.

I divided the creators into two groups: scientific and artistic creators.

The scientists and inventors constituted the smallest group, with only 20 representatives in all. The effect of formal education on scientific eminence is described by a curvilinear (inverted backwards J) relation with the peak occurring at 6.0—meaning some graduate work but no graduate degree. This outcome supports my conjecture that creativity in the scientific enterprise may demand more training than other creative endeavors. Nonetheless, the final attainment of a Ph.D. may not enhance one's prospects of making the grandest scientific contributions.

The remaining group in the Goertzels' sample consisted of 125 eminent creators in the arts and humanities. Two-thirds of these were authors of poetry, fiction, or literary nonfiction, over one-quarter were artists, composers, and film producers, and the rest were philosophers and religious thinkers. Significantly, achieved eminence in this group is a curvilinear (inverted backwards J) function of formal education, the peak appearing at 4.4, that is, between having some college and being a college graduate. In other words, the optimal amount of education for reaching the highest distinction in the arts and humanities falls somewhere between the junior and senior years of college. The concordance of this finding with the two previous studies could hardly be more perfect: this is precisely the same educational attainment of the most famous creators in the Cox study and the least dogmatic U.S. presidents. The only refinement over the two earlier studies is that the present indicator of educational level has more differentiating power on the lower end of the scale. As a consequence, it reveals that individuals with graduate degrees are more likely to achieve success than are persons with only a primary school education.

This replication using the Goertzels' sample shows that the curvilinear relation between creativity and education is in all likelihood transhistorically invariant. It holds across many nationalities and from the Renaissance to the present. Even though the peak point in the curve may differ for some areas of creativity, the curve's shape is very stable. This replication also yields another estimate of the size of the effect of education. Nearly 10 percent of the variation in the eminence of these 314 modern personalities is uniquely accounted for by level of formal education. It is rare in the behavioral sciences for effects of this magnitude to be replicated across such a diversity of disciplines, historical periods, nationalities, and even variable operationalizations. The effects of education cannot be ignored.

The curvilinear relationship appears to be reliable; the next question to ask is why it holds. I have suggested that the development of creative potential may be weakened by excessive formal training. An alternative explanation might be that creative geniuses select their own desired level of training. Perhaps the most securely directed and confident geniuses go to school only until they obtain the required knowledge and technical ability, and then quit. Creators of the highest rank tend to split off from conventional perspectives, and they may discover that higher education does not contribute to goals that lie outside the mainstream. Their less illustrious colleagues, who attain fame not so much by changing the course of history as by advancing it, find that formal education improves their opportunity for achievement. It is important to note that this alternative interpretation does not claim that graduate education is detrimental in any direct way to the development of the highest creative potential, but only that it may be irrelevant. The more impressive intellects simply may not need a doctorate. Einstein wrote to a friend just two years before publishing his paper on special relativity, "I shall not become a Ph.D. . . . the whole comedy has become a bore to me" (quoted in Hoffman, 1972, p. 55).

SCHOLASTIC SUCCESS AND SELF-EDUCATION

Alongside the Ph.D. diploma hanging on the office wall may be an elaborately framed certificate naming the room's occupant as a member of Phi Beta Kappa or another academic honor society. Such a certificate is sometimes viewed as no less crucial to adult success than the diploma. The desire to graduate with honors, to be valedictorian or summa cum laude, accordingly drives high school and college students to vie with each other for the highest grade-point averages. This competition at times reaches an intensity that may undermine the purpose of education. G. H. Hardy firmly believed that the competitive examination for the old Mathematical Tripos, which established who were the prestigious "Wranglers" among Cambridge students, effectively destroyed creative mathematics in England for a century.

There is little evidence to suggest that scholastic success has any impact whatsoever on long-term achievement. Research on contemporary populations indicates that scholastic honors do not predict occupational success (MacKinnon, 1960; Hoyt, 1965). Furthermore, the nonacademic or extracurricular creative accomplishments displayed in school, which often do contribute to eventual success, are uncorrelated with academic potential and achievement (Bednar and Parker, 1965;

Richards, Holland, and Lutz, 1967). For the most part, this picture holds for the eminent as well. The scholastic performance of students at Cambridge bore no connection to whether they attained Doctor of Science degrees or were ultimately elected Fellows of the Royal Society, the highest scientific honor in Great Britain (Hudson, 1958). Only 20 percent of the eminent in the Goertzel sample were honor students, and 8 percent failed. British author D. H. Lawrence, for instance, ranked only thirteenth out of 21 students enrolled in a high school composition class. Not surprisingly, 60 percent of the Goertzel personalities disliked school as compared to the mere 30 percent who were more favorably disposed. Those who got along well in school had the best chance of becoming politicians or scientists, yet even in these endeavors the linkage was far from perfect. According to one of Einstein's most distinguished professors at the Zurich Polytechnic Institute, Hermann Minkowski, "in his student days Einstein had been a lazy dog. He never bothered about mathematics at all." Einstein might not have graduated had he not been befriended by a brilliant classmate, Marcel Grossmann, who took meticulous lecture notes from which Einstein was free to cram for his examinations.

Einstein used his stolen hours of leisure to study, learn, and think about the big unsolved questions of turn-of-the-century physics. His case takes us to the heart of the matter: time spent in pursuit of academic honors is time lost for the acquisition of information and expertise not directly connected to schoolwork. It is time that also cannot be used for profound reflection. Many of the eminent are deeply involved in their own programs of self-education. At least half of the famous persons the Goertzels studied were early voracious readers, and their love of reading continued into adulthood. One study of contemporary creative adolescents found that they tended to read more than 50 books a year (Schaefer and Anastasi, 1968). Being well-read is not superfluous entertainment. By my own calculations, the achieved eminence of those in the Goertzels sample is positively correlated with their being omnivorous readers ($r = .12$).

This connection is not surprising. Research on the creative personality often points to the importance of wide interests, a breadth of perspective, and a need for novelty, diversity, and complexity (Stein, 1969). Innovation depends on the ability to see relationships between hitherto unconnected ideas or methods and then to fuse them into a new synthesis (Barnett, 1953; Koestler, 1964). Newton combined the latest developments in mathematics, Galilean mechanics, and Keplerian astronomy into a single wide-ranging synthesis. Similarly, Einstein, to effect the integration that became known as the special theory of relativity, had to immerse himself in two supposedly unrelated topics: Maxwellian electromagnetic theory and Newtonian mechanics. It was typical for Einstein to attempt to merge what other physicists of his day considered utterly disparate subdisciplines.

There of course are numerous first-class geniuses who got excellent grades and academic honors without apparently sacrificing their creative potential. Marie Curie was a couple of years ahead of her elementary school classmates in all subjects and received a gold medal at 16 upon graduation from the Russian lycée. Sigmund Freud was at the head of his class at the gymnasium and graduated summa cum laude. J. Robert Oppenheimer graduated summa cum laude from Harvard with the highest honors ever awarded an undergraduate. Clearly, academic and extracurricular knowledge acquisition are not necessarily inconsistent.

In the so-called hard sciences, such as physics or chemistry, the kind of education received at the college level is still very broad in scope. These sciences are so richly endowed with basic knowledge that the frontiers of the discipline are not usually glimpsed until the seminar blackboards of graduate school. It makes sense, therefore, that the peak for creative development in the sciences falls somewhere in the midst of graduate education. In other disciplines, such as the arts and humanities, the fork in the road occurs much earlier in the educational sequence. The process of just obtaining a bachelor's degree may squelch the development of creative potential in such fields.

It is also important to keep in mind the distinction I made earlier between revolutionizing a field and merely advancing it. Revolutionaries are likely to find much sooner than advancers that formal education has become tangential to their adopted course. Oppenheimer was a far better student than Einstein, but it was Einstein who transformed the field of physics.

It is possible that the greater the intellectual genius a person possesses, the more likely it is that he or she can burn the mental candles at both ends without jeopardy. After all, a genius is a person who can master more things in less time than those with less awesome capacities. Presumably it is this versatile quickness of grasp that makes possible both the childhood precociousness mentioned in the preceding chapter and the phenomenal adulthood productivity I will treat in the next chapter. Hence, the more brilliant an intellect is the more successfully that mind can juggle scholastic honors on the one hand and stimulating self-education on the other. Naturally, as an individual ascends the educational ladder, this juggling act becomes ever more difficult; at each educational level one's classmates come from more selective intellectual groups, and the competition becomes fiercer. Sooner or later a student is forced to choose either to relinquish the self-directed pursuit of general proficiency or else to abandon hope of academic rewards.

This choice is a crucial one. A student who subordinates everything to the goal of academic success may forfeit any chance of becoming a truly revolutionary innovator. But the alternative route is no safer: dropping out of the academic rat-race to concentrate on a self-ordained program of intellectual growth will not automatically allow one to become the hoped-for revolutionary. The fate might be to become neither revolutionary nor even advancer, but rather a noncontributor. A certain minimal competence is demanded in any endeavor, and that competence may have to be gained through formal training. The days are probably far over when a person as unschooled as Faraday can hope to make fundamental contributions to physics.

We are now in a position to understand why creativity in various disciplines may require different grades of intellect. The physical sciences tend to attract those with the highest IQs, the biological sciences those with somewhat less Olympian minds, and the social sciences those with still lower IQs (Roe, 1952; Harmon, 1961). The complex body of knowledge in the physical sciences requires intelligence of a very high order just to master the essentials. Even more intelligence is required if room is to be left over for the general self-instruction and reflection that nurture a revolutionary approach to problems. The accumulated erudition in the social sciences is far less demanding on the intellect. Consequently, one may not have to be as bright to make revolutionary contributions to the social sciences, and even less intelligence may be required to advance social scientific knowledge in already established directions. Thus it is not utterly preposterous to suggest that Einstein and Oppenheimer may have been equally bright and that both were the intellectual superiors of Freud. Both Einstein and Freud were revolutionaries, but Freud revolutionized a field that requires less intrinsic intelligence. Oppenheimer may have surpassed Freud in raw brain power, but the field of physics demands more, so Freud is a revolutionary, Oppenheimer only an advancer. Finally, even though Einstein and Oppenheimer may be equal in native genius, Oppenheimer used his to attain uncommon distinction from a first-rate university, Einstein to go his own deliberately original way.

The integrated, multivariable perspective I have outlined in this chapter compels the utmost caution when judging the value of higher education in the development of creative potential. To be sure, the evidence is strong that the relation between fame and education fits a curvilinear inverted-U form and that academic honors do not guarantee ultimate success. Even so, degrees and honors are not the sole parameters in the equation. A person's intrinsic intellectual power, the informational and technological richness of the discipline, even its ripeness for revolution as opposed to simple advancement—all these things must be weighed too. It is certainly possible for a person to graduate with honors, obtain a doctorate, and then proceed to revolutionize a field. Max Planck did. Awarded his doctorate summa cum laude when just 21 years old, Planck went on to revolutionize physics by inventing quantum theory. Einstein's disparaging remarks about education cannot be said to have universal applicability.

5

PRODUCTIVITY
AND INFLUENCE

THOMAS EDISON HELD 1,093 patents, which remains the record number granted by the United States Patent Office. Albert Einstein had 248 publications to his credit, Charles Darwin 119, and, within psychology, Sigmund Freud 330, Alfred Binet 277, and Francis Galton 227. Mozart had well over 600 compositions to his credit before dying at age 35, and Schubert composed more than 500 works before succumbing to typhus at 31. Bach's extant compositions, numbering over a thousand, fill 46 volumes. Bach averaged 20 pages of finished music per day, reportedly enough to occupy a copyist, working standard business hours, a lifetime just to write out the parts by hand. Such prodigious output recalls Thomas Edison's famous remark: "Genius is one percent inspiration and ninety-nine percent perspiration." The pen, the paintbrush, or the chisel never seems to rest. Rembrandt produced around 650 paintings, 300 etchings, and 2,000 drawings, and Picasso executed more than 20,000 works.

The focus of this chapter is an analysis of this phenomenal productivity and its links with eminence. Much of the discussion must concentrate on creativity rather than leadership, but some parallels can be drawn between creative productivity and the influence of leaders.

CREATIVE INEQUALITY

If a leader is one whose imprint on the group exceeds that of most group members, then certainly some creators are leaders within their own cultural realms. Wayne Dennis (1955) examined the distribution of productivity in seven fields: eighteenth-century American secular music, books in the Library of Congress as of 1942, gerontology and geriatrics, North American geology from 1929 to 1939, research on infantile paralysis from 1789 to 1944, chemists in the *Chemical Abstracts* for 1937 to 1947, and linguistic research from 1939 to 1947. Dennis determined the number of works contributed by each of 200 creators who were randomly selected from each field. In early American music he found that 64 percent of all works were created by the 10 percent who were the most productive. The single most productive composer, in fact, was responsible for 11 percent of all compositions, producing a total of 146 works during his career. In dramatic contrast, about 46 percent of these composers produced only one item each. Though the results are less skewed for the other six fields, inequality in productivity is nonetheless very pronounced. In the least skewed discipline, linguistics, the most prolific 10 percent of the researchers account for 34 percent of all published research, the top producer alone accounted for 5 percent of the total, and 71 percent of the contributors made only one contribution each. Across all seven fields, 10 percent of the creative workers contributed roughly 50 percent of all the work, 61 percent of the contributors made only one contribution each, and the single most prolific creator in each discipline is credited with 9 percent of the total. The most prolific creator in a given field tends to be 57 times as productive as the least productive creators. This unequal distribution of productivity also holds for psychology, as Dennis showed in another study (1954c). Ten percent of the psychologists publish between 37 and 47 percent of the total psychological research, whereas the least productive 50 percent contribute 15 percent or less of the total literature. Thus, the 10 percent in the productive elite turn out two or three times as much work as the 50 percent in the lower echelons of psychological creativity. Dennis points out that in fact his figures probably overestimate the contribution of the least active producers. Only those members of a discipline who published *something* were included in the analysis. Untold numbers of psychologists, linguists, geologists, and other professionals may have made no contribution whatsoever to the published literature.

Other researchers besides Dennis have observed the ultra-elite status of the top producers in a given endeavor. Moles (1958) reported that even though the number of classical composers runs into the thousands, only 250 are responsible for the pieces that are performed regularly in the concert or recital hall. A mere 36 composers account for three-quarters of all works performed, and just 16 provide half of all music listening. The top 10 composers give us 40 percent of the masterworks, while the top three composers—Mozart, Beethoven, and Bach—offer about 6 percent each or almost 20 percent taken together. In sum, fewer than 1 percent of the composers with extant compositions provide most of the classical repertoire.

This highly skewed distribution of creative contributions has been formulated as a social scientific law. Alfred James Lotka (1926), the father of demographic analysis (and the author of 95 technical papers and 6 books), formulated a principle that has become known as Lotka's law. According to this law, the number of scientists publishing exactly n papers is roughly proportional to $\frac{1}{n^2}$, where the proportionality constant varies with the discipline. Suppose, for illustrative purposes, that this constant equaled ten thousand: then the number of scientists producing exactly n contributions would be $\frac{10^4}{n^2}$. Then the number of scientists contributing only one publication each would be 10,000, two publications 2,500, three publications 1111, and 10 publications 100. Only one scientist would contribute as many as 100 papers. Lotka's law is remarkably similar to Pareto's law of income distribution (Price, 1963), by which cumulative figures for personal earnings, as assessed in several nations over a long period of time, tend to be proportional to $\frac{1}{n^{1.5}}$. It is this highly skewed distribution of wealth that permits a tiny percentage of the population in any economy to command an overwhelmingly disproportionate chunk of the economic power. There exists a provocative isomorphism between cultural creativity and economic leadership such that the intellectual hegemony of an Einstein compares with the material monopoly of a Rockefeller.

The accuracy of Lotka's law is high, but it does not fit the empirical facts perfectly. Such discrepancies have led several investigators to propose more refined formulations. One interesting alternative, formulated by Price (1963), is far simpler than Lotka's law, and thus a bit cruder, but nonetheless has considerable didactic value. According to Price's law, half of all scientific contributions are made by the square root of the total number of scientific contributors: thus, if there are 100 scientists within a given discipline, just 10 of them will account for 50 percent of all publications. Although both Price's and Lotka's laws were originally conceived as applying to scientific productivity, these principles probably apply to creative endeavors in the arts as well. Dennis (1955) found, for example, that the top 20 most prolific authors of books in the Library of Congress accounted for 53 percent of the catalogue listings; Price's law predicts that the top 14 most prolific authors would provide 50 percent. Returning to the Moles data on classical composers, if there are 250 contributors to the repertoire, then by Price's law $\sqrt{250}$, or 15.8, should be responsible for half of the music performed—a prediction in almost perfect concordance with the actual number of 16. Add to this interdisciplinary confirmation the fact that these principles of creative productivity hold for many nations and for several historical periods, and the conclusion must be that these are truly nomothetic rules. The inequality of productivity revealed in the highly skewed distribution of creative output is an undeniable law of historiometry.

QUANTITY AND QUALITY

Arthur Cayley was surely one of the most prolific mathematicians of all time, averaging a paper every two or three weeks for a total lifetime output of 995 publications. Henri Poincaré, by comparison, published "only" 500 papers and 30 books. But we cannot conclude that Cayley was almost twice as creative as Poincaré. Though Cayley's prodigious output was wide-ranging and significant—developing among other things the matrix algebra that is so central to quantum mechanics and multivariate statistics—Poincaré is judged by posterity to have had a greater overall influence on mathematics and allied endeavors. Bernard Riemann, the great nineteenth-century German mathematician, postulated one of the first non-Euclidean geometries, creating ideas that were drawn upon by Einstein to produce the general theory of relativity. And yet Riemann has only 19 contributions in his bibliography. Are we then to infer that Riemann is only one-fiftieth as creative as Cayley and around one-quarter as creative as Poincaré? What is the relation between quantity and quality?

Dennis (1954a) conducted one of the earliest studies to respond to such questions. He began by determining the lifetime productivity of American scientists eminent enough to have been elected to the National Academy of Sciences. Taking only those who had reached the age of 70 and thus had a full career, Dennis found that the least productive member had 27 bibliographic items and the most productive 768. The average was 203 works, only 36 percent having made fewer than 100 contributions, 27 percent having made at least 300. For comparison with this elite group, Dennis took a second sample of scientists from the *Catalog of Scientific Literature 1800-1900* published by the Royal Society of London. The productivity of this second sample ranged from 1 to 458 publications, a full 30 percent having only 1 publication each and 50 percent having fewer than 7 publications each. In fact, only 25 percent of the sample was as productive as Riemann, whose output is one of the lowest among eminent scientists. Dennis checked which members of this sample were honored with an entry in the *Encyclopaedia Britannica,* a distinction not easily attained. The most productive 10 percent, each of whom contributed

81

more than 50 publications, had about a 50-50 chance of being listed in the *Britannica,* whereas for the other 90 percent the probability of inclusion was only around 3 percent. This stark difference converts to a correlation coefficient of .46 between being in the top decile in productive rank and being acclaimed by posterity about a half-century later (Simonton, 1981b). Hence quality, as measured by eminence, is linked with quantity of output.

To be sure, the correlation is not perfect; exceptions exist to the general tendency. Dennis noted some instances. Gregor Mendel, one of the most famous of all nineteenth-century biologists, published only 7 scientific papers. This figure would place him just barely in the upper 50 percent of the sample, and certainly not in the top 10 percent. But Dennis indicates that Mendel's case is truly a rare exception. Of the more than 13,000 scientists in the Royal Society catalog with 7 or fewer contributions, not one has achieved fame approaching Mendel's. Then there is John Edward Gray, an English naturalist, who has 883 publications listed in the catalog, but whose name Dennis could not locate in any history of biology or in the *Encyclopaedia Britannica.* Gray is not an utterly obscure personage; I found him in the *World Who's Who in Science* (1968). For a biologist who died in 1875 to appear in a standard reference work almost a century later is no distinction to be spurned. When all is said and done, the exceptions to the rule do not undermine its validity.

Dennis's work on the relation between quality and quantity has been corroborated by other researchers. Zuckerman (1977) has shown that American recipients of the Nobel Prize for scientific achievement tend to publish twice as many papers as a matched sample drawn from *American Men of Science,* a group that cannot be said to consist of nonentities. Other investigators have found a high correlation between the number of publications and the number of citations received in the professional literature, the latter index correlating very highly with scientific eminence (see, for example, Ashton and Oppenheim, 1978; Myers, 1970). In psychology, for instance, the number of citations has a very high correlation ($r = .67$) with the eminence rankings provided by a panel of experts (Clark, 1957), and the citation count has a respectably high correlation ($r = .47$) with the number of publications (Helmreich et al., 1980). Furthermore, even though most of this research has been conducted in the area of scientific creativity, comparable results hold for artistic creativity. I have found the best predictor of the differential eminence of 696 composers to be melodic productivity

(β = .56) (Simonton, 1977b). It is clear that productivity is a major factor, even if not the sole one, in the attainment of eminence.

This demonstrated connection between quantity and quality is consistent with a "constant probability of success" model of creative productivity. Perhaps the odds that any single contribution will prove successful are constant across all creators and so those creators who are most likely to produce a masterpiece are precisely those who produce more works altogether. As W. H. Auden once observed, since major poets are so prolific, "The chances are that, in the course of his lifetime, the major poet will write more bad poems than the minor" (quoted in Bennett, 1980, p. 15). Or as Dennis more formally conjectured in the realm of science, "the correlation between fame and fecundity may be understood in part in terms of the proposition that the greater the number of pieces of scientific work done by a given man, the greater the likelihood that one or more of them will prove to be important . . . Other things being equal, the greater the number of researches, the greater the likelihood of making an important discovery that will make the finder famous" (1954c, p. 182).

This model is theoretically compatible with Campbell's (1960) blind-variation and selective-retention model of creative thought. According to Campbell, the course of cultural evolution is analogous to that of biological evolution. The "cultural fitness" of an individual creator is dependent upon his or her ability to generate big ideas, each representing a certain permutation of smaller ideas. The more permutations that are generated, the higher the odds that a particular permutation will survive the winnowing process imposed by posterity. A less prolific creator will simply have a lower chance of leaving intellectual progeny that will endure this selection process. This model clearly predicts that quality is a probabilistic consequence of quantity and thus provides a theoretical framework for the constant probability of success model.

PRECOCIOUSNESS, PRODUCTIVITY RATES, AND LONGEVITY

So far I have concentrated exclusively on total lifetime output. Obviously the phenomenon of creative productivity is much more complicated than this. At least three separate components directly contribute to lifetime productivity (Simonton, 1977b). In the first place, it is a great boon if a creator begins producing very early in life. Secondly, to reach an impressive lifetime total the creator must have a high average annual rate of productivity. Thirdly, it helps to have a long career in which creativity persists into old age.

The productive precociousness of genius is legendary. Mozart began composing at age 6, Pascal wrote an original paper on conic sections at 16 or 17, Galileo discovered the isochronism of the pendulum at 17, Freud published his first professional paper at 21, both Darwin and Einstein began to publish at 22. One investigation of nineteenth-century creators—personages like Balzac, Faraday, Goethe, Gauss, Maxwell, Pasteur, and Tolstoy—found that the *average* age for first publication was between 24 and 25 (Raskin, 1936). And in the twentieth century, American Nobel laureates in science averaged more than a dozen publications before their thirtieth year, about four times as many as scientists in general contribute in an entire lifetime; such laureates also published almost twice as much in their twenties as did a matched sample of colleagues drawn from *American Men of Science* (Zuckerman, 1977). And the psychologists who have been awarded the Distinguished Scientific Contribution Award by the American Psychological Association first published, on the average, at around age 25 (Albert, 1975).

Dennis (1956) calculated the correlation between early productivity and later productivity for 156 eminent scientists sampled from *Webster's New International Encyclopedia.* He first tabulated the number of scientific publications appearing each decade of life. About 38 percent of these distinguished scientists began making contributions before age 25, and the average number of contributions made in the twenties by all 156 scientists is about 8. More significantly, Dennis found that the number of publications in this first decade of the productive career correlated .57 with productivity in the thirties, .46 with that in the forties and fifties, .35 with that in the sixties, and .33 with that in the seventies. Thus, productive precociousness allows us to anticipate a continual productive output throughout a creator's career. It is invalid to suppose that those who begin the creative spark early will burn out early (Dennis, 1954b).

The productivity rate among eminent geniuses is also proverbial. Darwin averaged over two publications per year, Einstein almost four, Freud over seven, and Poincaré almost 16. In the arts, Schubert averaged over 30 compositions per year, Mozart over 20, and Picasso well over 200. Bertrand Russell normally composed around 3,000 words a day. American recipients of a Nobel prize for scientific creativity published an average of 3.24 papers per year in comparison to the

1.48 papers per year published by the matched comparison sample (Zuckerman, 1977). And psychologists who received the Distinguished Scientific Contribution Award averaged around 2.9 publications per year (Albert, 1975). In Dennis's sample of 156 scientists the average annual productivity rate exceeded two contributions per year, and in my examination of the 696 composers who contributed to the classical repertoire the average productivity rate surpassed two notable melodies a year (Simonton, 1977b).

This prodigious rate of output helps make it possible for a creator to attain the highest eminence despite an early death. Poets like Keats and Shelley, who died in their twenties, are examples. Indeed, when a high productivity rate is coupled with productive precociousness, a genius may die at an extremely early age and still leave an impression upon world civilization.

The third component of lifetime output is productive longevity. Bach, age 65, dictated his last composition on his deathbed; Buffon was still adding new volumes to his *Histoire naturelle* when he died in his eighties; Cervantes completed the second part of *Don Quixote* at 68; Benjamin Franklin invented bifocals to improve the poor eyesight he suffered at 78; Michelangelo was still chipping away at his *Rondanini Pietà* just six days before he died at 89; and Wilhelm Wundt, the founder of experimental psychology, finished the last revision of his voluminous *Völkerpsychologie* at almost 90 years of age.

The persistence of productivity even in the final years of a great creator's life, coupled with the tendency toward productive precociousness, implies that eminence may be associated with a long creative career. One study of eminent scientists and literary figures of the nineteenth century found that productive careers averaged around three decades (Raskin, 1936). Nothing prevents creativity from spanning even a half-century or more, as can be witnessed in the lengthy careers of Darwin and Einstein, Kant and Russell, Voltaire and Tolstoy, Handel and Verdi, Michelangelo and Picasso. Jean Piaget, the distinguished Swiss psychologist and developmental epistemologist, made his first scientific contribution at age 11 and was still productive some 60 years later. When Piaget received the Distinguished Scientific Contribution Award at the record age of 73 he had about 300 publications to his credit.

Given that the most eminent creators tend to begin their careers early, end their careers late, and produce at impressive annual rates, it should come as no surprise that eminence is strongly linked with a vast lifetime output. But what *is* surprising is that these three components of total productivity are themselves so highly correlated. There is no mathematical reason that precociousness has to be associated with either an exceptional rate of output or a career extended well into old age, nor is there any logical necessity for contribution rate to be connected with longevity. Yet all these factors are intimately related in empirical fact (Albert, 1975; Simonton, 1977b). Something appears to drive these creators to venture into the world of truth or beauty at an early age, to contribute masterworks at a hectic pace, and to continue their creative endeavors until late in life.

CUMULATIVE ADVANTAGE

Imagine a hypothetical situation where there are 100 potential creators all desiring to make a contribution to science. Assume that all 100 are of equal intellectual ability and scholastic accomplishment. All of them simultaneously submit research based on their doctoral dissertations for consideration by the editor of the most prestigious scientific journal in their field, a publication so selective that it rejects 90 percent of all manuscripts submitted. Even if all 100 manuscripts are roughly equal in quality, only 10 will be accepted and 90 will be rejected. This does not mean that the 90 will not be published elsewhere, but these rejected papers will receive less recognition than the 10 that appear in the most influential journal in the discipline. Hence, 10 young scientists are encouraged, 90 discouraged. The former group will then have a high probability of submitting later manuscripts with confidence that they will be well received at the editor's desk. Many of the less fortunate aspirants, in contrast, may despair of breaking into this top journal. Suppose that 100 percent of the privileged 10 submit a second manuscript to the top journal, but that only 50 percent of the unlucky 90 do so. The 10 submissions from the first group will have a higher probability of acceptance than the 45 submissions from the second group. The editor, after all, has already committed the journal to the publication of papers coming from the research programs of the first group. Perhaps 5 out of the successful 10 will find their second submissions accepted while only three out of the unsuccessful but persistent 45 will prove so fortunate. The twice-victorious 5 will be even more encouraged and the probability of acceptance of their subsequent manuscripts will be heightened, whereas the 42 two-time failures will be even more discouraged and any editorial prejudice against their third attempts more magnified.

As this process continues year after year, the differential between the well-published and the rejected will enlarge. Moreover, the more prolific contributors will begin to accrue other awards from their visibility in the most respected journals of the discipline: teaching appointments, funding, professional honors and awards. Advantage will accumulate for an elite group of initially successful scientists. And the expanding gap between them and their unsuccessful colleagues is especially poignant because it does not necessarily reflect any real disparity in merit when the original 100 first began to stalk elusive fame. All 100 aspirants may have begun the winnowing process with the same native ability and motivation; the inequality in accomplishment nonetheless expands because of the extreme selectivity of the reward system of science.

The distinguished sociologist Robert K. Merton first described this process and christened it "the Matthew effect" after a passage in the Gospel According to St. Matthew (25:29): "Unto every one that hath shall be given, and he shall have abundance: but from him that hath not shall be taken away even that which he hath." As Merton put it, "the Matthew effect consists in the accruing of greater increments of recognition for particular scientific contributions to scientists of considerable repute and the withholding of such recognition from scientists who have not yet made their mark" (1968, p. 58). When we take publication in the best professional journals as an index of scientific recognition, there is appreciable evidence in support of this effect. For example, several researchers have shown that the concept of cumulative advantage, when expressed in mathematical form, predicts the highly skewed distribution of lifetime productivity that is empirically observed (Simon, 1955; Price, 1976; Allison, 1980). The principle of cumulative advantage also may explain the empirical relationship among productive precociousness, productivity rate, and productive longevity. Those who manage to publish early will begin receiving further incentives early as well, acquiring more motivation for output and increased justification for achievement late in life. A primary cause of the differential in lifetime productivity is the large dropout rate among the less successful scientists (Allison and Stewart, 1974). The more prolific end up in universities that are more supportive of research in terms of teaching load and laboratory resources, and researchers from prestigious research-oriented universities tend to receive disproportionate credit relative to the actual merit of their work (Crane, 1965; Cole and Cole, 1973).

The Matthew effect, while pervasive in its influence, cannot provide the exclusive explanation of the differences in productivity. One mathematical model predicated on the principle of cumulative advantage suggests, not surprisingly, that not all creators start out at the same point in the race to eminence (Allison, 1980). Yet the Matthew effect does explain why two creators who commence their careers with absolutely equivalent skill and drive may end the grueling marathon miles apart.

LIFE SPAN

Judging from what has been said up to this point, a primary determinant of fame should be how long a creator lives. Eminence is a probabilistic consequence of prolific productivity, which is a function of productive precociousness, an impressive rate of output, and productive longevity. This last contributing component must be related to life span. Bernard Riemann surely would have published more than 19 papers had he lived past 40, and Arthur Cayley would have had fewer than 995 publications had he died at 30 years instead of at 73. And other factors may be brought into play when a creator lives a long life. The average age at which scientists receive the Nobel Prize is in the early fifties (Zuckerman, 1977), that at which psychologists receive the Distinguished Scientific Contribution Award the mid-fifties (Albert, 1975). While it is not unheard of for such honors to be bestowed upon younger scientists—the discoverer of the positron, Carl Anderson, became a Nobel laureate at just 31 years of age—the norm is to wait until a scientist passes the half-century mark. Consequently, those of premature mortality seldom have the opportunity to accumulate a list of honors and awards.

And yet the relationship between life span and influence is by no means simple. In my study of 696 classical composers I found that biological longevity had no linear correlation with eminence and only a modest effect upon creative longevity ($\beta = .25$) (Simonton, 1977b). There is something more to life span than just its relation to productivity and the receipt of contemporary kudos. Perhaps the association between life span and achieved eminence is curvilinear rather than linear. To be sure, a longer life implies more creative products and more honors, yet a short temporal existence can have its incentives too. It may be that posterity gives a sort of sympathy vote to creators who are struck down in their youth, and tends to overrate their accomplishments. It is dangerous to base eulogies upon potential rather than actual productivity, of course, since some creators run out of steam after an impressive early start. An example is Pietro Mascagni, who composed the popular opera *Cavallieria Rusticana* when he was only 26 and almost at once became famous. Mascagni never came close to duplicating the success of his first work. His creative output represented one continual decline, though he kept composing into his seventies. Mascagni himself lamented, "It is a pity I wrote Cavallieria first, for I was crowned before I became king." If Mascagni had died on the eve of his masterwork's premiere, his reputation might be much higher today. Perhaps he, and not Puccini, would have been proclaimed as the successor to Verdi.

These considerations lead to the hypothesis that a tragic early death may magnify a creator's impact far out of proportion to that creator's objective contribution. To test this hypothesis I returned to the 301 geniuses of the Cox (1926) sample. Again separating the leaders from the creators, I estimated the functional relationship between ranked eminence and life span (Simonton, 1976a). The outcome is exhibited in Figure 3. Notice that the achieved eminence of creators is a curvilinear U-shaped function of longevity. The most famous creators are

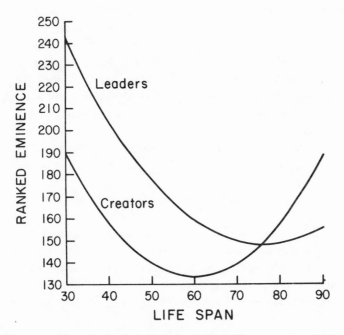

Figure 3. The relationship between achieved eminence and life span for the 301 geniuses of the Cox sample.

those who either died tragically in their thirties or lived to become octagenarians. The low point on the graph is at 60 years of age. Death at such a middling age comes too late to provoke a sense of tragic loss, and yet too early to allow the creator to become a living legend of artistic or scientific greatness. It would be unwise to extrapolate this curve too far, especially in the direction of shorter life spans. The curve shown in the graph is calculated for 192 creators who actually attained eminence for some aesthetic or scientific contribution to world culture. Contributions of lasting value are nearly impossible to make before age 20.

The second curve presented in Figure 3 shows the functional connection between life span and achieved eminence for the 109 leaders in the Cox sample. This curve is curvilinear like that for creators, but with one notable difference: the curve is dominated by an overall negative relationship. All in all, leaders are accorded more fame by posterity if they die young. Such leaders are likely to be glorified beyond what their contributions would warrant. Joan of Arc was still a teenager when she died at the stake. Our assessment of the presidency of John F. Kennedy may well be biased by his having been assassinated in his prime.

The major historiometric lesson to be gleaned from Figure 3 is that the attainment of eminence involves much more than the accumulation of accomplishments. Not only productivity but also the context of that productivity determines ultimate historical influence. Posterity's evaluation of a precocious work partially depends on whether the work's creator dies young. If the creator is long-lived, that early work may diminish in significance and be branded a piece of juvenilia of no more than biographical interest. But if the work is one of the last of a youthful genius whose career was nipped in the bud, it acquires an expanded significance as a certificate of achievement and not just promise.

LEADERSHIP AND INFLUENCE

Since a leader's historical impact does not directly depend on total lifetime productivity as is the case for creators, a brief life span has different repercussions for leaders. Much of this discussion of productivity may have no direct bearing upon our understanding of eminent leaders. Nonetheless, some of the results mentioned earlier may have analogues for leadership.

Let us first of all look at the highly skewed distribution of productivity in creative endeavors. Does the influence of leaders exhibit a similarly skewed distribution? I have already indicated that according to Pareto's law the distribution of wealth, which underlies economic power, follows this pattern. This same near monopoly of influence may be granted other types of leaders. When we call some historical figure a great reformer, it is likely that we are implicitly recognizing a highly lopsided distribution of reforms such that a small number of reformers account for a large number of political innovations. It may be that an elite 10 percent of all lawmakers are responsible for half of all new laws. Napoleon fought more battles than probably any other general in history. Lotka's and Price's laws may apply to the distribution of any reasonable index of leader influence or power, whether it be reforms, laws, or battles fought.

Precociousness, productivity rate, and creative longevity may be pertinent for leadership as well as for creativity. Napoleon first had an impact upon military history in the defeat of the British at the French naval base in Toulon in 1793, when he was an artillery captain only 24 years old. At 27 he was given his first major command, and before he was 30 he had won a remarkable series of great battles such as the Lodi bridge, Arcole, and the Pyramids. Alexander the Great began his conquests in his early twenties and conquered virtually all of the civilized portions of the Western world before he died at 33. And it is not just the precociousness these two leaders exhibited that is so exceptional, but the pace of their conquests as well. The rate at which Napoleon altered the face of Europe and the speed with which Alexander took over the massive Persian Empire rival the productivity rates of any creative genius. As for productive longevity, we might have to look at other examples than these two conquerors. And yet, although much has been made of the meteoric brevity of Alexander's career, he reigned over Macedonia for a dozen years, far longer than the average reign of Roman emperors (Sorokin, 1926). Research is needed to reveal whether productive longevity has the same effect on eminence for leaders as for creators, or whether, like biological longevity, it traces a different type of curve in the realm of leadership.

Last of all, it seems quite likely that the principle of cumulative advantage applies to leadership as well as to creativity. In Chapter 8 we will see that one of the chief predictors of tactical victory on the battlefield is the comparative length of the winning streaks of the generals leading the two opposing armies. Military success tends to encourage further successes; failure ushers in further failures. In politics generally, success brings power, and "the rich get richer and the poor get poorer" in overt power. In U.S. presidential election years, much is made of the advantage an incumbent president has over challengers. The attainment of a supreme power position usually follows a long series of mostly victorious elections and appointments, and at each step in this process there must be losers who drop out in discouragement. Thus the Matthew effect functions to create a small group of eminent leaders. In leadership, as in creative endeavors, an elite few accumulate more and more influence and power, and humanity is progressively stratified into the eminent, the also-rans, and the anonymous multitudes.

6

AGE AND ACHIEVEMENT

SHAKESPEARE WAS IN HIS late thirties and early forties when he wrote *Hamlet, King Lear, Othello,* and *Macbeth.* Tolstoy was 38 when he published *War and Peace.* Michelangelo completed the Sistine Chapel at age 37, Newton his *Principia* at 45, and Beethoven his Fifth Symphony at 37. Examples such as these have led many behavioral scientists to surmise that the fortieth year marks the high point—the Latin *floruit* or Greek *acme*—of a creative career. Yet it is just as easy to cite creators whose peak productive age occurred long before or after age 40. Einstein was 26 when he published his revolutionary papers on the photoelectric effect and the special theory of relativity, and Rossini was 23 when he wrote perhaps the finest comic opera ever written, *The Barber of Seville.* Kant published his *Critique of Pure Reason* when he was 57, about the same age at which Copernicus completed his *Revolution of the Heavenly Spheres.* My purpose in this chapter is to go beyond the mere citation of example and counterexample in order to unearth any nomothetic principles regarding the relation between age and peak achievement. I will begin by detailing the existing empirical results concerning the functional relation between age and achievement. Afterward I will review some theoretical explanations for the observed relationships.

EMPIRICAL RESULTS

Harvey C. Lehman's *Age and Achievement* (1953) must constitute the starting point for any treatment of the longitudinal fluctuations in creativity. Lehman put together the fruits of nearly 20 years of empirical labors. He not only established some of the chief empirical findings but additionally set out the principal substantive questions that have occupied subsequent researchers. Hence, my review of the results regarding the relation between age and achievement will pursue largely the same topics as did Lehman, the task being mostly to bring Lehman's book up to date. I will start by scrutinizing the specific age curve characteristic of creative contribution, then I will examine the connection between quality and quantity of creative output across the years. Next will come a discussion of how the age function varies from discipline to discipline, a subject related to the final topic of the relevance of age for achievement among leaders.

THE AGE CURVE

George Beard (1874) studied the biographies of more than a thousand eminent persons to ascertain at what ages they made their major contributions to history. Beard assigned metaphorical labels to the decades of life: 20 to 30 is the brazen decade, 30 to 40 the golden, 40 to 50 the silver, 50 to 60 the iron, 60 to 70 the tin, and 70 to 80 the wooden. Beard found that 70 percent of the world's best work is accomplished by persons under 45 years of age and 80 percent of it by those under 50. The absolute peak period of a career seems to fall between 30 and 45, though the half-decade from 35 to 40 is more productive than that from 40 to 45. On the average, moreover, the last score years of life tend to be unproductive. Thus, according to Beard, achievement tends to increase rapidly up to a peak just before age 40 and then decline very slowly to almost nothing by age 80.

Almost eighty years after Beard, Lehman (1953) published his own conclusions on this subject, this time with a much more systematic, objective, and quantitative approach to the biographical data. Lehman presented an impressive series of tabulations giving counts of major creative contributions as a function of age. For example, Lehman investigated the ages at which the world's greatest philosophers produced their most frequently cited contributions. The years of maximum productivity tend to fall between 35 and 39, and the average age for producing a philosophical masterpiece falls in the early forties. Furthermore, the age curves indicate that philosophical creativity rises rather quickly between 25 and 40 and then falls off gradually. The age functions are, in fact, virtually identical in shape to the one in Figure 4 of the previous chapter. Lehman found comparable curves for science, medicine, music, art, literature, and numerous other realms of human achievement, thus corroborating Beard's findings. In most instances the peak productive age occurs around age 40, plus or minus about five years; the creator ascends to this peak rapidly from around the mid-twenties and then descends more gradually, so that about half of all enduring contributions to world culture are produced by creators who are 40 years old or younger.

Other researchers have obtained similar results. My inquiry into the ages at which 696 classical composers produced the most frequently heard melodies found the decade from 33 to 43 to be the peak productive period (Simonton, 1977b). And in psychology the peak creative age for influential production has been repeatedly shown to fall between 35 and 39 (Lehman, 1966; Lyons, 1968; Zusne, 1976). Researchers since Lehman have also confirmed the broad outline of the age curve over the life span (Davis, 1954; Zusne, 1976). Examining the 10 greatest composers in classical music, for example, I found that the curvilinear age function accounted for about one-third of the agewise fluctuations in creative production (Simonton, 1977a). There does appear to be one modest exception to this pattern: on rare occasions more than one productive peak is observed in the age functions. Haefele (1962), for instance, has spotted a creative resurgence around the years 80 to 85 which he ascribes to youthful recollections in the final years. Dennis (1966) had observed a similar spurt of creative activity on the part of mathematicians in their sixties, a finding largely confirmed by Cole (1979). These departures from the overall shape of the age curve, however, are really quite diminutive in size. In fact, I have shown that a single-peak age function (to be discussed later in this chapter) predicts more than 90 percent of the longitudinal variance in creative productivity in tabulations by Lehman (1953), Dennis (1966), Cole (1979), and Zuckerman (1977) (Simonton, 1983a). The probability of conceiving notable creative products tends to diminish as the creator passes the peak productive age of around 40.

QUALITY VERSUS QUANTITY

Lehman has been criticized for building his analysis upon the most notable creative products of each creator and not looking at the creators' total output. This focus seems, on the face of it, to be quite consistent with my own current purposes: after all, it is the famous works on which a creator's reputation must rest. Beethoven's status with concert audiences and record buyers does not depend on the obscure canons and occasion pieces he dashed off for friends or for extra money. Nonetheless, there may be insights to be gained from considering all of a creator's works rather than just the major ones.

Wayne Dennis (1966) conducted an inquiry that included the inspection of total output without regard for the standing of the works with posterity. Like Lehman, Dennis studied a diverse array of creative endeavors in the arts and sciences. In general, he found that productive quantity does not decline so rapidly as productive quality. Creators in their sixties are normally as prolific as creators in their twenties, and between 6 and 20 percent of a creator's total output may be produced in the seventies. The precise figures depend upon the particular disciplines examined—the productive decline is far more precipitous for aesthetic enterprises than for scientific or scholarly ones—yet Dennis has shown that the drop-off in productivity can be minimal.

Other investigators have supported Dennis's chief conclusions. Cole (1979), as an example, examined the quantity of output for creators in six scientific disciplines and concluded that productivity gradually increases to about the age of 45 and then gradually decreases. He found in most of the six fields that the scientists over the age of 60 were almost as productive as those under 35. Zuckerman's (1977) study of Nobel laureates in the sciences essentially reiterates this conclusion: the peak productive age is in the forties for these distinguished scientists, and any decline afterward is negligible.

Lehman himself addressed the issue of quality versus quantity, and his inferences are comparable to Dennis's. When productions of lesser merit are included in the tabulations, the decline in productivity with age appears far more gradual. Moreover, all these investigators have found that the most productive decade in terms of quantity may be the forties rather than the thirties. The safest generalization is that the peak productive age is at around 40, but that the greater works may appear slightly before that age and the lesser works slightly after. Unfortunately, no researchers have looked at the decade from 35 to 45, the likely peak productive period for both quality and quantity. Rather, the fortieth year, the probable optimum point, has been selected as the boundary line between the thirties and forties, thus slicing the most crucial decade in two.

These findings raise the issue of the exact functional relationship between quality and quantity of productive output. Does the ratio of major to minor works per time unit increase, decrease, or remain constant as the creator ages? Each of these possibilities can be supported by a reasonable theoretical argument. If creators benefit from past experience so that they have an ever better idea about what works and what does not, then the proportion of historically successful creations should gradually increase over time. This position may be called a "learning model." Or it could be that the creative spark is primarily the prerogative of youth, more routine production being the bane of old age. Perhaps youth's ambition is what propels the creative process to its highest achievements, and later in life this ambition gives way to more pragmatic but far less bold aims. This "bold youth" model obviously predicts that the most influential creative products are likely to appear early in the career.

The third alternative model, a longitudinal version of the "constant probability of success" model advanced in Chapter 5, maintains that the proportion of top-quality products stays relatively constant throughout a creator's career. Since quality of output is a function of quantity of output, the more prolific periods of a creator's life will produce both more good *and* more bad works. This idea was first propounded by Dennis (1966) in defense of his position vis-à-vis Lehman. And the idea fits in well with Campbell's (1960) blind-variation and selective-retention model, outlined in Chapter 5.

Little empirical research has been done on longitudinal changes in the ratio of quality to quantity. For various reasons, the tabulations presented by earlier researchers will not do. As an example, the observation that quantity of output declines more gradually than quality cannot be interpreted as endorsement of the bold youth model. Different creators are involved in these comparisons, and the peculiarities of aggregation will render the tabulations of major works somewhat more sharply peaked than tabulations of total works. What is required is a study that looks at the agewise ups and downs in both total and notable productivity for the same batch of creators.

I performed such a study (Simonton, 1977a), investigating the careers of the 10 classical composers who were the most highly ranked by members of the American Musicological Society. I divided the productive careers of these composers into five-year periods, and devised two separate indicators of agewise productivity. The first was the number of melodies composed in each age period that are listed in a standard thematic dictionary; the second involved a weighted tabulation of all works produced, as judged by listings in catalogues of composers' published works. The weighting scheme took into consideration the differential effort required by various forms: masses were assigned 50 points, symphonies 40, concerti 30, sonatas 15, and instrumental solos 5, other musical forms receiving similarly appropriate weightings. The next step was to divide each of these two indicators of productivity into two parts, one consisting of major works, the other of minor works. A major composition had to be cited in at least 2 out of 15 sources, such as music appreciation texts, record anthologies, concert guides, and the like. The thematic indicator can therefore be divided into two sub-indicators of major themes and minor themes, and the index of total output can be likewise subdivided. By this criterion 80 percent of the total themes can be considered major melodies, while 35 percent of the total weighted work index can be considered major works. I then used these split indexes to construct two longitudinal measures of quality proportion, defined in each case as the ratio of major contributions (works or themes) to total contributions (works or themes). I also determined the age of the composer for each five-year age period, as well as numerous control variables.

I found respectable correlations between major and minor works ($r = .35$) and between major and minor themes ($r = .56$). The periods in which the 10 composers created their most notable compositions tended to be the same as those in which they created their more obscure compositions. Even when various extraneous factors are controlled, especially linear and curvilinear age functions, the association remains high ($r = .32$ for works and .45 for themes). Not just the overall trend but the period-by-period fluctuations follow the same path over time. Furthermore, the proportion of high-quality works according to both productivity indicators is largely constant over time. Some creative periods may yield a higher percentage of great compositions, other periods a lower percentage, yet the proportion of successes does not change in any systematic way as the composer matures. Even at the peak productive age the proportion of great works is about the same as at earlier or later phases of the composer's career. Those golden periods that see the birth of world masterpieces also produce pieces of only ephemeral value.

A striking implication of this result is that the composers themselves may not be aware of what their own best works are. Beethoven's favorite symphonies, the third and the ninth, are not necessarily those most favored in the concert hall, while two incredibly overplayed piano pieces, the Moonlight Sonata and the bagatelle Für Elise, were both subject to the composer's disdain. Creators cannot possibly view their own work with the same eyes as appreciators in generations to come.

Because the constant-probability-of-success model contradicts so many preconceptions about the creative process, it is necessary to emphasize that I have replicated the foregoing results for 10 eminent psychologists (Simonton, 1983e). This replication sheds added light on the common belief that truly revolutionary advances in science are the offspring of youth. The physicist P. A. M. Dirac formulated his relativistic wave equations when he was only 25, for which achievement he received the Nobel Prize at age 31. So many of the early quantum physicists were still in their twenties that the field became known as Knabenphysiks (boy physics). Thus it is not surprising that Dirac penned the following verse (quoted in Zuckerman, 1977, p. 164):

> Age is, of course, a fever chill
> that every physicist must fear.
> He's better dead than living still
> when once he's past his thirtieth year.

Dirac's testimonial notwithstanding, the evidence does not endorse the notion that scientific quality far precedes scientific quantity in the age distribution. Zuckerman (1977) has shown that the average age at which scientists create the work for which they eventually receive the Nobel Prize is around 39, an age close to the peak productive age for total output. In addition, taking data on the productivity and citation rates collected by Cole (1979) for scientists in six fields, I have calculated a correlation of .77 between quantity and quality. Those periods of a scientist's career in which the most papers are published also tend to see the publication of the most frequently cited papers. My analysis of Cole's data reveals, in fact, that the ratio of citations to publications remains more or less constant throughout a scientist's career—the same result found in my studies of 10 composers and 10 psychologists.

How then do we explain the youthfulness of revolutionary scientists? The answer lies in one of the primary lessons of the previous chapter: scientific geniuses of the highest historical order tend to begin their careers at unusually early ages. Yet these precocious intellects do not cease their contributions once they have begun to shake up the foundations of normal science. On the contrary, their endeavors to reform scientific thought continue almost unabated into the last years of life. Their later creative offerings may not be perceived by the scientific community to be nearly as innovative as the initial milestones, yet this perception may be partly an illusion of contrast. It may be precisely because the early efforts have revolutionized the field so thoroughly that the later works, being interpreted in the new context, may seem to lack any revolutionary quality. Einstein produced his special theory of relativity when he was only 26 and his general theory more than a decade later, and the general theory is a contribution no less revolutionary than the special theory once allowance is made for the shifted baseline for comparison. Because Einstein's 1905 contribution had changed the way scientists viewed the universe, his 1916 contribution may look less momentous than it was.

INTERDISCIPLINARY CONTRASTS

Numerous qualifications were left lurking in the preceding two sections. These qualifications stem from the fact that both the broad shape of the age curve and the specific location of the peak vary from one creative discipline to another. Dennis (1966) demonstrated that for scholarly activities such as history and philosophy the peak productive age may not be attained until the sixties, and that the output at that optimal age period is only barely superior to that observed for the forties and fifties and for the seventies. Artistic endeavors, such as music, poetry, and drama, normally peak decades earlier, in the thirties or forties, and then output drops far more sharply. While 20 percent of a scholar's lifetime production will come in the seventies, less than 10 percent of an artistic creator's contributions can be attributed to that late decade. Scientists generally fall somewhere between these two extremes. Like the artists, scientists are more prone to peak in the forties; like the scholars, scientists tend to preserve their rates of output longer so that around 15 percent of their total contribution may come from the seventies.

Although Lehman (1953) concentrated on historically significant creations rather than total output, his results essentially corroborate those of Dennis except that the peaks are slightly earlier. In addition, Lehman showed that even within a single discipline the age functions may vary dramatically according to the particular type of creativity attempted. Within classical music, for instance, the peak for producing great instrumental selections occurs between 25 and 29, the peak for symphonies between 30 and 34, that for chamber music between 35 and 39, and that for light opera or musical comedy between 40 and 44. In a similar vein, Dennis observed that the peak decade for producing chamber music is the thirties whereas that for opera is the forties. And my study of 10 great composers revealed that the world's most frequently heard classical melodies tend to be created by composers in their early thirties, while the production of works in such large forms as cantatas, oratorios, masses, and operas tends to maximize in the late forties.

I designed an inquiry to learn whether certain contrasts in the peak productive age are cross-culturally and transhistorically invariant and thus are secure nomothetic principles of human creative behavior (Simonton, 1975a). The specific focus was on the difference between poets and authors of prose in world literature. The youthfulness of poets is legend. Blake, though he lived to be seventy, composed his *Songs of Innocence* while yet a teenager, and Coleridge, who lived to age 82, wrote his *Lyrical Ballads* and *The Ancient Mariner* in his twenties. Great novels, by comparison, are the offspring of more mature minds: *Les Misérables* appeared when Hugo was 60, and *The Brothers Karamazov* when Dostoevski was 59. In line with these exemplars, Lehman (1953) discovered that the peak age for writing great poetry may precede that for writing great novels by a decade or so. Dennis (1966), too, observed a conspicuous age gap between the best work produced in these two literary genres. To test this age contrast, I drew a sample of 420 literary creators from 25 centuries of world literature. The age at which each literary figure conceived his or her best contribution was determined, and numerous control variables were also defined, such as life span and the fame of the contribution. The peak age for writing literary prose, whether fiction or nonfiction, was around 43, whereas the peak age for writing a poetic masterwork fell at around age 39 (though there is reason to believe that epic poetry is produced at later ages). An age difference of four years may not seem important. Even so, it is large enough to help explain why the reputations of poets may survive even if the poets die at younger ages than do novelists or historians. Twice as much of a poet's lifetime output comes from the twenties as is the case for novelists (Dennis, 1966).

Age differences between other disciplines may also represent invariant properties of creative development. For example, the finding that mathematical creativity tends to peak much earlier than, say, creativity in geology (Lehman, 1953; Dennis, 1966; Cole, 1979) may prove to be universal. Such differences in the peak productive age cannot be automatically ascribed to some cultural prejudice of our modern civilization. In the case of literary creativity, there may be something intrinsic to the content and form of poetic expression that renders it a more youthful preoccupation than the composition of literary prose. By the same token, there may be some attribute of mathematics that makes its production peak earlier than production in other scientific fields. This youthfulness of poetic and mathematical creativity makes it feasible for poets and mathematicians to die at tragically early ages and still find a place in the annals of history. The English poet Thomas Chatterton produced work of poetic genius even though he died at 17, and the French mathematician Evariste Galois made important contributions to mathematical thought before his death in a duel at the age of 20. I know of no creators in fields besides poetry and mathematics who died so young and yet accomplished enough to secure lasting reputations.

AGE AND LEADERSHIP

The examination of different life expectancies may provide us with a preliminary guide to the age function for leadership. A look at the average life spans of the 301 eminent personages studied by Cox (1926) is most provocative. Curiously, the leaders in this sample exhibit both the highest and the lowest life expectancies. As compared to the overall mean life span of 65.8 years, the famous statesmen on the average lived 70 years. Fully 30 percent of all statesmen lived 80 years or more, and only about 5 percent lived fewer than 50 years. By contrast, philosophers enjoy the most impressive longevity of all the creators in the Cox sample, with a mean of 68.4, and yet less than 14 percent lived to be octagenarians. The 84 years of Benjamin Franklin and the 91 years of John Adams are not atypical of statesmen. In contrast, the revolutionaries in the Cox sample have a life expectancy of only 51.4 years; not one lived to be 80, and more than 44 percent died before age 50. Among creators, the group with the lowest life expectancy is the musicians, with an average of 61.8 years. Even though not one of the composers in the Cox study reached 80, only around 28 percent died before attaining the half-century mark. Thus revolutionaries are unusually short-lived in comparison to other historical figures, whether creators or leaders. Revolution is, like poetry and mathematics, a preoccupation of youth. Half of all the eminent revolutionaries studied by Rejai (1979) were younger than 35 at the time they got themselves involved in changing history, and not quite 80 percent were younger than 45 years old. Thomas Jefferson was 33 in 1776, Fidel Castro 32 in 1959. By comparison, only around 13 percent of the world's leaders attained power before age 40 (Blondel, 1980). The only leaders who come anywhere close to rivaling the youth of revolutionaries are the famous soldiers in the Cox sample, only about 8 percent of whom lived to be 80 and around 18 percent of whom died before age 50. But even these soldiers had a life expectancy more than 11 years longer than that of the revolutionaries.

Lehman recorded that the great religious revolutionaries who founded various religions, sects, and religious societies tend to have launched their movements in their thirties, whereas the principal heads of established religious organizations have a distinct tendency to be "elders." More than 97 percent of the Popes were 50 or older when they took office, and 65 percent were well above the age of 65. The papal antagonist Martin Luther, by contrast, was in his early thirties when he nailed his revolutionary theses to the church door in 1517. Similarly, John Calvin was 27 when he published his *Institution Chrétienne*, George Fox began preaching the principles of Quakerism at 23, John Wesley was 35 when he founded Methodism, and Joseph Smith was 25 when he published the *Book of Mormon*. Mohammed was 40 when he took up his prophetic mission, the Buddha began teaching at 35, and Jesus was still in his thirties when he was crucified. We have here instances of the ritualization of charisma discussed by Max Weber (Eisenstadt, 1968). Young charismatic leaders found new faiths, then are succeeded by elders who routinize the religion into an established organization, substituting mature, orderly ritual and regulation for inspired revelation. Brigham Young was twice as old as Smith when he assumed command of the Mormon Church, and subsequent prophets of this established church have been older still. As Granville Stanley Hall put it in *Senescence: The Last Half of Life* (1922), "men in their prime conceived the great religions, the old made them prevail" (p. 420).

This same process can be witnessed in various political roles, as Lehman has amply demonstrated. Members of the U.S. House of Representatives and Senate have gotten older and older over the years, and so have House speakers, cabinet officers, Supreme Court justices, ambassadors, and army commanders. And the age contrasts are not small: the differences may be anywhere beween 10 and 20 years. Evidently, the charismatic leadership that provided the motivating force for the American Revolution became progressively routinized, the leaders of the federal institutions becoming ever more the guardians of the status quo rather than the instigators of further revolutionary measures. In the Soviet Union, which is not yet a century old, the average age of the politburo members is far higher than Lenin's age when he founded the Communist state. There is a broad tendency, however, for this trend to reverse when a nation faces political turmoil and threat. In such times, younger leaders once again come to the fore.

A question that deserves consideration is whether there exists any relationship between age and political success, power, or influence. Machiavelli warned that the capricious goddess of Fortune is "a lover of young men, because they are less cautious, more violent, and with more audacity command her." There has been astonishingly little research on the precise age function for political success. Lehman provided graphs and tables for leaders similar in appearance to the ones for creators, but the results are not strictly comparable. For example, his chart of the ages at which generals have the highest probability of leading armies into battle means nothing because victorious and defeated commanders are thrown together indiscriminately. It is one thing to determine the age at which a person is assigned a particular leadership role, quite another to demonstrate that a given age is associated with optimal success. The closest Lehman comes to discerning the role of age in the attainment of power or influence is his analysis of U. S. presidential elections. Winning presidential candidates are usually in their late fifties, whereas their unsuccessful opponents are most often either younger or older, with a particularly conspicuous tendency for the losers to be advanced octagenarians. The optimal age for winning a presidential election appears to be between 55 and 60. In fact, however, most of the defeated candidates also fall into this age range, even if at a smaller percentage than holds for the victors. Presidential candidates of whatever success tend to be in their late fifties. Also, it is important to recognize that electoral success is not necessarily equivalent to leadership ability. A president may win by a landslide and go on to earn a low rating as a leader.

In order to probe the connection between age and leadership, I investigated 25 hereditary monarchs who reigned in the age of absolute monarchy (Simonton, 1984a). This choice of representatives from a long-dead political institution and a bygone era had two rational justifications. For one thing, estimation of the age function requires looking at long political careers, and no other political position features terms of office as long as those found in hereditary monarchies. Secondly, absolute monarchs possessed far more power than do constitutionally circumscribed prime ministers or presidents. If we wish to ascertain how age relates to political achievement, we can do no better than to scrutinize rulers whose personal will was virtual law. In such peculiar test cases, the ups and downs of a nation's political fortunes should be most closely related to the developmental changes in its head of state.

I drew a sample of the 25 longest-reigning absolute monarchs from European hereditary monarchies between the Middle Ages and the Napoleonic era. Besides Louis XIV, this group included such personages as Frederick the Great of Prussia, Suleiman the Magnificent of the Ottoman Empire, Emperor Charles V of Spain and the Hapsburg dominions, and Ivan the Terrible and Peter the Great of Russia. Three queens were included in the sample: Elizabeth I of England, Maria Theresa of Austria, and Margaret of Scandinavia. Each of these monarchs reigned 36 years or more, with an average reign of 43 years.

I subdivided each reign into 5-year periods employing the same design used in my study of the 10 classical composers. These time units provided the basis for tabulating a wide range of measures of political accomplishments and failures, such as military victory or defeat and domestic stability or strife. Furthermore, a great many variables were operationalized to control for possible methodological artifacts. The outcome of a multivariate age-trend analysis indicated that the ruler's age has a considerable effect on the state of the nation. As an absolute monarch gets older, the nation becomes less likely to invade another country or to make any territorial gains if it does invade. Its armies also have a lower probability of emerging victorious on the battlefield, especially if the army is under the monarch's personal command. Diplomatically, increased age means a decline in the number of treaties that are successfully negotiated. And in the domestic sphere, disturbances both among the masses and among the members of the monarch's own household are more frequent in the ruler's later years.

Besides these linear age functions, several curvilinear relationships appear as well, all suggesting the existence of an age of peak power comparable to the age of peak productivity found for eminent creators. In military affairs the monarch has the smallest likelihood of suffering defeat on the battlefield at around 42 years old. At this optimum age the monarch is also less likely to lose territory to neighboring countries, either through negotiated settlements or through military force. Taken as a whole, the results show that the welfare of the nation does depend on the age of its ruler. Either the national condition declines as the monarch ages or a rise to a peak of power is followed by a rapid decline. By none of these measures do political matters consistently improve as a monarch ages.

Naturally, we cannot rush to extrapolate these results to the political leaders of the modern world. Still, the outcome is suggestive, particularly since the peak age for political success is remarkably close to the age-40 floruit for most creative activities. Creativity may be no less crucial to the achievement of an eminent leader than for a famous creator—if by "creativity" we mean a certain flexible imagination. And therefore age may have an important relationship to success for leaders, as it does for creators.

SUBSTANTIVE EXPLANATIONS

To my way of thinking, the chief weakness of Lehman's empirical work on age and achievement is its paucity of theoretical discussion. Furthermore, most subsequent research has been far more concerned to refute Lehman's empirical results than to advance our theoretical grasp of the phenomenon. Therefore, my review of the possible explanations must be tentative rather than conclusive. In the main, the causes underlying the age curve may be either extrinsic constraints—influences from outside that impinge on the individual's behavior—or intrinsic developmental processes.

EXTRINSIC CONSTRAINTS

Possible external causes of the ups and downs in creativity are many, but only two have attracted much direct empirical inquiry. One obvious possibility, suggested by Lehman, is that the age curve parallels the longitudinal trend for physical vigor. Certainly intellectual vitality requires some degree of biological health. For example, much of Beethoven's productivity in his final third period was blocked by sundry ailments, not the least being his ever deepening deafness. Yet as reasonable as this suggestion sounds, it cannot provide a complete explanation. In the first place, the peak for physical well-being may appear far too early to account for the peak in mental activity. Lehman found that the most successful athletes—the record breakers, professional team players, and sports champions—tend to be in their late twenties or early thirties. If we take their success as an indicator of the peak age of physical power, it comes a full decade too early to explain the creative acme at age 40. My study of 10 composers assessed the impact of physical illness upon creative output and failed to demonstrate the dominance of matter over mind (Simonton, 1977a). Though the composers' health did tend to deteriorate with age, and though this deterioration had an adverse effect upon the rate of composition, the age curve was largely unchanged even after this extrinsic factor was statistically controlled. The lack of biological fitness may make the final decline steeper than it would be otherwise, but the decline occurs regardless of health.

The principle of cumulative advantage, presented in the preceding chapter, has also been put forward as an explanation (Allison and Stewart, 1974; Cole, 1979). That is, awards, honors, and other positive events may reinforce certain behaviors associated with outstanding influence, while the lack of these social rewards may extinguish such behavior by disappointing and discouraging the aspiring creator or leader. As plausible as this argument sounds, the opposite is plausible as well: social recognition and fame may be goals rather than reinforcers. A creator may strive to win a Nobel Prize, for example, and once that goal is attained the motivation that propelled the creator to the top may be considerably weakened. In addition, fame and fortune often bring increased responsibilities and external demands that consume ever larger portions of time, thereby detracting from intellectual output (Roe, 1972). Hence, social rewards are a mixed bag of encouragement and discouragement.

I have empirically observed the influence of social reinforcers on creative productivity, and I found no effect one way or the other. In the study of 10 classical composers the receipt of honors and awards had no bearing whatsoever upon compositional output. An interesting agewise distribution of social rewards was observed, however: their occurrence is described by a J-curve; that is, most such honors come either very early in the career or much later toward its end, the latter period earning the most kudos. The early rewards are given to those who demonstrate productive precociousness, whereas the later rewards are given to those who have nearly completed a lifetime of admirable creative production. This curve, interestingly, is virtually identical to that for the relationship between eminence and life span. As noted in Chapter 5, the most famous creators and leaders tend to endure either tragically short or prodigiously long lives (see Figure 3). Those in the former group die in the midst of the first peak period of social rewards, while those in the second group die during the second peak period. In both cases they leave the world at the height of their contemporary recognition, a concurrence that may not be lost to posterity. Individuals who die at more middling ages, in contrast, will have suffered a decline in formal praise received from contemporaries, which may bias the judgments of later generations. Consequently, contemporary social rewards may exert a considerable influence upon the assignment of posthumous acclaim.

One potential explanation of the age curve can be discounted: any waxing and waning of productivity or influence with age cannot be reasonably attributed to gains and losses in intelligence. Though intelligence is indeed a potent agent of an individual's historical success, the agewise fluctuations in an individual's intelligence do not decline rapidly enough to account for the agewise changes in cultural or political contributions. Except in manifest senility, a descent from intellectual genius to mediocrity is unheard of. Further, the whole weight of the constant-probability-of-success model is against the proposition of intellectual decay. Since a creative product generated in the later years has the same probability of historical success as one produced during the supposed peak productive age, mental decline is not very useful as an explanation. The character in *Much Ado About Nothing* (written when Shakespeare was 34 years old), was clearly mistaken in saying, "When age is in, the wit is out."

INTRINSIC INFLUENCES

The bulk of the empirical research indicates that in fact the age curve for creative productivity is relatively immune from the impact of extrinsic events (Blackburn, Behymer, and Hall, 1978; Simonton, 1978a). Invariably the curvilinear age function explains far more variance in personal output than does any extrinsic factor. Thus, we must accept the possibility that some internal force, something intrinsic to the creative process, accounts for the observed developmental trends. Beard (1874) propounded just such a theory. According to Beard, creativity is a function of two basic variables, enthusiasm and experience. Enthusiasm provides much of the motivational impetus for continual effort, but enthusiasm alone yields nothing more than original work. Experience is what gives the creator the capacity to discriminate good from bad ideas and to articulate original ideas with greater effectiveness. But experience without any enthusiasm results in routine work. True creativity demands the right combination of enthusiasm and experience. By Beard's model, however, these two factors are postulated to exhibit contrary age distributions. Enthusiasm tends to peak rather early in life and then steadily decline, whereas experience gradually increases with age. Beard maintains that the proper equilibrium between these two forces is only attained between the ages of 38 and 40. Before that peak age period, a creator's output is excessively original, and afterward it is too routine. Thus the age-40 floruit is a consequence of this uniquely balanced juxtaposition of youth's rapture and maturity's sagacity.

Beard's model, for all its simplicity, has some explanatory power. It can explain, for example, why creativity peaks at different ages in various disciplines, if we assume that some types of creative products require more enthusiasm, others more experience. Take the well-established age contrast between poetic and prose literature. Poetry seems to require more enthusiasm, novels more experience, and so poets peak earlier than novelists do. Scholarly endeavors probably require a higher ratio of experience to enthusiasm, thus accounting for the virtually nonexistent decline with age in activities such as historiography. And if artistic creativity generally tends to peak earlier and decay faster than scientific creativity, the relative proportions of enthusiasm and experience may provide the hidden cause.

This argument may also apply to leadership. Enthusiasm may be the primary prerequisite for becoming a revolutionary, whereas success as a politician in a well-entrenched system may depend on experience. Likewise, the age contrast between the founders of religious faiths and the preservers of established religious institutions may be interpreted as a contrast between religious ecstasy and organizational expertise. And if leadership tends to peak at a later age than creativity, the relative proportions of enthusiasm and experience may be crucial. Benjamin Franklin was famous first as a scientist, then as a politician. Disraeli wrote his greatest novels before becoming prime minister. All in all, Beard's two-factor model appears to have a surprising amount of interpretative utility.

Whatever the explanatory success of Beard's model, its predictive precision leaves much to be desired. The model is conceptual rather than mathematical and thus is difficult to test. I have proposed a mathematical model of creative productivity that overcomes this liability (Simonton, 1983a). This model starts with the simple assumption that each individual creator begins with a certain "creative potential" defined by the total number of contributions the creator would be capable of producing in an unrestricted life span. This initial creative potential presumably varies across creators (the exact distribution underlying the individual differences being irrelevant). Each creator uses up this supply of creative potential during his or her productive career by transforming potential into actual contributions. Yet the translation of creative potential into actual creative products does not take place all at once. Instead, I postulate that the creative process consists of at least two steps. The first step involves the conversion of creative potential into creative ideations, or ideas for projects; in the second step these ideas are worked into actual creative contributions in a form that can be made public. The first step could be called ideation, the second step elaboration. If we assume that the rate at which ideas are produced is proportional to the creative potential at a given time, and that the rate at which such ideas are elaborated into finished products is proportional to the number of ideas in the works, then this simple two-stage process can be restated as a set of linear differential equations describing the cognitive transformations over time.

The solution to these differential equations gives us a new equation that predicts how productivity varies with professional or career age. The result is

$$p\ (t)\ =\ c(e^{-at}\ -\ e^{-bt}).$$

Here p is the number of contributions made in year t, where t is counted from the outset of a creator's career, and e is the exponential constant 2.718.... In addition, a denotes the rate of ideation, b defines the elaboration rate ($a<b$), and c allows for differences in productivity levels. Whereas the ideation rate a and the elaboration rate b are assumed to be characteristic of creativity in a given discipline, c is more a function of individual differences in initial creative potential. Thus the exact values of these three constants will vary from discipline to discipline (in the case of a and b) and from person to person (in the case of c). However, typical values are $a = .04$, $b = .05$, and $c = 61$ (Simonton, 1983a). A graph of the above function for these particular values is shown in Figure 4.

This function almost perfectly predicts the observed course of creative productivity with age; the correlation between predicted and observed values is in the upper .90s (Simonton, 1983a). Furthermore, one special feature of this model is that it can readily accommodate the different age curves found for various disciplines. In some fields, the rate at which a creative idea can be worked into a finished product (the elaboration rate, b) is quite slow. In historiography, for example, the lag between conception and publication can be immense. Gibbon took more than a dozen years to write *The Decline and Fall of the Roman Empire*. When the appropriate parameter in the equation is adjusted to recognize this temporal gap in the second step, the model predicts a very flat age curve for historiography in the later years with a minimal decline. For poetry, in contrast, the lag between idea and communication is far smaller, and hence the model predicts a much more rapid drop-off in poetic composition in the last years.

This model can also handle the specific age location of the peak of creativity. The key parameter here is the "ideation rate," a, associated with the first step. In fields such as poetry or mathematics, where the

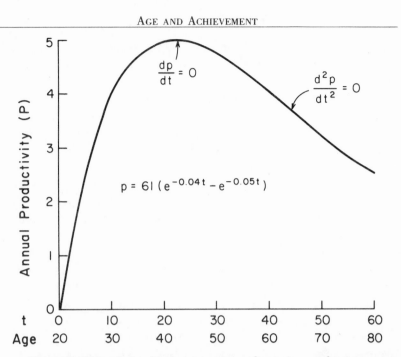

Figure 4. The relationship between age and creative productivity according to a two-step model of the creative process (from Simonton, 1983a).

rate of inspiration may be quite high, the peak is predicted to be much earlier than in fields such as geology or biology. Since this ideation rate also represents the speed at which creative potential is used up, and since the consumption of this potential takes the same form of exponential decay as found in radioactive substances, we can meaningfully speak of the "half-life" of various disciplines. The half-life is the amount of time it takes for a typical creator to transform 50 percent of the initially given creative potential into works-in-progress and finished contributions. By my own calculations, for instance, the half-life for artistic endeavors is 13.9 years, that for scholarly activities 34.6 years. That is to say, half of an artist's total creative potential will have been used up 14 years after the onset of his or her career; if the career begins at 25, the halfway mark will be at 39. By comparison, a scholar reaches the midpoint of his or her career, in terms of creative potential, after 35 years, meaning at age 60 if the beginning was at 25.

At the same time, according to the model, creative potential never totally dries up. Creativity, like radioactivity, approaches zero without ever reaching it. So even if this mathematical model suggests that the downturn in productivity is intrinsic to the creative process, it also holds that the potential for creative contribution need never vanish. In fact, the model implies that even when the peak productive period falls around the fortieth year, as in Figure 4, creators in their seventies will be more prolific than they were in their twenties. Furthermore, even an 80-year-old creator will have 26 percent of the initial creative potential still remaining for exploitation. Despite the fact that this model assumes that the potential for creativity cannot be replenished, it nonetheless holds that most creators die with anywhere between one-quarter and one-third of their genius still locked up inside their heads. Biological durability, not intellectual capacity, places the chief restriction on total lifetime output.

The model has one other asset, this time concerning creative productivity across creators rather than within careers. Recall that differences in creative potential across individuals are reflected in the constant c. A person with a high potential would have a large c in the personalized equation, and one with a minimal potential would have a correspondingly small c. If the equation is used to define a probability distribution for productivity as a function of age for each creator, those creators with the highest initial creative potential will be predicted to begin productivity earlier in life, to produce at higher rates of output per annum, to end productivity much later in life, and, naturally, to have a larger lifetime output. In other words, if this mathematical model is at all reasonable, the observed correlation (described in the previous chapter) among the variables of precociousness, productivity rate, longevity, and total contributions becomes a mathematical necessity rather than an empirical coincidence.

To date, the only theoretical treatments of the relationship between age and productivity are the two-factor model proposed by Beard and my own two-step model. Both models must be considered tentative, but their explanatory and predictive successes imply that intrinsic processes bear most of the responsibility for the age curve. Hence, not only have Lehman's findings about the shape of the curve and the peak age of productivity received empirical endorsement, but his work has also been given the beginnings of a theoretical foundation. Productivity over a career appears to fluctuate in a predictable way precisely because it is more dependent upon the requirements of the creative process than upon external constraints and pressures.

7

AESTHETICS AND CHARISMA

WHAT MAKES A LITERARY or musical composition attain recognition as a masterpiece? What enables a leader to capture the allegiance of the public and go down in history as great? The answer to the first question is a matter of aesthetics, and the answer to the second has much to do with the mysterious quality called charisma. Aesthetic judgments and charisma have in common an intense subjectivity; both depend upon the ability of genius to appeal directly to the emotions. Because of this nonrational quality, these two phenomena are quite resistant to the application of the scientific method. Consequently, the results of investigations into aesthetics and charisma have a preliminary and tentative character. Both of these topics are frontiers of the historiometric search for nomothetic principles.

THE CREATIVE PRODUCT

Aesthetics has always been one of the most elusive subjects in the behavioral sciences. Only recently have armchair philosophical aesthetics and art criticism been supplemented by empirical research. And to date such research has been dominated by the laboratory experiment. In a typical experiment, artificial stimuli are presented to volunteer subjects to ascertain the basis of artistic likes and dislikes (see, for example, Berlyne, 1971). This technique has a great deal to recommend it, particularly with regard to the rigor of causal inference that only laboratory experiments can provide, and yet of course responding to contrived stimuli in a university cubicle is a far cry from appreciating real aesthetic objects in an art gallery, recital hall, or reading room. An important goal of any scientific aesthetics must be to discern what attributes of Beethoven's Fifth Symphony or Shakespeare's *Hamlet* makes them masterpieces. It seems to me that the way to achieve this aim is to inspect directly, in an objective and quantitative manner, the actual masterworks of the world's greatest aesthetic creators, and to compare the products that have won immortality with other products that have left no mark.

Just as we can assess the relative fame of creative individuals, so can we gauge the fame, or presumed aesthetic impact, of various musical, artistic, or literary creations. The difficulty lies in evaluating the attributes of these objects that may contribute to their success. This very difficulty is what has motivated psychologists to experiment with actively manipulating the possible parameters with artificial, simplified stimuli. An alternative way to attack this problem is to exploit the arsenal of techniques that come under the inclusive heading of "content analysis." What makes content analysis an especially powerful tool is its susceptibility, in certain applications, to treatment by computers. Many sophisticated computer packages have been designed to analyze the content of messages. Though most of these programs are geared for use with written text, other forms of communications, especially music, also lend themselves to this sort of analysis. Computer analysis makes possible the objective assessment of many aesthetic characteristics all at once and with perfect reliability, and it also allows the analysis of a vast number of creative products, thereby permitting an immense expansion of the sample.

A fine application of computerized content analysis to aesthetic questions may be found in Colin Martindale's book *The Romantic Progression: The Psychology of Literary History* (1975). Martindale tested some theoretical conceptions about poetic creativity by analyzing the content of poems by 21 English and 21 French poets. He sought to tap such variables as primary and secondary process thinking, emotion, regressive cognition, and incongruous juxtapositions. Taking these measures, Martindale traced changes in poetic content over the history of these two national literary traditions, with special focus on the ways poets respond to the incessant pressure to be ever original.

It is impossible to do full justice here to the richness of Martindale's findings. My only real complaint about Martindale's ambitious project is the unit he selected as the foundation for his analyses. Instead of choosing the single poem as the analytical unit, he selected the individual poet, and even then he most often aggregated these poets into 20-year-long generational time-series units. This choice was useful in his attempt to understand the course of literary history—but for my purposes this unit is far too big. Even the greatest poets compose some bad poems, and an occasional great poem comes from an otherwise mediocre poet. A better method would have been first to discover the factors that determine the differential distinction of each poem, and then to ask whether the most famous poets are those who produce a higher percentage of the noteworthy poems. I shall pursue this method in the next two sections of this chapter, using examples from drama and music.

CLASSICAL MUSIC

Why is it that some tunes linger in the mind and are whistled as we walk down the street while others fade from memory as soon as their last notes die away? It is begging the question to say that melodic memorability depends on how often themes are played over the radio or in concerts, for why are some compositions performed more in the first place? The answer supposedly lies in the differential beauty or emotive force of various themes. Those melodies that possess the most potent aesthetic impact should be more likely to be heard, and hence remembered. The question is what qualities render a musical composition beautiful or powerful or memorable.

In search of an answer, Berlyne (1971), one of the pioneers of experimental aesthetics, developed an "optimal arousal" model. According to this model, aesthetic experiences stimulate the mind, raising the level of emotional arousal to some pleasurable level. The capacity to stimulate arises from the complexity, novelty, surprisingness, ambiguity, and other properties of an aesthetic stimulus. Very simple, banal, and predictable art objects are devoid of interest. At the same time aesthetic objects that are too rich in intricacies, unexpected turns, and an originality that defies the comprehension of would-be appreciators are likely to provoke an adverse reaction. The ideal is for an aesthetic work, such as a musical composition, to fall between these two extremes.

Laboratory experiments have generally endorsed Berlyne's model (see Heyduk, 1975). But because these studies employed artificial stimuli, we cannot know for sure whether this model applies in real-life aesthetic situations—though at least one musicologist has put forward a compatible theory (Meyer, 1956). What is required is a historiometric examination of actual music compositions, something I have accomplished in a recent study (Simonton, 1980d). The unit of analysis was the single melody or theme drawn from the repertoire of classical music; the sample consisted of 15,618 themes by 479 composers. No major classical composer, and no warhorse of the standard repertoire, was omitted. Using music appreciation textbooks, record-buying guides, collections of popular excerpts, general cultural histories, thematic dictionaries, and library guides, I rated the themes objectively along a 32-point scale from the most obscure to the most famous. This "thematic fame" scale has been shown to correlate with actual frequency of performance (Simonton, 1983c).

The next task was to assess the melodic originality of each theme. I used a computerized content analysis to calculate the two-note transition probabilities of each melody with respect to the entire repertoire. In the key of C, for example, the two-note transitions C to C and C to G are very common, whereas C to D sharp and C to G flat are far more rare. By taking the first six notes of each theme and estimating the probabilities for the corresponding five two-note transitions, I could define the "repertoire melodic originality" of the theme as the theme's improbability in the context of all melodies in the classical tradition since the Renaissance. Highly chromatic melodies with many accidentals are more original than those which never depart from the seven notes of the scale. And melodies in which consecutive notes jump unusual intervals are more original than those which proceed by thirds. Though it might seem desirable to look at higher-order transitions, this was found to be unnecessary; melodic originality scores founded upon three-note transition probabilities correlate very highly with those based on two-note transitions ($r = .81$), and the latter are far less expensive to calculate. A skeptic might doubt that much can be learned about a melody from just its first six notes, but previous research has discovered that even the first *four* notes of a melody usually suffice to betray the style of its composer (Paisley, 1964). If the first four notes can give away a composer's identity, the first six notes should tell us something about the melodic structure of that particular theme.

These two measures allow us to determine the functional relationship between thematic fame and melodic originality. In a manner quite in keeping with the optimal arousal model, fame is an inverted-J function of originality (see Figure 5). As melodic originality increases, the frequency with which a theme is played increases up to a certain maximum value and then declines. The least favored themes tend to be the most original; the listening audience favors trite tunes over atonal or serial note sequences. This curvilinear relationship was detected after controlling for a host of potential artifacts. For example, since instrumental melodies tend to be more famous than vocal melodies, and since

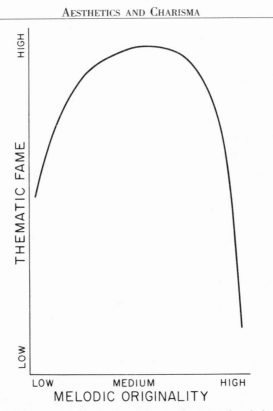

Figure 5. The relationship between thematic fame and melodic originality for 15,618 themes in the classical repertoire (from Simonton, 1983c).

concert pieces tend to be more popular than chamber, theater, or church work, some provision had to be made for the implied preference for orchestral music. Controls were also introduced for the fact that thematic fame is greater, on the average, for more recently composed melodies, and for melodies that are part of larger works such as symphonies or operas rather than part of smaller compositions such as piano pieces or art songs. The inclusion of many control variables in the 35-variable multiple regression equation provides some assurance of the accuracy of the curvilinear relationship between fame and originality. This historiometric study has shown that a model developed in experimental research—Berlyne's optimal arousal model—is indeed generalizable to the real world of music appreciation.

Melodic originality is not the only determinant of thematic fame, of course. As the constant-probability-of-success model would predict, the most notable melodies are likely to be composed by the most prolific composers, especially during the composer's period of peak productivity, namely around age 39 (even after controlling for the effect of competition).

These additional predictive factors notwithstanding, melodic originality plays an important part in the determination of a theme's aesthetic impact. Several factors can be mentioned that contribute to the repertoire melodic originality of a theme. For one thing, melodic originality is partly a function of the specific medium and form in which the melody appears. Because of the limitations of the human voice and the requirements of the written text, vocal melodies are less original on the average than instrumental ones. Additionally, in comparison to melodies drawn from concert music, those from chamber and church music are more original, those from the theater (ballet and opera) much less so. More significantly, melodic originality is also a curvilinear inverted-backwards-J function of the composer's age. As composers grow older the unpredictability of their melodies rises to a certain peak and then falls, though the melodies composed in their later years remain more original than their youthful compositions. Indeed, the peak for melodic originality falls not at age 39 as is the case for thematic fame, but rather at age 56. Only after age 60 does there appear any appreciable decline in a composer's melodic originality (compare Porter and Suedfeld, 1981). Curiously, Beethoven died when he was 56, and he composed his last six string quartets, which many music critics and listeners place at the pinnacle of his originality in this form (and among the greatest quartets of all time) between the ages of 53 and 56— precisely during the peak period for melodic originality.

Another determinant of melodic originality deserves an honorable mention: the predictability of classical themes has tended to decrease through history from the simple modal productions of the Renaissance to the atonal and serial note groupings of the twentieth-century avant-garde. This historical trend complies with what Martindale (1975) said drives the course of aesthetic creativity. Each generation of composers is under strong pressure to surpass its predecessors in originality, thus propelling the creators to ever more daring compositional feats.

Music also expresses emotion. Indeed, the structure of a melody may mirror the shape of our internal emotional states. For example, chromaticism, or the use of notes outside the diatonic scale defined by the key signature, has been said to convey anguish and sorrow. The quasi-chromatic notes in jazz are called "blue notes," symbols for the emotional condition of the blues. Interval leaps between notes, or otherwise uncommon intervals between notes, are often interpreted as symbols of intense and chaotic emotion (LaRue, 1970).

Since both chromaticism and odd interval transitions are included in the probabilistic definition of melodic originality, it is conceivable that the most original melodies come from those periods in which the composer is suffering the most extreme life stress. I designed a study to measure the amount of stress in 5-year age periods to see whether stressful events affected the nature of melodic composition (Simonton, 1980c). As I described in Chapter 1, the measurement of stress was accomplished by applying a life-change scale devised for research on psychosomatics (Holmes and Rahe, 1967) to relevant biographical data. I selected for study only the 10 most distinguished classical composers. These 10 composers created their most original melodies during those periods in which they were facing the most intense life challenges—the death of family members, job changes, geographical dislocations, marriages, legal hassles, and the like. This result provides direct evidence that the structure of a melody may be affected by the composer's private emotional states. Even more critically, because stress affects originality and originality is related to fame, thematic fame is partially grounded in the creator's biography.

These inquiries have as yet barely scratched the surface of what makes a musical masterpiece. Melody is only one facet of a composer's success with audiences. Still, historiometry must begin somewhere, and the individual melody, as a composition's building block, is a good place to begin.

DRAMA

Hamlet and *Oedipus the King* are acknowledged masterpieces, frequently read, discussed, produced, and quoted. Yet both Shakespeare and Sophocles created less distinguished dramas as well. How often is *Titus Andronicus* produced? Who reads the *Trachiniae?* Clearly, it is something more subtle and elusive than the author's name on the title page that makes us label certain plays greater and consign others to obscurity.

To address the question of what makes a play become a classic, I examined 81 plays created by 5 of the world's most famous dramatists: 7 by Aeschylus, 7 by Sophocles, 19 by Euripides, 11 by Aristophanes, and 37 by Shakespeare. A detailed content analysis of all these plays is included in *Great Books of the Western World* (Hutchins, 1952). From this valuable reference source I determined the 42 major themes of these classic dramas; a major theme was defined as a subject discussed by all five playwrights in at least one play each. An example of such an issue is "The conflict of love and duty." I calculated the proportion of each play devoted to each issue, and then ran a factor analysis to consolidate these issues into 19 key questions. I also used these content factors to operationalize the "issue richness" of each play: the number of key questions each play addresses. To assess a play's greatness, I factor analyzed five distinct citation measures, among them the frequency of occurrence in anthologies, literary digests, plot summaries, and literary histories. The result was a measure of dramatic greatness that had a high degree of reliability (coefficient alpha .82). Several other attributes of the plays were also assessed, among them each play's quotability, or wealth of memorable lines. I also considered the age of the playwright at the time of composition, as well as several variables concerning the contemporary political context, to throw light on the developmental and sociocultural basis of dramatic creativity. Finally, several control variables were introduced.

The best-known plays of these five dramatists were shown to feature many more quotable passages ($r = .39$) and to survey a richer array of major issues ($r = .26$) than do their lesser-known works. A path analysis revealed that issue richness exerts no direct effect upon the lasting success of a drama; rather, this content trait makes its effect felt through its impact upon a play's quotability. The broader the range of significant philosophical questions a drama presents, the more impressive its supply of memorable lines. Curiously, the specific philosophical debates tossed about in a play have very little to do with the play's success with audiences. Great plays cannot be distinguished from obscure plays on the basis of the particular themes addressed. A love interest can no more salvage a bad play than it can a bad movie. The number (richness) of issues treated is what finally counts, and then only insofar as the issues are expressed in memorable passages.

This content-analytical study has no more than scratched the surface of the question of what makes some plays masterpieces. Yet this preliminary inquiry does provide an illustration of how the differential greatness of literary creations can be examined in terms of attributes of content. Future investigations will no doubt bring us closer to discovering what qualities add up to aesthetic greatness.

THE EFFECTIVE LEADER

Few personality traits are more resistant to precise definition than is charisma. To be charismatic is to possess some mysterious attribute that provides the foundation of exceptional influence, whether that influence is exerted in intimate interpersonal contacts or before immense crowds of people. It is far easier to offer exemplars than to operationalize this construct in any definitive manner. Napoleon was evidently a charismatic leader, and so was Hitler. Just what was it that made them so?

The one researcher who has made some progress in the direction of assessing the different levels of charisma displayed by various heads of state is Charles Cell (1974). Concentrating on male heads of state, Cell devised a scale of pertinent indicators: a leader accumulates points for charisma if the leader's picture is conspicuously posted both in public places and in homes, if a statue of the leader appears in the nation's capital during the leader's tenure in office, if the leader is seen as unifying the country behind some grand purpose and as leading the country to military victory against dangerous foes, if the leader gives long speeches and exhibits a lack of appreciation for basic economics, if people are willing to make personal sacrifices for the leader, and if the leader has some claim to impressive sexual prowess. Cell applied his 11-point charisma scale to 34 modern heads of state. Receiving the top score of 10 points are Hitler, Kenyatta, Mussolini, and Ataturk; at the bottom with zero points are such figures as Ben Gurion, Frei, and Adenauer. In between fall such leaders as Sukarno at 9, Mao at 8, Castro at 7, De Gaulle at 5, Lenin at 4, Nyerere at 3, Churchill at 2, and Khrushchev at 1. The only two American presidents among the 34 are Franklin D. Roosevelt at 6 points and John F. Kennedy at 4.

Cell's attempt to objectify the concept of charisma is unusual. Most of the research related to this topic does not even try to assess charisma directly, although that trait is always lurking in the background. Instead, the concentration is usually on aspects of leadership that seem more amenable to scientific measurement. I will explore these various indirect alternatives by focusing on a subclass of leaders, the presidents of the United States. I will first look at the factors that affect presidential popularity and election success, and then examine the determinants of presidential performance and greatness.

PRESIDENTIAL POPULARITY

Ever since the presidency of Harry Truman, pollsters have been fond of asking the American public what they think about the performance of the current president. Since these opinion surveys show marked fluctuations in the approval ratings over time, both across and within presidencies, they provide a useful indicator of how the American people have altered their perceptions of the head of state. Among the first to begin exploiting this information was John E. Mueller (1973), who set out to discover the factors responsible for the ups and downs in presidential popularity from Truman to Johnson. One such factor is a tendency for a president's approval rating to decline during the course of his term, from the honeymoon immediately after the election to the doldrums some four years later. If a president is reelected, his popularity resurges upon the second inaugural, only to fall again. So inexorable is this pattern that some political scientists have suggested that approval ratings may not depend at all upon a president's actual performance in office (Stimson, 1976).

Another factor is that whenever an international crisis occurs a rally-around-the-flag effect boosts the president's popularity. For example, the Bay of Pigs fiasco of 1962, in which American-supported Cuban exiles tried to overthrow the well-entrenched Fidel Castro, actually raised President Kennedy's standing with the people. On the negative side, the president's popularity is hurt when the economy goes sour, as when unemployment increases. Curiously, though the president is blamed for an economic slump, he does not receive any comparable credit when the economy prospers (also see Bloom and Price, 1975; Kenski, 1977). Finally, war can affect a president's popularity. Truman's approval rating deteriorated as a consequence of his engagement of American forces in the Korean War.

Mueller's pioneer research has come under some criticism. Kernell (1978) has argued that popularity does not simply decline after election or reelection, but rather that this apparent loss of support can be attributed to specific events, especially to consequences of particular presidential decisions and actions. But even more critically, Kernell demonstrated that a president's approval rating according to one poll has a positive autocorrelation with the rating in the previous poll. That is, there prevails a certain inertia in public opinion about how well the president is doing in office, an opinion that can be changed only gradually. What Mueller and his critics agree on is that a president's popularity is tossed about by the viscissitudes of political fate. Of the five presidents between Truman and Nixon, only Eisenhower's popularity seems to have been largely immune to such extraneous influences.

SUCCESS IN ELECTIONS

The popularity of a president has a lot to do with the outcomes of presidential elections (Sigelman, 1979). Electoral success might appear to be a useful indicator of leadership ability, perhaps even of charisma. It is commonly believed that success in the polls requires considerable skill in commanding the attention and admiration of the voters. But in fact elections are at best only very imperfect indicators of such interpersonal skills. Policy often overrides personality in the voting booth, and electoral victory says as much about the inferiority of the defeated candidate as it does about the superiority of the victor. The landslide defeat of George McGovern in 1972 may say more about the public's reaction to the anti–Vietnam War peace movement than about any great infatuation with Richard Nixon.

What little research has been done on electoral success indicates the immense significance of apparently situational or contextual factors. For instance, Grush (1980) studied the determinants of success in the 1976 Democratic presidential primaries and found that almost 80 percent of the variance in voting outcomes could be attributed to just three predictor variables. First, candidates who have regional exposure—who have held some public office, such as senator or governor, that makes them already well-known to voters in the region in which the primary takes place—have a certain edge. Second, a bandwagon effect occurs such that victory in one primary improves the odds of another victory in the next primary. As predicted by the Matthew effect (see Chapter 5), the rich get richer and the poor get poorer, expanding the gap between victorious and defeated candidates and leaving fewer and fewer candidates at the end of the campaign trail. Grush's third finding is that campaign expenditures significantly affect the primary outcomes, especially at the beginning of the race for the nomination. It takes money, and plenty of it, to expose the candidate to the voting public through newspaper advertisements and television or radio spots. Once success comes at the polls and momentum is established, less money can be spent in the later primaries. The bandwagon or cumulative advantage effect will take over.

The fact that success in presidential primaries largely depends on regional exposure, prior election outcomes, and campaign expenditures does not mean that personality, even charisma, plays no part in the process. These three variables may serve as proxy variables for underlying individual characteristics. For instance, since to have regional exposure a candidate must have held office as a governor, senator, or representative, the candidate must already have evidenced some leadership skills. In the same vein, campaign expenditures, unless the candidate is extremely wealthy, presuppose donations from numerous supporters, and these donations may serve as rough monetary quantifiers of the candidate's charismatic qualities. Of the three predictors, only the bandwagon phenomenon appears almost entirely devoid of personological content. The inequality of primary outcomes may begin as a reflection of different leadership abilities in the pool of candidates, but through cumulative advantage the series of primaries eventually exaggerates any initial disparities.

Once a presidential candidate has won the nomination, the general election is still ahead. Emerging victorious from that campaign is no easy matter. Interestingly enough, success as a presidential candidate is not unlike success as a revolutionary. In Chapter 3 I discussed the shift in the conceptual complexity of revolutionaries from pre- to post-takeover phases; Tetlock (1981b) has shown that a similar shift occurs in successful presidential candidates once they take office. During the campaign, the candidate's rhetoric is decidedly simplistic. Simple and easy solutions are suggested for complex and difficult problems, and policy ideas are presented in a nonrelativistic and dichotomous fashion. Yet once the president is inaugurated and sets up a functioning administration, his rhetoric exhibits an appropriate transformation. This change in integrative complexity might reflect the president's cognitive adjustment to the realities of governing, but Tetlock shows otherwise. The simplicity or complexity of the president's rhetoric is more a matter of impression management. Tetlock found that a president's policy statements do not gradually become more complex with the passage of time in office but rather that the change from simplicity to complexity occurs almost immediately upon inauguration—far too sharp a shift to fit a slow learning process. Even more telling is the fact that when the president runs for reelection his policy statements regress to the simplicity that dominated his public addresses four years before. That the public is evidently fooled by this oscillation between simple-minded campaign rhetoric and worldy-wise presidential excuse-making is one of the peculiarities of American democracy.

PRESIDENTIAL PERFORMANCE AND GREATNESS

Historiometric researchers have attempted to find a way to predict, taking into consideration the wealth of information available about the background and political experience of each candidate, which aspirant will make the more competent president. Alas, these attempts have not been fully successful. For example, I made a comprehensive study of the 38 presidents from Washington to Carter (Simonton, 1981c). I defined two sets of variables. First, a large number of prepresidential biographical variables were operationalized to serve as potential predictors. They included family background, formal education, various personal attributes (such as age at inauguration), prior occupation, and previous political experience. Next a second set of variables were operationalized as objective criteria of presidential performance. These criteria included various aspects of the president's legislative and executive power, such as the use of the veto, treaty negotiations, and appointments to the cabinet and Supreme Court. The number and range of these variables were every bit as great as those of the predictor variables.

Only one prepresidential biographical variable had any general predictive utility with regard to objectively assessed presidential performance: those chief executives who succeeded to the office from the vice-presidency upon the death or resignation of their predecessor prove to be much less successful than other presidents. Such unelected presidents tend to experience more cabinet resignations, to have more Supreme Court and cabinet appointments rejected by the Senate, to have more vetoes overridden by Congress, and to be denied their party's nomination to run for the presidency in the next election. Of the 9 vice-presidents who unexpectedly became president—Tyler, Fillmore, Andrew Johnson, Arthur, Theodore Roosevelt, Coolidge, Truman, Lyndon Johnson, and Ford—only 4 were elected to serve another term. By comparison, only 8 of the 30 duly elected presidents were defeated for renomination or reelection: John Adams, John Quincy Adams, Van Buren, Cleveland, Benjamin Harrison, Taft, Hoover, and Carter. And Cleveland hardly counts, since he lost the election to Harrison even though he won the majority of the popular vote, and since he defeated Harrison in the next election, thus becoming the only president to serve two nonconsecutive terms. So unelected presidents are about twice as likely as elected presidents to be defeated in their quest for another term. Given their relatively poor performance, those differential odds are not amazing. But why do they perform less well than their duly elected counterparts?

On the one hand, it may be that a president who succeeds to the office without being elected is not perceived as a legitimate leader. This unexpected president must face a Congress consisting of elected senators and representatives who can confidently claim to have some constituency behind them. This perceived difference in legitimacy may make the Congress ill-disposed to approve the president's appointments to the cabinet and Supreme Court and more inclined to overturn presidential vetoes. On the other hand, it is equally possible that these political defeats merely reflect the fact that such presidents lack leadership skills. The unelected presidents may attempt to appoint incompetent or otherwise unacceptable persons to high office, and may lack the charisma or acumen required to convince Congress to sustain a presidential veto. After all, a vice-presidential nominee is often chosen to balance the ticket ideologically or geographically, and there is no guarantee that leadership will figure prominently in the selection process.

Perhaps the reason we have not found an objective equation that will predict presidential performance is that the criterion variables have been too objective. The rejection of a Supreme Court or cabinet nominee is no more than a surface phenomenon, a mere repercussion of some more fundamental deficiency in personal influence on the part of the president. Such measures may be too remote from the original subject under study, namely, presidential charisma. A more subjective criterion of competence might work better. In earlier chapters I mentioned a survey by Maranell (1970), who had 571 American historians rate 33 presidents on seven dimensions of leadership. I took Maranell's ratings and consolidated them, using a factor analysis, into a single dimension which I called presidential greatness (Simonton, 1981c; see also Wendt and Light, 1976). The greatest chief executives are those who score high on general prestige, strength of action, presidential activeness, and administration accomplishments, characteristics that bear a closer prima facie relevance to charisma than do simple counts of vetoes overturned or nominations rejected. The greatest American president by this measure is Franklin D. Roosevelt, who also was highly rated on Cell's charisma scale. This greatness measure correlates very highly with other ratings of the American presidents and with variables that Cell considers evidence of charismatic leadership. The greatest presidents are more likely to have monuments built in their honor in the nation's capital, to have a county seat or state capital named after them, to appear on low-denomination paper currency, and so on. Thus this measure merges academic and popular consensus.

I then employed multiple regression analysis to determine the best predictors of greatness by this more subjective criterion. About 75 percent of the differential greatness of the 33 American presidents could be successfully predicted. The four most important predictors are as follows. First, the worst-rated presidents are those whose administrations were plagued by major scandals ($\beta = -.20$). Grant, Harding, and Nixon are the only three chief executives who presided over scandals that reached cabinet level. Second, those presidents who were targets of unsuccessful attempts at assassination tend to be rated as greater by subsequent historians ($\beta = .30$). Truman was one president who survived a serious assassination attempt. Curiously, presidents who fell victim to an assassin, such as Lincoln or Kennedy, did not similarly gain in assessed greatness. Third, the presidents rated as greatest tend to have had the longest tenures in office ($\beta = .24$). Franklin D. Roosevelt, who served 12 years and 39 days in the White House, received the highest greatness rating. Most of the poorly rated presidents—Tyler, Andrew Johnson, Arthur, Harding—served less than a full term or just one term. This result suggests that the assessments of historians tend to be in approximate agreement with those of contemporaries who refuse to elect inferior presidents to second terms.

The fourth predictor seems to contradict what was shown to be true for popularity: even though the approval ratings of Truman and Johnson were damaged by the Korean and Vietnam Wars, presidential greatness is positively linked with being a wartime leader ($\beta = .36$). The greatest presidents tend to lead the nation through more years of war. All of Lincoln's 4 years and 42 days in office were preoccupied with the Civil War, and Roosevelt devoted a comparable length of time to winning World War II. Perhaps the reason Lincoln and Roosevelt are rated as great while Truman and Johnson lost in popularity is that the former pair won their wars and the latter pair, if they cannot be said to have lost, still only fought to a stalemate. I strongly suspect that wars are far more popular with historians than with the contemporaries who must fight in them and pay for them. We tend to forget that the War of 1812 was also extremely unpopular. In New England especially, Americans sometimes aided the British. Even worse, the war was never really won. The Treaty of Ghent settled none of the issues that had brought about the war, and the only decisive American victory, that of Andrew Jackson at New Orleans, could hardly compensate for the burning of the nation's capital. Yet President Madison, who had to put up with hearing the unpopular conflict called "Madison's War," has not suffered a depreciation in his greatness rating that equates with the loss in popularity experienced by Truman and Johnson. So in the long run the latter two presidents may gain in the eyes of history from their military entanglements.

One possible interpretation of the finding that these four factors predict greatness is that a president's greatness rating depends not so much upon individual traits as upon the situation in which he served. Take the finding that wartime presidents tend to be seen as greater chief executives. It is significant that it is the number of war years during which a president was commander-in-chief that best predicts assessed greatness. A president has very little control over how many years the nation is at war. To be sure, a president can deliver a war message to Congress, yet this behavior is far inferior as a predictor of greatness than the number of war years or even the congressional passage of a declaration of war. And many presidents were dragged into wars they had tried hard to avoid. McKinley was pushed into the Spanish-American War and Wilson into World War I by the force of public opinion. Only Polk can be considered to have deliberately provoked a war, whereas Franklin Roosevelt tried to involve the United States in a second European war but did not attain this goal until the Japanese attacked Pearl Harbor. All in all, the president's length of tenure as a wartime commander-in-chief seems to be a far more situational than individual factor.

The other predictors may also be largely situational. The occurrence of a major administration scandal or an assassination attempt is not something over which a president has a great deal of control, even though such events may result from negligence in standards or security. And certainly how long a president serves in the White House is not very susceptible to personal control either. It is not just a simple matter of getting elected and reelected, for length of tenure may depend on such chancy circumstances as the death of one's predecessor or one's own death. In addition, personality and biographical variables do not fully predict length of time in office. Significantly, the chief predictors of a long stay in the White House are whether the president was a dark-horse candidate ($\beta = -.46$), whether his father was also a politician ($\beta = -.44$), whether he was a Democrat ($\beta = .28$), and whether his party controlled the House of Representatives, that part of the Congress which most accurately mirrors public opinion ($\beta = .41$). Excepting perhaps the first two, these predictors have a much more situational than individual aura. It is true that a long stay in office is also associated with a host of other events that make the president look very active: a larger number of acts signed, bills vetoed, treaties negotiated, cabinet appointments and resignations, Supreme Court appointments, military interventions, and war declarations. But these events have no relation to presidential greatness once administration duration is controlled. The conclusion is inescapable that presidential greatness, much like presidential popularity, is mostly a product of events over which the president has little personal control. Many presidents might concur with what Lincoln wrote in a letter in 1864: "I claim not to have controlled events, but confess plainly that events have controlled me."

Someone committed to the explanatory value of personality variables might object that the situational nature of presidential greatness has been far overstated. Perhaps many of the contextual factors are nothing more than surrogates for underlying personality constructs. The discussion of the power motive in Chapter 3 revealed that the president's need for power is associated with his willingness to involve the United States in military actions and even with his danger of being the target of an assassination attempt, whether successful or not. Accordingly, it may be that these events are indicators of a president's power motivation, and that the putatively situational predictors are actually proxy variables for the true causal personality dimension. Yet the need for power exhibited in a president's inaugural address does not predict presidential greatness once war years and the other variables are controlled (Simonton, 1981c). Moreover, much other evidence exists that seems to subordinate individual factors to situational ones, evidence I will discuss in the next chapter.

In Chapter 4 I pointed out that presidential dogmatism, or idealistic inflexibility, is not correlated with the attributes that compose presidential greatness. A good president can be just as dogmatic as a bad president; it matters more what the ideals are than how tenaciously they are held. The dogmatism of American presidents tends to fluctuate in a very odd way: the autocorrelation is negative, which signifies that dogmatic presidents tend to follow undogmatic presidents and vice-versa. The very pragmatic and flexible Lincoln is succeeded by the impractical and inflexible Andrew Johnson, the supremely ivory-tower Wilson by the more easy-going Harding. This pendulum swing suggests that the American voters tend to react to one type of presidency by electing a president of another type to compensate, and also that running mates on a single ticket tend to be counterbalanced on this dimension. It appears that dogmatism, rather than being a personality variable that shapes historical events, serves as a situation criterion by which voters select the next occupant of the White House.

The scores the presidents received on the greatness scale are displayed in Table 1, along with the scores that were predicted by the equation (using the predictors mentioned earlier, namely, scandals, assassination attempts, tenure in office, and years of war) and the difference between actual and predicted scores. This table provides useful insights about the American presidency. W. Harrison and Garfield were not rated because of their exceptionally brief tenures in office, and Nixon, Ford, and Carter were not rated because Maranell's was published in 1970. Of the 33 presidents who were rated, the three greatest are F. D. Roosevelt, Lincoln, and T. Roosevelt, in that order, and the three worst are Harding, Pierce, and Fillmore. For the most part, the predicted greatness scores are in accord with these ratings: the correlation between predicted and actual scores is .87. Encouraged by this close correlation, I have used the equation to predict scores for the 5 unrated presidents. The scores for W. Harrison and Garfield are far below average. It is likely that these low scores would have held even had they served out their terms, as can be surmised from the low ratings of their successors, Tyler and Arthur, who served under similar situational conditions. The only difference would be that Garfield, if he had survived rather than succumbed to an assassin's bullet, would receive a higher score. For the 3 more recent unrated presidents, the scores are also low. Note that Nixon rates lower than his hand-picked successor, Ford. This result is founded on two facts: Ford was twice the target of unsuccessful assassination attempts, and Nixon suffered the most disgraceful administration scandal in U.S. history, becoming the first president to be forced to resign.

Table 1. Observed, predicted, and residual scores for greatness ratings of 38 American presidents.

PRESIDENT	GREATNESS RATINGS		
	OBSERVED	PREDICTED	RESIDUAL
1. Washington	5.69	−.66	6.35
2. J. Adams	1.99	.38	1.61
3. Jefferson	5.98	4.71	1.27
4. Madison	.43	2.75	−2.32
5. Monroe	−.09	−.66	.57
6. J. Q. Adams	−.43	−.18	−.25
7. Jackson	5.66	2.78	2.88
8. Van Buren	−1.97	−2.99	1.02

Table 1—*Continued*

PRESIDENT	GREATNESS RATINGS		
	OBSERVED	PREDICTED	RESIDUAL
9. W. Harrison	—	−3.45	—
10. Tyler	−4.15	−2.99	−1.16
11. Polk	1.68	−.04	1.72
12. Taylor	−4.91	−3.92	−.99
13. Fillmore	−6.49	−2.99	−3.50
14. Pierce	−6.89	−2.99	−3.90
15. Buchanan	−5.85	−2.01	−3.84
16. Lincoln	8.26	6.76	1.50
17. A. Johnson	−.95	−2.99	2.04
18. Grant	−5.66	−5.13	−.53
19. Hayes	−3.72	−2.99	−.73
20. Garfield	—	−3.92	—
21. Arthur	−3.73	−2.99	−.74
22. Cleveland	.45	−1.13	1.58
23. B. Harrison	−5.19	−2.99	2.20
24. McKinley	−1.57	−.61	−.96
25. T. Roosevelt	6.61	8.87	−2.26
26. Taft	−.30	−2.05	1.75
27. Wilson	5.94	5.05	.89
28. Harding	−6.92	−7.45	.53
29. Coolidge	−5.10	−1.59	−3.51
30. Hoover	−.51	−1.58	1.07
31. F. D. Roosevelt	9.04	11.88	−2.84
32. Truman	5.45	4.74	.71
33. Eisenhower	−.81	.32	−1.13
34. Kennedy	3.91	−1.11	5.02
35. L. B. Johnson	4.10	3.78	.32
36. Nixon	—	−.68	—
37. Ford	—	1.39	—
38. Carter	—	−2.25	—

SOURCE. Simonton, 1981c.

NOTE. The observed greatness ratings are based on a survey of 571 historians conducted by Maranell (1970). The predicted ratings are based on a multiple regression equation containing such variables as length of tenure, years of war, assassination attempts, and scandals—these variables proving to be the best predictors of assessed greatness. The residual is the difference between the predicted and the observed score, or the error of prediction.

The third column of the table presents the residual errors of prediction. Notice that four presidents seem to be underrated by the historians, namely, Fillmore, Pierce, Buchanan, and Coolidge. Far more remarkable than these small negative residuals are the large positive residuals for Washington and Kennedy, signifying that these two presidents may be overappreciated. Washington is perhaps unfairly borrowing a few extra points for having been the "father of his country"—for achievements that occurred prior to his becoming the first president of the United States. We may attribute Kennedy's high rating to the "Kennedy mystique," that is, to his supposed charisma, an effect that might diminish over time until Kennedy settles down to a rating fairly close to that of McKinley. Whatever the interpretation, it is clear that the criteria by which historians rate Washington and Kennedy are not identical to those used to rate the other presidents.

The discussion of Table 1 gives some indication of the value of applying historiometric techniques to presidential leadership. Though this application is yet in its infancy, it may eventually make it possible not only to predict greatness but also to throw light on other aspects of leadership, for example by establishing specific objective criteria of presidential performance. By elaborating the theoretical basis of the predictive equations and incorporating biographical and personality factors, we may one day be able to understand just what characteristics make for good or bad leadership in the American chief executive.

CONCLUSION

All of the historiometric studies reviewed in this chapter represent admittedly incipient efforts. Even so, the little work that has been done on aesthetics and charisma does reveal a few things about the way emotions affect the judgments of history. In the case of the arts, we have seen how one of the apparent purposes of a musical composition is to evoke the proper level of emotional arousal in the listener. Also, the melodic originality that generates this arousal is in part the composer's response to personal life crises and changes. Dramas, too, gain power by conveying a rich array of themes concerning the central issues of human existence—and doing so with the maximal amount of memorable lines. Inquiries into charisma have been far more oblique in attack, but they do seem to indicate that presidential popularity and ratings of greatness reflect a high degree of irrationality. The way war affects these judgments, the asymmetrical effect of economic slump versus prosperity, the repercussions of assassination attempts and international crises, all point to unobjective judgments on the part of historians and public alike. It will be useful for future inquiries to delve deeper into the emotional foundations of both aesthetic communications and charisma.

8

ZEITGEIST

IN THE COURSE of Western civilization, the most eminent thinkers in the sciences have tended to be contemporaries of the greatest creators in philosophy, literature, and music. Germany around 1800 saw the creative emergence of Alexander von Humboldt, Hegel, Schiller, and Beethoven, all born within a dozen years, who together imbued Germany with the special luster of a classical age. This type of grouping of talent I have termed a "discursive" cluster. Illustrious painters, sculptors, and architects together compose another type of cluster, a "presentational" one. The famous Attic painter Polygnotus of Thasos was an older contemporary of Phidias, who was responsible for the sculptural decoration of the Parthenon, an edifice built for Pericles by the architects Ictinus and Callicrates. Curiously, these two types of clusters are not associated with each other. The flourishing of the visual arts in Athens was not simultaneous with any comparable creative surge in discursive activities. Aristotle, Plato, and Euripides all came later. All types of cultural activities, in other words, do not necessarily thrive at the same time—but it is undeniable that certain creative endeavors do appear to cluster in some mysterious way through history (Simonton, 1975b).

Such conspicuous concurrences make it seem that the individual genius has very little control over which times are most opportune for a creative contribution in a particular endeavor. Sometimes the world is ripe for a major discovery in physics or a new philosophical treatise; other times the conditions are far less favorable, but may welcome some novel development in the visual arts. Perhaps it is the spirit of the time—the zeitgeist—that determines how genius shall manifest itself. Perhaps individual greatness is accorded to those who best fulfill the expectations of the age. Hegel made this claim in *The Philosophy of Right:* "The great man of the age is the one who can put into words the will of his age, tell his age what its will is, and accomplish it. What he does is the heart and the essence of his age, he actualizes his age." And Goethe said in *Faust:*

> What you call "spirit of the ages"
> Is after all the spirit of those sages
> In which the mirrored age itself reveals.

Leadership, too, may be pushed into certain channels by the political or military zeitgeist. According to Machiavelli, "he will be successful who directs his actions according to the spirit of the times." Tolstoy, treating military rather than political leadership, concurs; in *War and Peace,* after analyzing Napoleon's career, he defends the proposition that leaders do not lead at all, but rather follow their followers: "But we need only penetrate to the essence of any historic event—which lies in the activity of the general mass who take part in it—to be convinced that the will of the historic hero does not control the actions of the mass but is itself continually controlled" (1865–1869, p. 563).

To examine the validity of the theory that the zeitgeist determines historical genius, I will begin with a look at various timewise trends and corresponding models that describe how the spirit of the times changes over the course of history.

TIMEWISE TRENDS

The zeitgeist is thought to reveal itself in patterns or regularities that are exhibited by historical events over time. Some thinkers believe the movement of history is progressive; others see history as cyclical. In Hegel's philosophy of history, for example, the course of human events features a definite direction governed by the spirit of the times, the outcome being a world that is an ever better place with respect to the development of human freedom. Marx, too, thought that the patterns of history evince progress, in this case progress leading to the control of the workers over the means of production. Another nineteenth-century philosopher, Herbert Spencer, took a very different approach that was eventually developed as the sociocultural analogue of the changes in biological systems documented by Charles Darwin. Societies, like living organisms, evolve over time, pressured by the need to adapt to the environment. It was Spencer, in fact, who coined the term "survival of the fittest" to describe the force of these selective pressures. This evolutionary process is thought to assure that societies will never cease changing for the better. "Progress, therefore, is not an accident, but a necessity," said Spencer.

These social philosophers did not collect pertinent data in any systematic manner, let alone subject the data to objective and quantitative verification. What little research has been done on this topic is inclined to focus on exponential trends in the growth of science and technology, rather than on direct indicators of material progress. Most notably, Price (1963) has surveyed the exponential growth of science since the Renaissance, an increase that even exceeds the exponential growth of the general population over the same time period. In addition, Taagapera (1979) has suggested that the processes underlying scientific and demographic increases may be interconnected in a more subtle way. Besides the fact that scientific progress must depend on the basic reservoir of potential scientists and inventors in the general population, population growth is dependent in part on an enhanced technological base in agriculture, transportation, communication, and industry and on progress in medical diagnosis and treatment. Taagapera shows how the interaction between technological progress and population advance helps explain the phenomenal increases in population over the last few centuries.

In contrast to the dearth of good inquiries into progressive change, a veritable cornucopia of investigations have focused on cyclical changes in the spirit of the times. The possible existence of cycles in history exerts a profound fascination for many social philosophers and behavioral scientists. The ancient Chinese philosophers interpreted history in terms of the oscillations of yin and yang—of passivity and quiescence versus activity and strife. The medieval Moslem historian Ibn Khaldun spotted a cyclical rhythm in the rise and fall of political systems. And the Italian philosopher of history Giambattista Vico discerned a recurrent cycle in the histories of Greco-Roman and modern Western civilizations. Such historical cycles, if they can be shown to exist, seem to contradict the notion of smooth, uninhibited progress. History may be just as capable of retrogression as of progression.

In fact, progressive and cyclical interpretations can be complementary rather than antagonistic. According to Kuhn's (1970) theory of the structure of scientific revolutions, for instance, a given theoretical and methodological paradigm, after commencing with a series of notable empirical triumphs, often starts to run aground with the discovery of new phenomena that do not fit paradigmatic expectations. As these anomalies grow in number, science appears increasingly noncumulative and controversial rather than progressive and solidly monolithic. Eventually a new scientific revolutionary arrives to propound a more comprehensive synthesis that will provide the framework for another enthusiastic phase of scientific advance—until such time as another batch of anomalies appears to challenge the new paradigm. In Kuhn's scheme, science progresses only haltingly, through cycles of revolutionary, normal, and anomalous science, and yet the overall direction is toward the accumulation of systematized knowledge.

Recent research has tried to provide empirical evidence about historical cycles. This research distinguishes various cyclical conceptions along three dimensions. First, some cyclical processes exhibit relatively fast periodicities, and others take place in massive slothful sweeps centuries long. The ups and downs of scientific discovery and invention may be rather quick and fickle (Rainoff, 1929), whereas cycles in ideological systems or in the appearance of creative geniuses are much more sluggish, lasting centuries if not millennia (Sorokin, 1937–1941; Kroeber, 1944).

Second, cycles can be truly periodic with a well-defined wave length or can be more irregular. In truth, the overwhelming majority of empirical studies indicate that historical cycles are aperiodic or quasi-periodic in nature. Only a handful of investigators believe otherwise (for example, Dewey, 1970). Kroeber's (1944) cultural "configurations"—consisting of creators clustered into contiguous generations—may endure less than a century or as long as a millennium, with interludes of creative stagnation equally variable. As noted in Chapter 2, the fact that the number of creators in generation g is a function of the number in generations $g - 1$ and $g - 2$ implies that the distribution of creators over time will display a quasi-periodic configurational form that is by no means deterministic. All in all, the sinecoidal cycles seen in physical phenomena and the reliable circadian rhythms seen in the biological world have no exact parallels in the social domain.

Third, cycles may be produced by an intrinsic process or may be the outcome of underlying causes that just so happen to have a quasi-periodic or even periodic temporal distribution. Gray (1958, 1961, 1966), in attempting to provide a theoretical explanation for Kroeber's configurations, proposed a curious "epicyclical" model of cultural evolution. By this model, creativity is a function of aperiodic cycles in economic, political, and cultural circumstances. In a more mundane example of an extrinsic model, Rainoff (1929) has suggested an economic foundation for oscillations in scientific discoveries and technological inventions; this model would make the explanation of such scientific cycles a problem in economics rather than in creativity. Sheldon (1980) is equally interested in explicating the ups and downs in scientific output, but he considers such quasi-cycles to be caused by intrinsic processes. Specifically, he believes that modeling and recruitment influences operating across consecutive generations of scientists yield a complex but regular temporal pattern. It is important to recognize the difference between intrinsic and extrinsic causes of cycles, but in fact it is likely that the quasi-periodic cycles in history are compounds of both types of factors. For example, I have shown that Kroeber's cultural configurations result from both the intrinsic mechanism of role modeling across generations and the extrinsic factor of timewise trends in certain political circumstances (Simonton, 1975c).

The most ambitious historiometric inquiry into cycles to date is Pitirim A. Sorokin's *Social and Cultural Dynamics* (1937–1942). Sorokin believed that history moves in slow pendulum swings between two great ideological systems, which he called the sensate system and the ideational system. The sensate system is characterized by empiricism and nominalism; it holds matter to be the sole substrate of a reality that is in constant though deterministic flux (materialism, temporalism, and determinism); and it maintains that the individual is the primary social entity (singularism) who must be guided by hedonistic or utilitarian moral schemes (ethics of happiness). The ideational system, by contrast, sees reason (rationalism) and especially revelation (mysticism) as primary sources of knowledge about a world composed of spiritual substance (idealism) that is immutable and eternal (eternalism) and in which abstract ideas have real existence (realism). It grants the individual free will (indeterminism) within the confines of a social system that enjoys supremacy over the individual (universalism) and within the boundaries of moral strictures predicated upon abstractions or altruism (ethics of principles or ethics of love). According to Sorokin a sensate zeitgeist is associated with realistic and secular art forms, an ideational one with iconic and religious styles of aesthetic expression, and each system features distinctive political, legal, and social structures. Scientific creativity and economic entrepreneurship are the products of a sensate rather than ideational spirit. Hence, for Sorokin the sensate and ideational systems represent two comprehensive ways of defining modal personalities or favored sociocultural mentalities of a given civilization at a particular moment in its history.

Sorokin maintained that sensate and ideational systems have alternated over the course of Western history. Thus a sensate zeitgeist presided over the world of the Minoans and Mycenaeans, Hellenistic

Greece and Republican Rome, and modern Europe since the Renaissance; an ideational zeitgeist reigned over the Dark Ages of Greece
after the Dorian invasions and over the Dark Ages of Europe. Sorokin
hypothesizes that the movement back and forth between sensate and
ideational worlds is inherent in the nature of human thought so that
such change is always imminent. Neither system is completely satisfac-
tory in meeting human needs, and therefore the dominance of either
system breeds discontent, reaction, and eventually the emergence of
the diametric opposite. The triumph of Christianity, for example, was a
reaction to the psychological insufficiencies of Greco-Roman hedo-
nism, materialism, and individualistic pragmatism.

Sorokin amassed a prodigious quantity of data to document his thesis. This evidence looks impressive, but when I did a statistical analysis
of Sorokin's data I found that the data actually *disprove* his theory (Simonton, 1976c). It turns out that sensate and ideational philosophies
are not antagonistic systems. Those periods in Western civilization that
produce the most sensate philosophers are precisely the same periods
in which the supply of ideational philosophers is highest. The timewise
distribution of adherents of these two systems is virtually identical ($r =$
.98). From 540 B.C. (when Sorokin's data begin) the total count of
thinkers, sensate or ideational, increased to a primary peak during the
Golden Age of Greek philosophy, then gradually declined with inter-
mittent small revivals until the end of the Roman Empire ushered in the
Dark Ages. The advent of High Scholasticism and the eventual ignition
of the Renaissance initiated an upward trend that persists to the present day. As for the connection between the prevailing zeitgeist and scientific creativity, it is true that scientific genius is more likely to appear
when sensate ideas—especially empiricism, materialism, and determinism—are on the rise, but a rise in ideational ideas does not necessarily doom the prospects for science. Similarly, even though the
appearance of religious leaders is positively associated with an ideational zeitgeist, a sensate zeitgeist bears no relationship whatsoever,
whether positive or negative, to religious activity. Science and religion
are more orthogonal than antagonistic.

Sorokin's theoretical contention that a sensate philosophy emerges
as a reaction to the insufficiencies of an ideational zeitgeist, in some intrinsic dialectical process, has been undermined by more recent evidence that external forces can produce a sensate zeitgeist. As we will
see a bit later in this chapter, a political milieu called "political fragmentation" is a causal antecedent of the key beliefs that make up the

sensate mentality. And the next chapter will point out that warfare may inhibit the emergence of a sensate orientation. There is no current evidence that the zeitgeist oscillates between sensate and ideational ideologies in some dialectic process immune to extraneous forces.

As a matter of fact, by following Sorokin's data through history I discovered that although a pure ideational zeitgeist may be possible, the sensate ideology never stands alone but always coexists with an ideational contingent. In Greece just before the Persian Wars, for example, the sensate mentality constituted only 21 percent of the whole zeitgeist, the times being thus predominantly ideational. By the last generation of the fifth century B.C., at the height of the Peloponnesian Wars, sensate mentality had reached a peak of 70 percent, with the remaining 30 percent being ideational. This 30 percent is the lowest proportion ever attained by the ideational mentality throughout the 25 centuries surveyed by Sorokin. Except for a temporary resurgence of 67 percent in the last half of the third century B.C.—in the midst of the Hellenistic period—sensate culture declined after this all-time high, and struck rock bottom at the onset of the Dark Ages. For the next half millennium the zeitgeist was entirely ideational; not a single sensate thinker was to be found. Toward the end of the eleventh century, sensate ideas began to revive, and by the time of the Enlightenment sensate culture attained a new peak. Still, this peak was only 55 percent sensate, the remainder being ideational. During the Romantic period in the first half of the nineteenth century, sensate philosophy dipped below 30 percent because of the heavy influx of German Idealists. At the beginning of the twentieth century the two systems commanded approximately equal shares of the zeitgeist. Hence, a pure sensate zeitgeist has never existed in Western history. The ideational monopoly during the Dark Ages is also suspect: the number of thinkers in that period was very small, only 40 philosophers spread over 25 generations. Apparently the reason ideational culture can be "pure" is that there are very few philosophers at all. As soon as more thinkers appear, sensate philosophers join the ideational ones.

My own theoretical account of these ideological movements begins with three assumptions: first, that some sociocultural environments are more favorable than others to the emergence of thinkers; second, that as the number of philosophers increases the number of schools or sects increases; and third, that ideational philosophers are able to survive under adverse sociocultural conditions but sensate philosophers require a supportive setting of intellectual freedom and diversity. This third assumption is consistent with Sorokin's assertion that most so-called primitive cultures are highly ideational, while sensate ideologies thrive in more economically and politically developed societies. These three assumptions make possible an extrinsic model for changes in the zeitgeist. When the milieu is not particularly conducive to philosophical creativity, and thinkers are thus extremely rare, what few philosophers there are will be committed to ideational positions. But as the environment improves and more thinkers appear, philosophical controversy gives birth to rival schools, some of which will be sensate in orientation. Eventually, when the milieu is most conducive to intellectual ferment, the full repertoire of philosophical possibilities will be represented. Thus empiricism will co-exist with mysticism, materialism with idealism, temporalism with eternalism, nominalism with realism, singularism with universalism, determinism with indeterminism, and the ethics of happiness with the ethics of principles or love—just as they do now in our own era of ideological conflict. This interpretation explains why ideational philosophers are always well represented in supposedly sensate times while an ideational zeitgeist can exist in pure form. It also handles the near identity of the time trends for the two ideologies: a milieu favorable to thinkers will generate both sensate and ideational minds, and when creative decline sets in both ideologies will lose representatives, though ideationalism at a slower rate so that when only one or two thinkers emerge in each generation their philosophies will be ideational.

MATERIAL CONDITIONS

Karl Marx was in many ways a disciple of Hegel, but whereas Hegel was a preeminent idealist, Marx was a thorough materialist. Contrary to Hegel's philosophy that the Spirit, or Idea, provides the impetus behind material changes in sociocultural systems, the father of dialectical materialism believed that such ideas are the repercussions of specific material conditions, especially economic forces. In the Marxist view it is the struggle between economic classes, not the conflict of ideologies, that guides the course of human history.

SOCIOECONOMIC MILIEU

Many historians have propounded the idea that economic prosperity is the basis of sociocultural achievements. A civilization's Golden Age is just that, an age in which gold purchases the leisure for greatness. Pericles was able to adorn the Acropolis with the Parthenon because he had at his disposal monies deposited into the Athenian coffers by the allies of Athens in the Delian League. And yet there are counterexamples of extreme wealth being simultaneous with a dearth of cultural activity. The Byzantines were far richer than the Athenians, and yet except in the realm of architecture and mosaics, the accomplishments of these latter-day Greeks do not bear comparison with their predecessors of the Golden Age.

There have been very few historiometric inquiries to test the hypothesis that prosperity is associated with creativity, and those few tend to test the hypothesis only very indirectly. For instance, one investigation showed that monetary investment in basic research and development contributes to technological invention, as gauged by patents (Schmookler, 1966). There have, however, been a number of provocative studies of the way economic prosperity or depression affects the prevailing ideologies. In particular, religious activity appears to bear some connection with economic conditions. Religious activity is associated with economic decline, while prosperity tends to draw people away from worship of God to the quest for material goods. The first historiometrician to demonstrate this generalization was Sorokin (1947), who counted the frequency of major religious figures versus distinguished businesspersons over the course of Western history and concluded that creativity in ideational systems of religion and creativity in sensate systems of business are mutually exclusive.

Sales (1972) has indicated that this negative relationship between prosperity and religion holds not only for the eminent but for the general population as well. He studied the rates of conversion to authoritarian and nonauthoritarian churches as a function of economic conditions. An authoritarian church is one that demands absolute obedience, even to the point of condemning supposed heretics and practicing some kind of excommunication of the wayward. Nonauthoritarian churches allow their members more latitude of conscience in both belief and behavior. Sales studied conversion rates in the United States as a whole from 1920 to 1939 and also in the city of Seattle during the 1960s. As indicators of economic conditions he used per capita disposable income for the United States and unemployment statistics for Seattle. He found that economic good times brought about an increased conversion rate for nonauthoritarian churches, while economic bad times ushered in an increased conversion rate for authoritarian churches.

A more recent inquiry, looking at Germany between the two world wars, has described a comparable association between economic depression and the popularity of astrology and mysticism (Padgett and Jorgenson, 1982). Another study found that the amount of authoritarianism in the television programs shown in the United States from 1950 to 1974 correlated significantly with economic hardship over the same years (Jorgenson, 1975). Many nations responded to the Great Depression by appealing to authoritarian leadership; even in the United States, Franklin D. Roosevelt was given powers never before granted a president in peacetime. In times of economic insecurity people seem to need something definite to believe in—whether it be a dogmatic religion, irrational superstition, or a strong authoritarian leader.

A more pervasive consideration than unemployment and per capita income is social stratification, a characteristic of society that incorporates both economic and political power. In some times and places stratification is minimal, yielding relatively egalitarian systems in which everyone has fairly equal access to resources and to the political process. Other societies are much less democratically constituted, a small elite commanding a disproportionate share of the material goods and political clout. Researchers have found that social stratification has an impact upon the art produced in a society. For example, Dressler and Robbins (1975) made a detailed analysis of the formal design elements of Greek vase painting from 1000 to 450 B.C., and found that greater stratification in Athenian society was associated with greater stylistic complexity, more complete utilization of space, and more frequent enclosure of figures. These design characteristics mirror aspects of the concurrent social structure: a stratified society is a more complex one, and the power elite tends to be isolated from the populace by various symbols of distinctive status. Thus however purely decorative a vase decoration may seem, its design conveys information about the society in which the painter lived.

POLITICAL FRAGMENTATION

Ancient Greece during its Golden Age was fragmented into numerous independent city-states, such as Athens and Sparta. Alexander the Great did consolidate the eastern Greek states into a single political unit, but that empire was short-lived, and considerable political fragmentation persisted in Hellenistic times. Then came the Roman conquest, followed by the conversion of the Eastern Roman Empire into a thoroughly Greek Byzantine Empire, and yet this political revival of the Greeks did not bring about a comparable resurgence of cultural creativity. A massive, impersonal state had replaced the abundant diversity of small city-states. This historical pattern is also seen elsewhere. The Italy of the Renaissance was also sliced into small political units that provided centers of cultural activity. This politically fragmented culture produced such geniuses as Leonardo, Michelangelo, Raphael, Dante, Petrarch, Boccaccio, and Machiavelli. Political fragmentation appears to be conducive to creative upsurgence in non-Western civilizations as well: one modern historian of Islamic culture, for instance, finds that creativity was highest during the period of principalities, when the caliphs were weak and princes were fighting one another (Armajani, 1970). In more recent times, Hegel and Marx, Goethe and Schiller, Mozart and Beethoven were all born in a Germany made up of myriad little states that had been set adrift from the overlordship of the Holy Roman Emperor. When Bismarck united Germany under the Kaiser, he may have rung the death knell for the Golden Age of German creativity. Gladstone may have been correct indeed when he said of Bismarck, "He made Germany great and Germans small."

Do we have here a genuine nomothetic lesson of history? Are eminent creators more likely to emerge in civilizations divided into small political fragments? Is political unification into large empires a death warrant for creative genius? A pioneer inquiry conducted about a decade ago attempted to address this very question (Naroll et al., 1971). Using the lists of creators contained in Kroeber's (1944) classic work, Naroll and his students measured the number of creators active each century in the four major world civilizations, China, India, Islam, and Europe, from around 500 B.C. to A.D. 1899. They also counted the number of independent states in each civilization in each century. Political fragmentation and creative activity were shown to be positively correlated ($r = .29$). About 9 percent of the variance in number of creators was so accounted for. Besides political fragmentation, these investigators examined the impact of wealth, geographical expansion, governmental centralization, and warfare, but only political fragmentation exhibited any significant effect.

Because Naroll used a temporal unit an entire century long, the analysis may not have been fine-grained enough to yield a precise idea of how political fragmentation affects creativity. A few years after the Naroll study I made a similar inquiry using 20-year periods (Simonton, 1975c). I scrutinized Western civilization from 700 B.C. to A.D. 1839, slicing this period into 127 20-year units. Political fragmentation emerged as the single best political predictor of creativity. Further, I found some reason to suspect that political fragmentation operates as a developmental influence. That is, growing up in an environment characterized by numerous sovereign states tends to increase creative potential, and that potential is then actualized in adulthood no matter what may have happened to the political situation. Political unification may cause a decline in creativity 20 years later, but the initial stages of empire building may be graced with creators who grew up under more fragmented political conditions. Aristotle was the teacher of Alexander the Great, but tiny Athens and not the Macedonian Empire must take credit for Aristotle's intellectual development.

It appears that creative development depends on exposure to cultural diversity. But the construction of a large empire usually brings pressures toward cultural homogenization and uniformity. Alexander tried to unify Persian and Greek cultures into some overriding synthesis. Where Alexander failed, the Roman Empire largely succeeded, spreading a single language, legal system, and general culture over most of Europe and the Near East. Similarly, when the Ch'in Emperor Shih Huang-ti unified the sinic peoples into a single state known as China, he ordered the standardization of virtually everything—writing script, weights and measures, even the width of carriage axles—and he had every book in the empire that was not to his liking confiscated and burned, including practically all philosophy and history. I found further endorsement of this effect of political unification on cultural diversity in a study that measured one indicator of cultural heterogeneity, namely the number of rival schools of thought in the Western philosophical tradition. Decreases in political fragmentation were followed 20 years later by declines in ideological diversity (Simonton, 1976d). Rival philosophical schools disappeared as sovereign states vanished until, under large empires, ideological diversity became virtually nonexistent.

What can be done to diminish the stifling influence of imperial homogenization? The answer is simple enough: rebel! Nationalistic rebellions against imperial political systems tend to bring about the resurgence of creative activity—at least in such discursive endeavors as science, philosophy, literature, and music—some 20 years later (Simonton, 1975d). Apparently such civil disturbances serve as reminders that alternative points of view do exist besides the dominating imperial viewpoint. Revolts against imperial authority are strongly associated with the resuscitation of ideological diversity ($r = .41$) (Simonton, 1976d).

Many social scientists and historians have suspected a connection between nationalism and creativity. Toynbee (1946) found a negative relationship between the growth and expansion of a "universal state" and the creative activity of a given civilization. Kroeber (1944) noted the rarity of high achievements by suppressed nationalities. Sorokin (1947) said that many nations attain the climax of their creativeness in various fields after their liberation from foreign domination. The naturalist and philosophical historian Danilevsky made it his "second law of the dynamics of great cultures" that "In order for the civilization of a potentially creative group to be conceived and developed, the group and its subgroups must be politically independent" (quoted in Sorokin, 1947, p. 543).

Political fragmentation has a crucial influence on the history of ideas. Besides the fact that philosophical creativity grows in the fertile soil of political diversity, the existence of many nations contributes to the emergence of a very specific set of philosophical beliefs. About 20 years after an increase in political fragmentation there appear more philosophers who advocate the sensate positions of empiricism, skepticism, fideism, materialism, temporalism, nominalism, singularism, and the ethics of happiness (Simonton, 1976g). These attitudes belong to the broader syndrome of sensate individualism, which can thrive only in a civilization made up of small amounts of autonomous political units. Any empiricism, skepticism, materialism, temporalism, nominalism, singularism, or hedonism-utilitarianism in the writings of Machiavelli or Marx may be natural outgrowths of the political zeitgeist in which their intellects received nourishment. Just as the decorations on an Attic vase may mirror the social stratification of the Athenian state, so may *Il Principé* or *Das Kapital* reflect a civilization's political confusion.

GENIUS VERSUS ZEITGEIST: FIVE CASE STUDIES

The message of this chapter so far seems to be that the zeitgeist governs genius. The spirit of the times decides both the quantity and the character of creative activity. The eminent genius is a mere mouthpiece for the age, or a funnel in which diverse sociocultural causes are collated and concentrated. Needless to say, many scholars would take issue with this subordination of individual to situation. Some scholars believe that the genius is an active agent who transcends and transforms the times. Thomas Carlyle propounded this position in 1841:

"Universal History, the history of what man has accomplished in this world, is at bottom the History of the Great Men who have worked here." I will delve into these two rival accounts of historical behavior by presenting five case studies of the interaction of genius and zeitgeist. These five cases concern political greatness, military success, philosophical fame, musical originality, and scientific discovery.

LEADERS AS EPONYMS

In an extensive study of rulers throughout history, Sorokin (1925, 1926) found that great monarchs live longer than average ones. Taking just those kings and queens who died of natural causes, the average life span of the 78 most prominent rulers is 62 years, that of their more obscure colleagues only 54. Elizabeth I of England lived to be 70; Frederick the Great of Prussia 74; and Louis XIV of France, arguably the most eminent hereditary monarch in European history, 77. Why should the great monarchs be the ones who live to be old? One possibility is that the long-lived rulers may provide history with "eponyms," that is, with convenient names for the epochs of history. In the world of hereditary monarchs, a long life is often virtually synonymous with a long reign. Louis XIV was king of France in name for 72 years and actually ruled for 54 years once we discount the time he spent under a regency. That long reign makes Louis an exceptionally good label for the events of European history in the second half of the seventeenth century and the first decade or so of the eighteenth. "The Age of Louis XIV" serves as a label for that whole epoch, not only a political label but a cultural one besides.

If the fame of rulers depends on their usefulness as eponyms for historical periods, a usefulness that in turn depends on the length of their reigns, then the rulers must surely have very little individual control over how much fame they achieve. Eponymic theory must join Tolstoy in maintaining that "A king is history's slave . . . In historic events, the so-called great men are labels giving names to events, and like labels they have but the smallest connection with the event itself. Every act of theirs, which appears to them an act of their own will, is in a historical sense involuntary and is related to the whole course of history and predestined from eternity" (1865–1869, pp. 343–344).

The previous chapter's discussion of greatness among American presidents seems to support Tolstoy's eponymic assertion. The key predictor of presidential greatness, duration of time in office, may have more situational than individual causes. But testing the eponymic theory on American presidents faces the drawback that the length of a particular presidency may depend partly on personal influence, namely on the president's ability to get himself renominated and reelected. An investigation of monarchs may permit a more conclusive test of the eponymic hypothesis, since hereditary monarchs seldom ascend to the throne or step down from power except for situational reasons.

My examination of 342 European absolute monarchs, which I discussed in Chapters 2 and 3, yielded some support for the eponymic viewpoint (Simonton, 1984b). Between two-fifths and two-thirds of the variance in the fame of these monarchs could be ascribed to the number of significant historical events that occurred during their reigns. The more battles, revolts, reforms, laws, and the like, the greater the eponymic value of the ruler, and hence the larger the ruler's assessed distinction. This richness of the historical record was indeed a direct result of the length of the reign, and the primary determinant of length of reign was indeed life span. Those monarchs who lived longest tended to reign longest, and the length of reign then determined the amount of historical activity during the reign, historical activity that provides the foundation of that eponymic prominence called eminence.

Two further findings make the case for the eponymic theory even more convincing. First of all, it does not matter whether the events were positive or negative so long as they were transcribed in the annals of history. The number of battles lost in a reign contributes about as much fame to the monarch as the number of battles won. Likewise, territorial losses count about as much as territorial gains, and invasions by other nations about as much as invasions of other nations. Even such events as famines and massacres contribute to the composite of historical activity that underlies a monarch's assessed greatness. Secondly, events over which a monarch has more personal control do not count any differently in the determination of fame. For instance, the battles fought during a reign can be broken down into those that involved an army under the ruler's personal command and those that did not, but this distinction makes not one iota of difference. Impersonal quantity of historical events, not quality or personal accountability, is the primary factor behind a monarch's eminence.

I have already presented evidence for the influence of individual characteristics on the eminence of monarchs. In Chapter 3 I showed that the fame of a leader is a U-shaped function of morality and a positive function of intelligence, and that intelligence affects length of reign and life span, two important indirect determinants of a leader's eponymic greatness. I also showed that intelligence is positively associated with highly rated leadership. Besides all this, the richness of the historical activity in a given reign is a U-shaped function of the leader's morality. Those monarchs whose reigns feature the most impressive supply of events tend to be either extremely immoral or utterly virtuous. The iniquitous monarchs are likely to launch campaigns of aggression abroad and oppression at home, provoking rebellion and economic distress; the more saintly monarchs may pursue holy wars in foreign lands and domestic reforms against corruption and venality, interventions that also may destabilize the political situation. Less moralistic and less egotistical monarchs do less to rock the boat and accordingly leave little mark upon history.

One other personality characteristic appears germane to greatness: length of reign is associated with the possession of the qualities of leadership. Woods (1913) long ago rated the leadership abilities of European monarchs in an attempt to prove that such an individual variable is correlated with a nation's economic, political, military, and even cultural well-being. He actually found that "Strong, mediocre, and weak monarchs are associated with strong, mediocre, and weak periods respectively," the correlations for more than a dozen nations ranging between .60 and .70. Whatever suspicions we may have about Woods' holistic assessment of national welfare, his leadership ratings display respectable reliabilities (Simonton, 1983b). More critically, these leadership ratings are one of the principal predictors of life span.

The influence of the individual factors of intelligence, morality, and leadership on eminence, an influence exerted both directly and through the eponymic predictors of monarchal fame, implies that genius may play as crucial a role as zeitgeist in shaping history. The relative contributions of genius and zeitgeist to historical image-making are summarized in Figure 6. Notice that besides the three individual factors (intelligence, morality, and leadership) and the four variables composing the eponymic causal chain (lifespan, reign span, historical activity, and leader eminence) three situational factors have been added to the diagram. Historical time affects both the amount of historical activity in a reign and the length of that reign: the more recent leaders tend to enjoy longer reigns that have a higher density of events. Related to historical time is dynastic rank, or a monarch's place in the list of successive rulers in a given royal family: the early monarchs in a dynasty tend to live less long but also to reign longer, a paradox that may be explained by the fact that as a dynasty becomes more firmly established

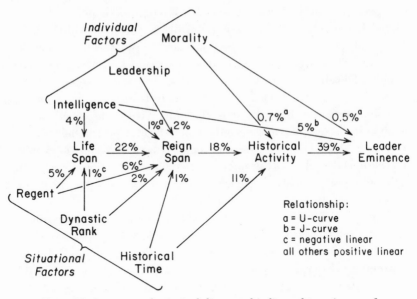

Figure 6. Summary of principal direct and indirect determinants of eminence of leaders, showing both the form of the function and the percentage of variance explained (from Simonton, 1984b).

its rulers can ascend the throne at younger ages without fear of usurpation, whereas in the early phase of the dynasty the rulers must be more mature, and hence older and shorter-termed, to maintain the throne against rivals (see Sorokin, 1925, 1926). The third situational factor is whether the leader was a true monarch or just a regent who governed during the minority of the rightful heir. Regents tend to reign less long but to live longer as well, perhaps because their unthreatening position as temporary caretakers protects them from assassination.

The amount of variance explained by each predictor variable is indicated in the figure by the percentages beside the causal arrows. For the most part, the individual factors account for the least variance, intelligence being the best of the lot, morality by far the worse. Intelligence explains 4 percent of the variance in life span and 5 percent of the variance in eminence; morality explains less than 1 percent of the variance in both eminence and historical activity; leadership accounts for about 2 percent of the variance in length of reign. The three situational factors explain somewhat more variance on the average. But the highest amount of variance is handled by the eponymic causal chain. Some 39 percent of leader eminence can be uniquely attributed to historical activity and 18 percent to reign span, and life span accounts for 22 percent of the variance in reign span. All of these proportions are calculated in a multivariate framework that controls for anomalies in the way a king or queen ascended to or descended from the throne. The results support a weak form of the eponymic theory, a form that permits some modest infusion of individual characteristics. Louis XIV may be a handy eponym because of his long life and his long reign enriched with notable events, but his intellectual gifts, his talents of leadership, and perhaps his morality did affect the eponymic causal sequence. His unique genius can be said to have sprinkled a little spice on the zeitgeist.

MILITARY GENIUS: CARLYLE OR TOLSTOY?

Battles can be turning points in history. A battle may decide the success or failure of a rebellion, as in Lee's defeat at Gettysburg; the survival of a nation, as in the English victory over the Spanish Armada; or the fate of a leader, as in Napoleon's defeat at Waterloo. To some historians, these encounters are moments when the will of individual genius reigns supreme. Thomas Carlyle again stands out among these hero-worshiping historians, and it is no accident that he included Napoleon in the exclusive list of world-making geniuses discussed in his classic *On Heroes*. Carlyle is not the only historian who places Napoleon so high: Napoleon enjoys the highest ranked eminence of all 301 geniuses in the Cox (1926) sample. And the Duke of Wellington remarked about 15 years after his defeat of Napoleon at Waterloo: "I used to say of him that his presence on the field made the difference of forty thousand men."

Many other theorists take issue with assigning so much importance to a solitary personage. Among them is Leo Tolstoy; *War and Peace* can be read as a diatribe against the genius interpretation of history in general and Napoleon in particular. After portraying the epic battle of Borodino, Tolstoy concludes, "And it was not Napoleon who directed the course of the battle, for none of his orders were executed and during the battle he did not know what was going on before him. So the way in which these people killed one another was not decided by Napoleon's will but occurred independently of him, in accord with the will of hundreds of thousands of people who took part in the common action" (1865–1869, p. 448).

Who is right? Is Carlyle justified in placing Napoleon among his historic stars? Or is Tolstoy correct in subordinating Napoleon to the broad impersonal movements of the times? I examined Napoleon's career and found that both positions have some merit (Simonton, 1979b). On the one hand, Napoleon's rate of success on the battlefield was almost double that of his fellow French generals fighting over the same years. During the French Revolution and the Napoleonic Wars, Napoleon's victory rate was 85 percent, whereas his colleagues averaged around 47 percent. This gap in competence means that being Napoleon accounts for 9 percent of the variance in French military success between 1796 and 1815. On the other hand, an inspection of the victory rates over time, year by year, gives some support to Tolstoy's explanation. Over the 14 years in which Napoleon was active on the field of battle, the correlation between his success rate per year and that of his colleagues is very high ($r = .50$). This result strongly implies that all French generals succeeded or failed depending on the strength or weakness of the French war machine. Tolstoy may be right in ascribing this strength to the collective spirit of the rank and file, or economic and technological factors may play a central part; either way, the military zeitgeist provided the necessary preconditions for French victory or defeat. About 25 percent of the yearly fluctuations in French military fortune may be ascribed to the workings of this zeitgeist. Carlyle may be right, but Tolstoy is perhaps more so.

It would be hasty to decide the issue according to a single case study of a single general's career. In another historiometric inquiry I went beyond the Napoleonic era (Simonton, 1980a). First I operationalized two sets of potential predictors of military success, one set entailing individual characteristics of the opposing commanders and the second set consisting of the situational attributes of the opposing armies. The relative age and experience of the two commanders were among the individual factors assessed, while chief among the situational factors were home defense and comparative size of army. Then I gauged success on the battlefield in two distinct ways, namely by actual tactical victory and by relative number of casualties. Suitable data could be obtained for 326 battles when the tactical victory criterion was used, and for 205 battles when the number of casualties served as a criterion.

The tactical victor on the field of battle could be correctly identified 71 percent of the time using merely four variables. First, the victorious general has more years of experience than his opponent. Second, the victor comes into battle with an unbroken string of victories that is nine times longer, on average, than his opponent's. This finding fits the principle of cumulative advantage discussed in Chapter 5. (In fact, the length of a general's winning streak is so highly correlated with his total battle experience as to make these two variables nearly equivalent ($r = .98$): the only way a general will fight many battles is to win them, for losers are fast replaced.) The third predictor is the general's willingness to take the offensive. The victorious commander tends to be the one who attacks first. By taking the initiative, he obliges his opponent to assume a defensive posture. Alexander the Great, Julius Caesar, Genghis Khan, Frederick the Great, and Napoleon were all disposed to attack first.

These first three predictors of tactical victory are all attributes of the general himself. However, the fourth predictor is more situational in nature—divided command. When two or more armies from separate nations combine to form a single allied force, the separate commanders may form a partnership rather than subordinating one to another. A famous example of this situation is the duo formed by the Duke of Marlborough and Prince Eugene of Savoy to lead the allied British-Dutch-Austrian forces against the French armies of Louis XIV. This combination was a winning one, fatal to the Sun King's ambitions in Europe. And this victorious partnership illustrates a historical tendency: armies commanded by two or more collaborating generals tend to win battles. This single situational factor accounts for only 14 percent of the total predictive power, however, whereas the three individual factors together are responsible for 86 percent of the prediction. By this criterion of military prowess, Carlyle seems to have won out over Tolstoy.

Oddly, relative army size is *not* a crucial predictor of tactical success. Voltaire was mistaken when he said, "God is always on the side of the big battalions." One reason army size does not predict victory is that the sizes of the opposing forces are almost invariably close to equal: the correlation between the sizes of opposing armies is .74. There do exist striking instances of daring commanders leading their men against fearfully superior forces—Alexander against Darius at Issus, Julius Caesar against Vercingetorix at Alesia, Charles XII against Peter the Great at Narva, Frederick the Great against Prince Charles at Leuthen—but these instances are exceptions, in which the smaller force had some advantage in technology, geography, or timing that compensated for the discrepancy in size.

Since a modest correlation exists between the relative size of a general's forces and his propensity to take the offensive ($r = .16$), the number of soldiers on each side does exert some indirect effect on military success. Commanders who know they have a size advantage are somewhat more likely to strike first. Yet it remains true that superiority in numbers does not make any independent impression upon the outcome of the battle.

If success in battle is measured by the second criterion, fewer battle casualties, then relative army size furnishes the single best predictor of military success ($\beta = .27$). Even though the casualties inflicted on each side tend to be highly correlated ($r = .74$), the winning side comes out better: the average number of killed, wounded, and missing for the victor in a given battle is 5,326, that for the loser 8,841, which amounts to losses of 14 percent for the winning side and 23 percent for the losing side. The fact that army size predicts advantage in number of casualties is not inconsistent with its failure to predict tactical victory—even though having fewer casualties is a predictor of victory. In fact the correlation between casualty advantage and victory is far from perfect ($r = .51$). Some victors win by displaying a willingness to sustain huge casualties, whereas some losers manage to avoid heavy loss of life by beating a hasty retreat.

Most of the remaining predictors of casualty advantage also differ from those of tactical victory. The only predictor they have in common is divided command. Otherwise, a casualty advantage is a function of two additional predictors, one situational and one individual. The remaining situational variable is the date of the battle. In ancient times the discrepancy between the numbers of casualties suffered by the two sides was normally quite large, as the victor often pursued and slaughtered the defeated army. With the advent of modern weaponry, mass warfare, and enhanced military discipline, such routs have become far less frequent. The two armies now share the horrifying experience of mutual annihilation, in which the victor may suffer almost as many casualties as the loser.

Together, the situational factors of army size, divided command, and date predict 83 percent of the explained variance in casualty advantage. The remaining predictor is individual, however: the relative numbers of cumulative victories of the opposing generals. The commander who has won the most battles in the past will suffer a smaller proportion of casualties. Moreover, the number of career victories at the moment of battle is correlated with the disposition to take the offensive ($r = .25$). It is very likely that being assertive in battle ultimately serves to diminish casualty counts, since being the aggressor predicts tactical victory, and most casualties occur after the battle has been decided. The reason adopting the offensive does not emerge as an individual predictor of casualty advantage is that initiative saves lives only if the attack succeeds. Because cumulative victories constitutes the only individual factor out of the four predictors that together explain 18 percent of the total variance in battle casualty advantage, Tolstoy defeats Carlyle according to this criterion of military success. Situation takes precedence over the individual in deciding which side in a battle will suffer more casualties.

In light of the discussion in Chapter 6, it is intriguing that the respective ages of the two commanders do not predict military success by either criterion. Age does have some indirect effect on military achievement, however. The closer a commander is to the apparent peak age of 45 years, the more experience he has, and the longer his winning streak and his list of cumulative victories can be. In fact, the willingness to take the offensive in battle is a small negative function of age ($r = -.14$): older commanders are somewhat less likely to initiate an attack. Thus the influence of age lends some support to Carlyle, yet not enough to overthrow Tolstoy's position. The reality of the matter is much too complicated to assign victory to either theorist. On the battlefield at least, Carlyle and Tolstoy have fought to a draw, neither managing to conquer the explanatory domains of his adversary.

PHILOSOPHICAL EMINENCE: THE AGE OF VOLTAIRE?

Voltaire was one of the most eloquent and influential exponents of the French Enlightenment. Highly prolific in many genres, from history to poetry and from light philosophy to polemic lampoons, Voltaire dominated his age. Though long exiled from his native land, he returned to Paris in triumph at age 83, and died at the height of his glory. Of the 301 geniuses in the Cox sample, only Napoleon surpassed Voltaire in ranked eminence. The source of such prominence may lie in Voltaire's relation to his zeitgeist. He functions as a valuable eponym for the Age of Enlightenment. He attains a secure place in history for being the spokesman and representative of his age. Is Voltaire's case typical, or are other great philosophers less apt exemplars of the prevailing zeitgeist? I addressed this and related questions in a study of 2,012 European philosophers from Ancient Greece to the twentieth century (Simonton, 1976f). I examined each thinker simultaneously as an individual creator and as a member of a generation with characteristic ideological and political properties. The beliefs of all of these thinkers had already been rated by a team of professional philosophers under the direction of Sorokin (1937–1941), and these ratings of individual beliefs could also be utilized to operationalize the ideological zeitgeist of each generation. In simple terms, the spirit of the times was defined by those beliefs that were advocated by the plurality of thinkers of each generation. The first two decades of this century, by this definition, were dominated by, among other beliefs, empiricism, nominalism, determinism, and the ethics of happiness. Defining measures of the philosophical zeitgeist of each 20-year period makes it possible to determine how representative a thinker is of his or her time, the extent to which the thinker is behind or ahead of the times, and even the degree of ideological modernity in the thinker's philosophical system. In addition, I devised a single measure of philosophical eminence that had high reliability and face validity.

Quite contrary to Voltaire's example, the greatest thinkers in the Western philosophical tradition have tended to be unrepresentative of their times. It is, in fact, their less distinguished colleagues who most accurately match the spirit of the times. The truly impressive thinkers are ruggedly independent of what the zeitgeist dictates for their generation. Philosophers of the caliber of Aristotle or Descartes are not mere mouthpieces, but rather are striking out on their own.

If great minds are not tied down to the zeitgeist, are they perhaps precursors of the next generation's zeitgeist? Surprisingly, the analysis indicated quite the opposite: rather than being harbingers of a new ideological age, the most eminent thinkers are oddly backward-looking in their ideas. They are more representative of the previous generation's ideological consensus than of those of present or succeeding generations. Monumental intellects struggle to consolidate the ideas of the recent past into some grand overarching synthesis. Aristotle was just such a synthesizer, and so was Thomas Aquinas. The latter, for instance, attempted to integrate the doctrines of the Christian church with the newly revived infatuation with Aristotle, and created a comprehensive system that became the foundation of Roman Catholic orthodoxy.

The stereotype of the great mind being ahead of his or her time is evidently mistaken. The reason seems to be that the most eminent thinkers of European intellectual history also tend to espouse the most modern ideas; that is, philosophical fame is a function of a high concordance with our own zeitgeist. Obviously this relationship reflects a strong epochcentric bias. When the zeitgeist changes, so will the assessments of the thinkers in the past.

The most notable thinkers are thus products of the previous generation's zeitgeist, the zeitgeist of their youth. For one thing, the political milieu in which thinkers develop their creative potential influences their probability of philosophical success. The most eminent philosophers are more likely to grow up in times of political fragmentation, for example, and are less likely to develop during periods of paralyzing political instability or anarchy. Furthermore, the availability of role models in the previous generation has a *negative* consequence for the emergence of first-class thinkers. The great philosophers develop in times of relative intellectual stagnation, where less distinctive colleagues more often follow a generation of philosophical superfluity. This result at first glance seems incompatible with the generalization, from Chapter 2, that the number of philosophers in generation g is a *positive* function of the number of philosophers in generation $g - 1$. But this apparent contradiction dissolves upon closer inspection. The probability of philosophical activity is enhanced if the preceding generation is intellectually active, because of role-modeling effects, but creativity of the highest order must mature in a relative philosophical vacuum. With an abundance of role models available, the potential genius is likely to become a disciple of some prominent thinker in the older generation. A dearth of available models, by contrast, obliges the thinker to pursue his or her own unique route to distinction. A similar process has been found for classical composers, whose creative productivity is a negative function of role-model availability once we control for the fact that such availability exerts a positive impact upon creative precociousness (Simonton, 1977c). Yet in musical creativity, too, the number of composers at generation g is a positive consequence of the number of composers at generation $g - 1$. The determinants of the differential fame of individual creators must be distinguished from the determinants of the variation in the aggregate counts across generations. What made Aristotle more eminent than Xenocrates need not be identical to what made both Aristotle and Xenocrates emerge in the middle of the fourth century B.C.

Besides the influences of the ideological, political, and cultural milieu, certain individual characteristics also facilitate the attainment of distinction. These personal factors all have to do with the belief structure of the individual thinker's philosophical system. First of all, the most renowned thinkers are those whose philosophical systems are broad enough to deal with a wide range of issues. Whereas less celebrated thinkers may devote their lives to discussing just ethics or epistemology or ontology, their more illustrious colleagues attempt to cover all the big questions in some grand synthesis. Aristotle, Aquinas, and Kant illustrate the scope of the most prominent thinkers. Secondly, lesser thinkers tend to take rather moderate or middle-of-the-road positions, while the most substantial thinkers are likely to advocate extreme viewpoints. The most eminent philosophers put forward ideas that are maintained by less than 10 percent of all two thousand thinkers in the Western philosophical tradition. Third, the eminent thinkers put their beliefs together in highly original ways. That is, the most highly esteemed philosophers combine positions that the majority of thinkers have implicitly stated do not belong together.

These three qualities of the most noteworthy philosophical systems—breadth, extremism, and combinatorial originality—make the great philosophical mind appear to be an artist seeking to provoke. Viewing these traits in the light of the fact that the greatest philosophers are atypical of their times, we realize how genius can rise above the dictates of the zeitgeist. A philosophical genius is a lone figure in the history of ideas, independent of contemporary consensus and boldly willing to revolutionize human thought with synthetic achievements of vast originality and scope.

MUSICAL ORIGINALITY: COMPOSING FOR ANOTHER AGE?

One of the inquiries into aesthetics discussed in Chapter 7 yielded discoveries quite compatible with the portrait of the master thinker as one who provokes and stimulates by promulgating broad, extreme, and apparently incongruous belief systems. That study had to do with the differential fame of 15,618 themes by 479 classical composers (Simonton, 1980d). The "repertoire melodic originality" of each theme was calculated according to the two-note transition probabilities for the first six notes. This variable was shown to predict the fame of each theme, via a curvilinear relationship in keeping with an optimal arousal model of aesthetic appreciation. Furthermore, the melodic originality of a theme was shown to be partly a reaction to stressful events in the life of the composer. This finding suggests that we must take a creator's biography into consideration when assessing the products of genius. At the same time, certain periods of history are clearly characterized by more melodic originality than other periods. As already noted, the originality of themes has generally increased since the Renaissance, a trend that suggests that the zeitgeist may be a better backdrop than biography against which to interpret a composer's creativity.

Actually, although the overall trend is that of an increase in originality, the details of that trend betray cycles superimposed over the broad
tendency. I performed a trend analysis on the melodic originality of the
themes and obtained the function that is graphed in Figure 7. Starting
at the low point in the modal melodies of the Renaissance, melodic
originality begins to increase, attaining a peak in the middle of the seventeenth century. Monteverdi's themes are immensely more complex
than those of Josquin des Près about a century earlier. After this peak,
melodic originality declines as new sources of aesthetic stimulation—
especially the development of fugue and sonata forms and the evolution of the orchestral sound—take precedence over melody. By the
time of Beethoven toward the end of the eighteenth century, melodic
originality bottoms out. The themes in Beethoven's symphonies are
among the simplest of all classical masters. The opening of his famous
Fifth Symphony is so rudimentary that the members of one orchestra,
first rehearsing the piece shortly after it was written, thought the composer was joking. While melodic originality does fall to a low point in
the classical period, it remains higher than it was in the Renaissance.
After this trough, melodic originality begins an ascent that continues
throughout the nineteenth century. Melodic originality becomes con-

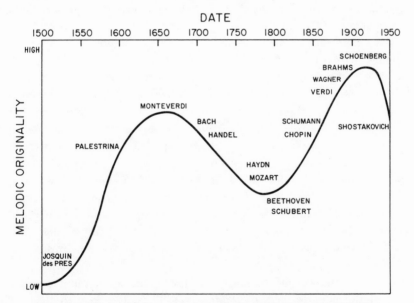

Figure 7. The trend in repertoire melodic originality over time for
15,618 themes by 479 classical composers (from Simonton,
1980d).

spicuous with Chopin and is transformed into almost an article of dogma in the "New Music" of Wagner. In the early twentieth century this unpredictability attains a new peak, one much higher than the first maximum around 1650. This high point marks the advent of atonal and serial music. Schoenberg's revolutionary, atonal *Pierrot Lunaire* was written in 1912, when he was 38 years old, and his "Method of Composing with Twelve Tones" came a decade later. Melodic originality began to retreat from this extreme very quickly, however, so that by the middle of this century the average originality of melodies was about at a level with the mid-seventeenth and mid-nineteenth centuries. This cyclic curve is a graphic depiction of the musical zeitgeist as regards melodic predictability.

Just as the most famous philosophers are those who are unrepresentative of their times, so also the most distinguished melodies depart from the expectations of the era in which they are composed. Departures in both positive and negative directions—toward more and less originality—increase the chances for success, though a strong preference exists for melodies that are more original than the average for their era. Perhaps this aesthetic disposition explains why the overall trend in melodic originality is ever upward. The discrepancy between the melodic originality predicted by the zeitgeist and the actual melodic originality exhibited by the theme can be called the "zeitgeist melodic originality" of that theme.

How does the zeitgeist's melodic originality of a composer's themes change with the composer's age? Recall from Chapter 6 that the world's best-known melodies tend to have been produced by composers between 33 and 43 years old, and from Chapter 7 that the most famous themes have the highest odds of appearing when the composer is 39, yet also that the repertoire melodic originality of these same themes does not peak until around age 56. It turns out that the zeitgeist melodic originality of a composer's output is a positive linear function of the composer's age. Increased age brings with it ever more independence from the spirit of the times. This trend can be traced in the piano concerti and symphonies of Mozart, for example, or in the operas of Wagner. Bach ended his career with the "Art of the Fugue" and "Musical Offering," works far different from the compositions of his contemporaries. And perhaps the best illustration of this gradual escape from the limitations of the musical zeitgeist can be seen in a comparison of the compositions of Beethoven's Third Period with those of his First. A great creative career begins in the zeitgeist and ends with genius.

MULTIPLE DISCOVERY AND INVENTION: IS SCIENTIFIC
PROGRESS INEVITABLE?

The English astronomer J. C. Adams in 1845 and the French astronomer U.-J.-J. Leverrier in 1846, working in ignorance of each other, exploited Newtonian gravitational astronomy to predict the existence of a planet beyond Uranus, a prediction that was soon verified with the discovery of Neptune. Elisha Gray notified the United States Patent Office of his intention of filing a patent for the telephone on the same day that Alexander Graham Bell filed for just such a patent, launching a bitter court battle. Newton believed Leibniz had stolen the idea for the calculus, and denounced Leibniz as a plagiarist and a liar, although, as we now know, Leibniz had conceived the calculus independently. A more amicable situation arose when Charles Darwin, who had been laboring at his *Origin of Species* since 1844, learned in 1858 that Alfred Russell Wallace was submitting a theoretical paper enunciating the same principle of evolution by natural selection. Friends intervened and arranged for Wallace's paper to be read along with an abstract of Darwin's forthcoming book at a meeting of the Linnaean Society.

The frequent occurrence of independent and simultaneous discoveries may be taken as evidence of the overwhelming importance of the zeitgeist, as opposed to individual genius, in the realm of scientific creativity. Ogburn and Thomas (1922) listed nearly 150 cases in order to give an affirmative response to the question "Are inventions inevitable?" It seems that when the times are ripe for a particular discovery or invention, it is certain to come forth. A recent distinguished proponent of this viewpoint is one of Sorokin's students, Robert K. Merton, the discoverer of the Matthew effect. Merton compiled a list of 264 multiple discoveries to make his case, and asserted: "It is the singletons—discoveries made only once in the history of science—that are the residual cases, requiring special explanation" (1961, p. 477).

If scientific advances are for all practical purposes inevitable, then individual creators must be little more than interchangeable agents. But the data on this question deserve a closer look. In the first place, true multiples are much rarer than the lists would lead us to believe (see Constant, 1978). The calculus of Newton was not identical to that of Leibniz, nor did Adams and Leverrier both make the same predictions, in that their calculated orbits for a planet beyond Uranus did not coincide. To infer the occurrence of a multiple requires a high degree of abstraction. And even when we accept abstraction enough to grant the existence of at least some bona fide multiples, many independent contributions are hardly simultaneous. Newton preceded Leibniz by a half-decade or more and Darwin anticipated Wallace by more than a decade. Merton (1961) reports that 34 percent of the multiples he studied were separated by 10 years or more, while only 18 percent took place within a 2-year time span. Furthermore, if scientific contributions are so much a product of their times, why does it often take so long for a contribution to gain acceptance? Such time lags strongly suggest that a scientist can conceive ideas that are totally out of step with the zeitgeist, though recognition of these unconventional ideas may have to wait until the times have changed. To evaluate the view that the zeitgeist rather than the individual genius determines scientific discovery, I applied historiometric methods, subjecting the zeitgeist position to four empirical tests (Simonton, 1978b, 1979a). The first test concerns the fact that multiples are seldom simultaneous. It is usually quite evident who got there first. The test is to discover how the scientists who make the discoveries first differ from the latecomers. A belief in the power of genius might inspire one to predict that the really great intellects of science are those who make the discovery first. Yet my scrutiny of multiple discoveries showed that the more eminent scientists are actually less likely than their more obscure colleagues to have made the discovery first (Simonton, 1979a). This connection between eminence and priority seems to fit with my earlier finding with regard to philosophers. Just as the most notable thinkers tend to be behind their times, serving as consolidators of past achievements, so may the scientists of the highest magnitude be synthesizers, and in the act of synthesizing these geniuses may accidentally arrive at ideas already conceived by less conspicuous scientists. These superior minds may thus usurp the credit due to those who could claim a less well-advertised priority.

The second test derives from the finding that the most eminent philosophers did not conform to the intellectual zeitgeist of their times. Might not the same relationship hold for scientists? If multiple discoveries are proof that the scientific zeitgeist is operating, and if the most distinguished scientific minds tend not to conform to that prevailing spirit, then such scientists should have lower odds of participating in multiple discovery. In contrast, a zeitgeist interpretation of events would predict that since the most notable scientists are eponyms who intimately symbolize their times, scientific eminence should correlate positively with participation in multiples. And in fact empirical tests endorse the zeitgeist interpretation: the most famous scientists are conspicuously more likely to participate in independent discoveries and inventions (Simonton, 1979a). Scientists are evidently more dependent than philosophers upon being in tune with the zeitgeist for sociocultural success.

Yet this result cannot be taken at face value. There is a third alternative viewpoint that can contaminate the testing process. Chapter 5 demonstrated most emphatically that quality of productive output is firmly entrenched in quantity. Similarly, the more prolific scientists should have higher odds of chancing upon a multiple. According to Merton, "great scientific genius will have been repeatedly involved in multiples . . . because the genius will have made many scientific discoveries altogether" (1961, p. 484). The eminence of a scientist correlates .25 with the number of multiples that scientist is involved in, but creative productivity correlates .32 with eminence and .42 with the number of multiples (Simonton, 1979a). Thus we must control for creative productivity to avoid confounding the results. Partialing out creative productivity reduces the correlation between fame and multiple participation to .14, indicating that only 2 percent ($.14^2$) of the variance in eminence and multiple discovery is shared. Indeed, creative productivity explains twice as much variance in participation in multiples as does the zeitgeist account. Since such productivity is a sign of genius, an individual factor can be said to be crucial to the emergence of multiples. The most acclaimed geniuses may participate in multiples in part because they are more in phase with the zeitgeist, but most of this participation can be attributed to their prolific output, which makes the probability of creative redundancy far greater.

The third test concentrates upon the differential probability of multiples appearing in various disciplines. In science, the zeitgeist partially consists in what Kuhn (1970) called a paradigm, a well-defined though often implicit body of theoretical approaches and methodological strategies. Some scientific enterprises are more paradigmatic than others. In the hard sciences such as chemistry or physics, the paradigmatic influence may be much more extensive than in softer disciplines such as biology. So the question is whether multiples are more likely to occur in the more highly codified disciplines. I investigated contributions in several scientific disciplines and found, in rough accord with expectation, that 16 percent of advances in mathematics, 8 percent in astronomy, 8 percent in physics, 3 percent in chemistry, 2 percent in biology, 14 percent in medicine, and 2 percent in technology entail multiple discovery or invention (Simonton, 1979a). In a more thorough mathematical analysis, however, I cast doubt on the idea that the probability of multiple discovery varies in any intelligible fashion across disciplines (Simonton, 1978b, 1979a). Instead, multiples may be distributed more or less randomly across the disciplines according to some sort of chance mechanism, and chance rather than the zeitgeist may be the primary explanatory variable in multiple discovery and invention.

The fourth test concerns the fact that multiples differ in "grade." Some are doublets involving two independent scientists or inventors, others triplets, and so on. The higher the grade, the lower the frequency. Merton's (1961) study of 264 multiples, for example, counted 179 doublets, 51 triplets, and 17 quadruplets, 6 quintuplets, 8 sextuplets, 1 septuplet, and 2 nonaries. In my own sample there were 449 doublets, 104 triplets, 18 quadruplets, 7 quintuplets, and 1 octuplet (Simonton, 1979a). Price (1963) was the first to suggest that this skewed distribution follows what would be anticipated from what is termed a Poisson probability process, and I have shown this conjecture to be valid (Simonton, 1978b, 1979a). Even when these overall frequency distributions are broken down into the various scientific disciplines, a Poisson model still holds. For example, in the Ogburn and Thomas (1922) sample there were 11 doublets in astronomy, 4 triplets, and 1 quintuplet—*exactly* as would be predicted on the basis of a Poisson process. This fit is fascinating from a theoretical standpoint because the Poisson model normally applies to the occurrence of *rare* events. As an example, it predicts very well the number of nineteenth-century Prussian military officers killed in any given time unit by a kick of a horse. The implication is that multiples may be extremely rare events that take place more by happenstance than by any pervasive power of the zeitgeist. According to the Poisson model, singletons should be considerably more common than multiples, as in fact they are. Contrary to what Merton claimed, it is multiple discoveries that constitute the special events of science, singletons being the more typical case.

Merton argued that the number of multiples may be immensely underestimated. Even if they are, this fact by itself does not overthrow a Poisson model so long as the probability distribution for the various grades remains unchanged. I carried out a detailed analysis, premised upon the Poisson process, that implicated the existence of a vast number of hitherto unrecognized multiples (Simonton, 1978b). This probability model actually seconds Merton's claim while concomitantly denying that these hidden multiples would make the zeitgeist position any more secure. That same analysis also suggests that singletons are more frequent than multiples and, worse, that "nulltons" are far more common than doublets. A nullton is a nondiscovery or noninvention, a potential contribution that never sees the light of day because the probability of any given discovery is so tiny. Even if dozens of scientists are all working toward the same end, they may never quite develop a given idea. The existence of these unrealized possibilities is in accordance with the proposal made by other analysts (for example, Schmookler, 1966) that the occurrence of multiples is not unequivocal evidence that scientific and technological progress is inevitable. There is an impressive uncertainty in the operation of both zeitgeist and genius. Zeitgeist and genius both have parts to play, but they are members of the supporting cast in a creative drama in which chance has the lead role.

THE INTERACTIONIST PERSPECTIVE

I have presented ample evidence that both genius and zeitgeist make integral contributions to creativity and leadership. The zeitgeist participates as linear or cyclical trends, as economic or political conditions, and as a backdrop of events that determines the eponymic significance or sociocultural success of a political, military, philosophical, aesthetic, or scientific leader. At the same time, the impact of the situational context is tempered by such individual attributes as intelligence, morality, leadership qualities, productivity, aggressiveness, age, and belief structure, depending on the specific area of endeavor. "Being the right person" is almost as important as "being in the right place at the right time." So far I have largely treated this genius-versus-zeitgeist debate as if it were a simple matter of ascertaining the relative influence of individual and sociocultural influences. This stress on "main effects" ignores the possibility of (in the parlance of the analysis of variance) individual-by-situation interaction effects. That is, it may be a matter of "being the right person in the right place at the right time." A certain type of genius may have a higher probability of accomplishment when the spirit of the times takes one form, whereas another type of genius may have an advantage when the zeitgeist shifts to another emphasis.

The possibility of such interaction emerges in a curious study by Stewart (1977) on the relationship between birth order and political zeitgeist. As mentioned in Chapter 2, first-borns may have superior odds of success, with the proviso that middle children may be more disposed toward political leadership and later-born children toward revolution. These tendencies may arise from childhood patterns of sibling relationships. Stewart elaborates this point by looking at the differential developmental experiences of the only child, the first-born son, the middle-born son, and the last-born son, and describing how these different experiences prepare the adult leader for contrasting political circumstances. The only child is more likely to rise to the top when social functions have collapsed and civil conflict breaks out, the first-born son during times of international crisis and warfare, the middle-born son when a nation is at peace and is engaged in the fine adjustment of internal affairs, and the last-born son when revolution is the order of the day. Lincoln was an only son elected during the domestic crisis that led immediately to the Civil War, while Jefferson Davis was the youngest of ten children. Winston Churchill, a first-born son who was a political maverick prior to World War II, became prime minister when his nation needed someone to serve as a vigorous counterweight to the designs of Adolf Hitler, designs that had only been encouraged by the appeasement policies of the peacetime ministry of Neville Chamberlain, a second-born son and third-born child of six. As tenuous as such assertions may seem, Stewart has systematically and objectively tested his theory on both American presidents and British prime ministers, and the results are intriguing. Stewart demonstrates, for example, that the chief presidential candidates in the United States in any given election year tend to have the same ordinal position in their families. Stewart's research illustrates how individual and situational characteristics may interact in the emergence of historical genius—and his work is an example of a direction in which historiometric research should travel.

9

POLITICAL VIOLENCE

GIBBON SAID THAT HISTORY is "little more than the register of the crimes, follies and misfortunes of mankind," and Voltaire agreed that "History is little else than a picture of human crimes and misfortunes." If we were to enumerate those crimes and misfortunes that most scar the historical record, war would surely be foremost on the list. History is more than anything else the narrative of conquests and conspiracies, battles and revolts. It seems natural to expect that historiometry might be able to exploit this record to answer many crucial questions concerning the place of creators and leaders in history. The prospects of this application look especially promising given how successful historiometric methods have been thus far. It is important, however, to choose substantive questions that are susceptible to historiometric inquiry. The question I will ask here is, What are the antecedents and consequences of political violence? What variables are responsible for civil conflicts and international warfare? What are the repercussions of such outbreaks of mass aggression? My review of the research cannot exhaust all that can be said on this subject, for I must restrict the discussion to results that are relevant to creativity and leadership. Clearly political violence provides unique opportunities for the emergence of eminent leaders; it should become apparent that the creative genius is also to some extent affected by the experience of war.

CIVIL DISTURBANCES

Political violence on a domestic level operates sometimes on a grand revolutionary scale that demolishes dynasties, despotisms, or democracies, other times on the microscopic level of the city riot or the palace conspiracy. The causes and consequences of civil disturbance are complex and as yet only partly understood, but historiometric research has shed some light on this phenomenon.

SOME DETERMINANTS OF RIOT AND REVOLT

Recall from Chapter 2 that revolutionaries of the stature of Lenin tend to be later-born children from large families. This finding is connected to a theoretical model of revolution that was developed by Matossian and Schafer (1977), which may be summarized by the following four points. First, a primary precondition for the outbreak of civil disturbances is an exceptional spurt in population pressure—an increase that is far out of proportion to the increments that can normally be accommodated by a socioeconomic system. The baby boom that hit the United States after World War II is a recent example of such a population spurt, and it may be no accident that the baby-boom generation led the youth rebellion of the 1960s. Second, the most significant facet of the increase in population is the sharp increase in the proportion of young adult males. This sudden influx of alienated males provides a reservoir of potential revolutionaries—for males dominate revolution almost as much as they dominate warfare. Third, the population pressure is responsible for greater hostility between father and son and among siblings while at the same time intensifying the positive relationship between mother and son. High fertility rates lead to large families, and such overpopulated households are breeding grounds for future revolutionaries. Fourth, the lag between population pressure and domestic political violence is about 25 ± 4 years, or approximately one generation. Young males exposed to inharmonious relations with their fathers and siblings develop a rebellious personality that must await early adulthood to come forth in violent behavior directed against those that govern society.

Matossian and Schafer tested their model in a somewhat unorthodox fashion, combining historical population and political data with information about familial relationships from the lives of French and English literary figures. Literary persons were selected because of the wealth of information available about their early lives. In exploiting this biographical information, we do not have to assume that the degree of family tension is the same for literary creators as for revolutionaries, but we do have to postulate that the ups and downs in family tension across history run parallel in these two groups. If we accept this assumption, the data more or less endorse the Matossian-Schafer thesis. In French history, for example, the revolutions of 1830, 1848, and 1871 all followed spurts in population pressures that had occurred 23, 26, and 29 years earlier, respectively, and family tensions appeared to provide the intervening causal connection.

Matossian and Schafer make some provocative observations linking their model with other theories in the behavioral sciences. For example, they claim that their model is compatible with the idea that political violence ensues from disappointed expectations. To offer a contemporary illustration, the American baby-boom generation lived in a period of rising expectations, of economic expansion corresponding to the burst in fertility. But as members of this optimistic generation reached their teens and twenties, reality became more hardfaced, and expectations jerked downward, producing frustration. According to Matossian and Schafer such a cohort is likely to become violent at 25 ± 4 years of age—to rebel against authority figures. America in the 1960s saw conflicts such as the student takeovers at Columbia, Harvard, and Berkeley and the demonstrations in Chicago at the 1968 Democratic Convention and at Kent State University after the Cambodian invasion of 1970. All these events may reflect more personal forms of conflict within the individuals involved—conflicts arising out of the families in which they grew to adulthood.

Riot and revolution are no doubt events with multiple causes, excess population growth being but one factor out of many. A factor that influences the specific timing of domestic political violence is temperature: civil unrest has an affinity for the hotter months of the year. In France, for example, the storming of the Bastille took place on July 14, 1789, thus symbolically initiating the first of several summer revolutions in Paris, including the July Revolution of 1830 and the June Days of bloody civil war during the Revolution of 1848. To be sure, civil strife is not always a summer pasttime: the Chinese Revolution of 1911 and the Russian Revolution of 1917 were both October happenings. But historiometric inquiries into this phenomenon indicate that civil disturbance does become more likely in the hot months of the year (Baron and Ransberger, 1978; Carlsmith and Anderson, 1979). The 1960s saw not only a period of youth revolt but also a prime period of black revolt in American inner cities. And the tendency of these urban revolts or riots to occur on the hottest days of the year led many to blame a "long, hot summer" effect. Although some disagreement exists about the precise shape of the functional relationship between ambient temperature and civil violence, the weight of the evidence suggests that as the heat becomes more unbearable, the probability of urban violence heightens. Ambient temperature may thus be a catalyst in the specific timing of the violent expression of civil discontent. Social injustice, economic frustration, and political alienation had been chronic in the black ghetto of Watts in Los Angeles, but it required a hot summer night in August of 1965 to ignite an explosion that sent thousands of people, mostly males "25 ± 4" years of age, on a six-day rampage of looting and burning.

SOME CONSEQUENCES OF CIVIL DISTURBANCES

Just as an outburst of domestic violence will lag about a generation behind an increase in population pressure, so can the repercussions of such an outbreak take a generation to manifest themselves. In other words, just as the tensions within larger families serve as developmental antecedents of the emergence of rebellious personalities, so do the actions of those rebels serve as developmental experiences for yet another generation. What exactly are the effects of that "stubborn and rebellious generation," to use the Biblical phrase, upon the next generation? For one thing, as I observed in Chapter 8, revolts directed against the homogenization of large imperial states tend to nurture the appearance of creative genius one generation later. The collapse of controls during periods of social upheaval does seem to open the way to innovation (Barnett, 1953). But political violence is not always positive in its effect on creativity. Recall from Chapter 1 that the number of major discursive creators—creators in science, philosophy, literature, and music, as opposed to painting, sculpture, and architecture, which are the presentational disciplines—in generation g is a *negative* function of the intensity of political instability in generation $g - 1$ (Simonton, 1975c).

Political instability as defined here means anarchy among a nation's leaders: such events as military coups, dynastic conflicts among rival members of a royal house, political assassinations of rightful heirs or rulers, and sundry other indicators of violent dissention among the power elite. Political instability must be distinguished from civil disturbances, which engage the participation of the populace, not just the elite. Sometimes struggles among those in power may enlist the masses, yet in instances of true political instability it is still those in high political positions who call the shots. Anarchy in a nation's leadership is a battle among the powerful; civil disturbances involve conflict between the powerful and the powerless.

Political instability has an adverse effect only on discursive creativity—not on presentational creativity—and then only on the emergence of the highest-caliber creators. In fact, I have shown that for one discursive discipline, philosophy, the fame of an individual creator active in generation g is a negative function of the amount of political instability that prevailed in generation $g - 1$ (Simonton, 1976f). Apparently political instability not only depresses the absolute number of great philosophical minds but also decreases the proportion of great genius relative to lesser talent. Furthermore, political instability exerts this influence in the developmental period, not affecting adult creators in any noticeable way.

The difference between discursive and presentational endeavors is important to an understanding of these findings. Discursive activities involve a high degree of logic and linguistic analysis arrayed in a serial format over time, whereas presentational activities entail more juxtapositional, visual thoughts configured in a simultaneous format across space. In a literary, philosophical, or scientific work, ideas are offered in a temporal sequence with a logic altogether different from the all-at-once presentation of ideas in a painting, sculpture, or work of architecture. Even music consists of a horizontal succession of notes whose linear sequencing to form melody dominates the vertical and simultaneous presentation of notes that defines harmony. In a sense, the scientist, philosopher, writer, and composer have more control over how a reader or listener will process the incoming information, while the painter, sculptor, and architect must leave the scanning sensory processes pretty much up to the perceiver.

Perhaps the creative process behind significant discursive genius cannot develop in an atmosphere where one regime succeeds another without rhyme or reason. Young potential geniuses who grow up under anarchic political conditions may acquire a sense that the universe is not a rational, coherent place in which a person can master the laws of nature and of society and gain control over his or her personal fate. Discursive creativity depends heavily upon a trust in order and in the efficacy of personal effort when conceiving the logico-linguistic symbol sequences of science, philosophy, literature, and music—sequences that mimic causal chains in which one thing leads to another in a rational pattern. Thus the probability of a great discursive creator developing in times of high-level political anarchy may be low.

Civil disturbance—political violence that involves the masses—also has consequences for creative development. For one thing, the intensity of civil disturbances in generation g is causally related to the amount of political fragmentation in generation $g + 1$ (Simonton, 1976g). This effect makes sense because many of the civil conflicts that occur are nationalistic revolts. Since political fragmentation, as noted in the previous chapter, encourages creative development in all varieties of endeavor, popular revolt may be said to exert an indirect effect upon the emergence of creative genius after a two-generation delay. Far more direct is the impact of such civil unrest on the *content* of creativity, especially in philosophy. Sorokin has put forward a historical generalization called the "law of polarization." He claims that revolution has opposite effects on different elements of the population:

> The overwhelming majority of the population in normal times is neither distinctly bad nor conspicuously virtuous, neither very socially-minded nor extremely antisocial, neither markedly religious nor highly irreligious. In times of revolution this indifferent majority tends to split, the segments shifting to opposite poles and yielding a greater number of sinners and saints, social altruists and antisocial egoists, devout religious believers and militant atheists. The "balanced majority" tend to decrease in favor of extreme polar factions in the ethical, religious, intellectual, and other fields. This polarization is generated by revolutions in all fields of social and cultural life. (1947, p. 487)

I tested Sorokin's assertion in a follow-up study examining the prevalance of various philosophical beliefs and the fluctuations in civil disturbance in Europe across 122 20-year generations from 540 B.C. to A.D. 1900 (Simonton, 1976g). Using the cross-lagged correlation technique, I found that the data basically confirm Sorokin's inference. Twenty years after a major outbreak of popular revolt there appears a salient polarization of the philosophical controversy on virtually every central issue in the history of ideas. That is, potential philosophical geniuses who are exposed to civil strife during the developmental period will, in their productive phase some two decades later, take extreme stands on various philosophical questions. They will argue, for example, either that only our sense organs can provide us with knowledge or that viable knowledge can be obtained by pure reason and even revelation; either that matter is the primary substance of reality or that the substrate is ultimately spiritual; either that reality suffers interminable transformations or that there exists a fundamental eternal constancy behind such epiphenomenal appearances; either that abstract concepts are mere names for things or that such ideas really exist in a Platonic world beyond their material manifestations; either that the individual is the central social unit or that society takes precedence over all individual acts and dispositions; either that events are totally determined by a mechanistic fate or that the will of human beings stands free of the constraints of cause-effect sequences; either that morality must be guided by the pleasure principle in a hedonistic or utilitarian way or that higher principles and altruistic commitments must rule individual ethical choice. In other words, two decades after the occurrence of marked civil disturbance, both sensate and ideational ideologies recruit stalwart adherents.

It cannot be stressed too strongly that the law of polarization involves an intergenerational effect. Civil disturbances polarize beliefs in the succeeding generation rather than in the concurrent one. The political conflicts of one generation become the philosophical conflicts of the next. Admittedly, civil disturbances do exhibit transient effects upon the thought processes of those citizens who must endure such strife as full adults. In the study of the plays of Aeschylus, Sophocles, Euripides, Aristophanes, and Shakespeare, discussed in Chapter 7, I found that plays written in times of civil upheaval tend to treat certain topics, such as the individual good versus the common good and the conflict of duty and desire, of loyalties and loves (Simonton, 1983b). Another inquiry has shown that the integrative complexity of the thoughts expressed in the letters of great British novelists tends to increase during times of civil disturbance (Porter and Suedfeld, 1981). Yet these are temporary repercussions; after civil order reappears, the playwrights and novelists revert to more typical themes and styles. The polarizing effect of civil unrest upon the youth of the next generation is far more indelible. A pattern of thinking that will define a philosophical career is shaped by some key historical events that occurred in the phase of early development.

INTERNATIONAL WAR

War between nations is the worst scourge on the face of the earth. Its consequences are usually much larger in scope than those of violence within one nation—and therefore the need to study its antecedents is all the more urgent.

SOME DETERMINANTS OF INTERNATIONAL WAR

Political scientists have shown considerable interest in investigating the causes of war by applying quantitative methods to historiometric data. Some pioneer attempts in this vein can be found in a book entitled *Peace, War, and Numbers* (Russett, 1972). These inquiries tend to aim at relatively abstract, systemic factors, an analytical level that may grant scant latitude for the intervention of individuals. The bipolarity of an international system of alliances, the relative military capacities of contending nations, and geographic location are among the variables investigated. For example, when clusters of alliance become more defined and firm, both the likelihood of occurrence and the duration of wars will increase (Bueno de Mesquita, 1978). This situational factor may thus be seen as imposing constraints on the operation of political or military genius.

We are inclined to think of wars as the perverse products of some "evil genius." Louis XIV was supposedly the instigator of the Dutch Wars, the War of the League of Augsberg, and the War of the Spanish Succession; Frederick the Great the culprit behind the Silesian Wars, Napoleon the villainous and eponymic agent behind the Napoleonic Wars, and the Hitler-Mussolini-Tojo trio the vicious perpetrators of World War II. But not all wars happen this way. Though the Treaty of Versailles asserted otherwise, no one evil genius lurked behind the First World War. The leaders on the opposing sides, if anything, were comparative mediocrities who lacked the perspicacity to avoid war. They were pulled by ever tightening alliance configurations into a system so touchy that an event that should have been relatively minor in the international scheme, the assassination of the Archduke Ferdinand by Serbian nationalists, could ignite a disastrous chain reaction.

Unhappily, the success of such quantitative research into the antecedents of war has been less than outstanding. Even J. David Singer (1981), the director of the ambitious Correlates of War Project at the University of Michigan, has noted that much of the literature is inconsistent and confusing, with only a vaguely discernable tendency toward convergence on a cumulative body of knowledge. The historiometric laws of war have proven elusive. Perhaps more attention should be paid to psychological variables. One likely candidate is integrative (or conceptual) complexity, which was discussed in Chapters 3 and 7: recall that the ability of revolutionaries to stay in power in the posttakeover phase is dependent on an ability to switch from a simplistic, black-and-white pattern of thinking to a more complex, relativistic, and multidimensional pattern (Suedfeld and Rank, 1976). Other research has shown that this cognitive or intellectual function may be germane to both the foreign policy considerations that provide the diplomatic backdrop to war and the decision-making processes that lead directly to the eruption of international war. For example, Tetlock (1981a) has indicated that the advocacy of an isolationist foreign policy by U. S.

senators in the 82nd Congress is associated with their integrative complexity levels. Isolationists such as Dirksen and McCarthy tended to view the world in simplistic and polarized ways, whereas the less isolationist senators, such as Humphrey, Kefauver, and Fulbright, displayed more elaborate and differentiated perspectives on issues in foreign affairs. The isolationists also tended to express more positive in-group and negative out-group attitudes: they believed the United States to be always right, the Soviet Union invariably wrong. In Chapter 3 I pointed out that the policy recommendations of presidential advisers are patterned after their styles of interpersonal relationships; another crucial source of input into foreign-policy decisions, the members of the Senate, may choose their policy stances according to their individual ways of processing information. We cannot deny the place of the individual personality in the formation of foreign policy.

The integrative complexity variable is even more important for the decision-making processes behind the outbreak of warfare. Suedfeld and Tetlock (1977) scored the integrative complexity of diplomatic communications exchanged during international crises. In two instances these crises led to war: the outbreak of World War I in 1914 and of the Korean War in 1950. The remaining three situations—the Moroccan crisis of 1911, the Berlin blockade of 1948, and the Cuban missile crisis of 1962—were resolved without bloodshed. The parties involved in the crises that were peacefully resolved tended to exhibit higher levels of complexity in their communications, whereas the parties engaged in the crises that led to warfare displayed a greater conceptual dogmatism and rigidity. Moreover, the evidence suggests that the complexity of thought of the world's leaders increases when a crisis is resolved peacefully; those crises that could only be settled by force of arms saw a decrease in the complexity exhibited by those leaders making the key decisions. In the Cuban missile crisis, both the United States and the Soviet Union became more sophisticated and less propagandistic in their diplomatic exchanges. In contrast, the communications traded after assassination of the Archduke Ferdinand in 1914 tended to decline in integrative complexity. The increased tightness of the alliance structures came to be mirrored in the augmented tightness of thought.

A second study corroborates this one by focusing on the Middle East, which has seen four wars since the state of Israel was born in 1948 (Suedfeld, Tetlock, and Ramirez, 1977). This time, speeches in the United Nations General Assembly were scored for integrative complexity. All nations directly or indirectly involved, except for the Soviet Union, displayed a marked decline in the complexity of information processing prior to the outbreak of war. Curiously, the United States and Israel, who exhibit the highest baselines of complexity under peacetime conditions, show the largest reductions in complexity just before war breaks out.

Does declining integrative complexity cause a crisis to result in war, or are such decreases consequences of a crisis irretrievably headed toward violence in any case? At this point there is very little evidence on this question. A recent study has shown, however, that the integrative complexity in the correspondence of five eminent British novelists decreases during times of war (Porter and Suedfeld, 1981). Since these novelists were not making the crucial political decisions, and since the scorings were done on private communications, it would seem that war may instill a certain simplicity in the information processing even of those who are not directly involved. So perhaps it is a matter of a war-directed crisis injecting simple-mindedness into political leaders rather than the leaders stumbling into war because of a lack of conceptual complexity in policy at the crucial time.

Other influences may also affect the integrative complexity of leaders. One such factor is "groupthink," which may compel otherwise sophisticated thinkers to reason simplistically. Tetlock (1979) has applied historiometric methods to establish the participation of groupthink in significant historical decisions. The classic case is President Kennedy's decision to support the Bay of Pigs invasion of 1961, an invasion that ended as an embarrassing fiasco. Groupthink occurs in tightly knit groups of self-confident policymakers who are loyal to their leader. In such circumstances the desire for consensus may overpower the need for rational deliberation. It is a happy fact of history that Kennedy learned from this mistake and introduced measures to avoid groupthink dynamics when the Cuban missile crisis arose. The emphasis in group discussion shifted from achieving unanimity to solving a problem.

One additional causal factor deserves mention. The previous section indicated that political events partially determine the philosophical zeitgeist. There is reason to believe that this process sometimes works the other way: that a particular ideological context may increase the likelihood of warfare (Simonton, 1976g). International war tends to erupt about a generation after materialistic and skeptical beliefs have dominated the zeitgeist (partial r's are .26 and .20 respectively).

Growing up under materialism and skepticism may nurture a militaristic mind—or at least a mind that will not shy away from the deployment of military might when diplomacy falters.

SOME CONSEQUENCES OF INTERNATIONAL WAR

The economic and political effects of war are vast and complex and have been much studied by historians; I will not touch on many of them here. But I have discovered one political after-effect of violent international conflict that has not received much discussion: the amount of war in generation g is related to the intensity of civil disturbances in generation $g + 1$ (Simonton, 1976g). Thus, for example, the civil storms of the 1960s all over the globe—from American and European universities to the streets of Peking and Tokyo—may be interpreted as a generational time-lagged response to the Second World War. It is not clear just why the two principal forms of political violence (and hence two kinds of leadership) are causally connected nor why the causal arrow goes from the foreign sphere to the domestic (and thus from the military to the revolutionary leader). The Matossian-Schafer model discussed earlier in this chapter may provide a clue. Perhaps the upsurge in fertility that follows any postwar demobilization injects the population pressure needed to destabilize the civil environment. The men come home from the front, millions of babies are conceived, and a generation later society feels the strain. It is perhaps more than coincidence that the first truly global manifestation of civil turmoil came in the 1960s, just a generation after the first really worldwide military conflict.

Naturally, war has other effects that do not wait a generation to manifest themselves. In particular, international political violence may exert an immediate influence upon creativity. It is often thought that war quickens cultural development in some way: the fact that the Age of Pericles in Athens coincided with the onset of the Peloponnesian Wars is one possible case in point. But for the most part history seems to indicate the opposite: that warfare has a negative effect on cultural and intellectual activity. For example, the greatest plays by Shakespeare, Aeschylus, Sophocles, Euripides, and Aristophanes tended to be written in peacetime, while their lesser plays tended to appear during times of war (Simonton, 1983a). *Antigone, Oedipus Rex,* and *Medea* were all composed in a brief lull in the struggle between Athens and Sparta, and *Hamlet* and *King Lear* came after England and Spain had sheathed their swords for the first time in a dozen years.

Scientific discovery and technological invention in Europe since the Renaissance have also been adversely affected by international violence (Simonton, 1980b). About 5 percent of the yearly fluctuations in scientific contributions can be accounted for by warfare, even after controlling for various potential artifacts ($\beta = -.12$). Even medical knowledge is not advanced by warfare. War draws would-be medical researchers away from their laboratories to the battlefields and hospital ships. What little information is gained from the examination of mutilated human flesh—such as surmising the localization of psychoneurological functions by observing the crippling effects of having certain portions of a brain blown away—comes nowhere near to compensating for the lost basic and applied research of a more systematic nature. And, in fact, it is a lesson of historiometry that the casualty counts in war are *negatively* correlated with the number of medical discoveries made over the same time period (Simonton, 1976e).

Care must be taken when studying the adverse consequences of war upon creativity; many early investigations, because of methodological limitations, failed to demonstrate any such effect (see Naroll et al., 1971; Simonton, 1975c, 1976b, 1977a). It is important to distinguish among different types of warfare: wars among European nations and defensive wars where the people of European civilization are being attacked by people from a non-European civilization both have an adverse effect on European scientific output, while European civil wars and imperialistic wars of European nations against non-European cultures have no effect whatsoever (Simonton, 1980b). One probable reason for this difference is the scope of the national involvement in the war, including the number of casualties. Furthermore, the analytical time unit is of central significance. The impact of warfare is far too transitory to manifest itself in studies using time units as long as a generation. An outbreak of war may depress creativity for the moment, but the recovery is quick and in some cases even compensates for the wartime losses. Short wars may simply force creators to redistribute their creative output over their careers so that the masterpieces will appear in more peaceful times. Only if a war is long enough to smother the entire peak productive period of a generation will an entire generation of genius be lost to the world. Fortunately, such wars are scarce.

My study of Shakespeare and the four Greek dramatists (Simonton, 1983a) gives some indication that war may be more devastating to creativity if it occurs at a creator's peak productive age than if it occurs at either end of the creator's career. War tended to occur at the beginning and end of the careers of these five great playwrights rather than during their thirties and forties. A creator whose country is at war during what should be his or her most productive period may lose opportunities for achievement that can never be recaptured.

Warfare can also leave an imprint on the content of cultural creativity. One example that has been documented concerns the appearance of the Don Juan figure in a nation's literature. Winter (1973), whose work on the power motive was discussed in Chapter 3, has studied Don Juan as an archetype of the need for power. The Don Juan legend is rich in power imagery; the central character comes from an ancient line of conquerors but chooses to substitute sexual for military accomplishments. Though Don Juan originated in popular legend, he first attained a literary form in 1630 in a play attributed to the Spanish dramatist Tirso de Molina. From that time on, versions of the story proliferated in many literatures, and in many genres. The extensive bibliography allowed Winter to investigate whether the appearance of a new version is partially a function of the political milieu, particularly the course of national conquests. Winter found that the gain or loss of colonial territory by England and France preceded by two decades the publication of new renditions of the Don Juan legend in the national literatures. Even more to the point, participation in war by 15 Western nations between 1830 and 1959 is associated with the creation of Don Juan stories about a decade later. Indeed, Tirso's original drama succeeded, by about a decade, Spain's misguided entry into the Thirty Years' War in Germany and the equally ill-advised reopening of the war with the Netherlands. It seems that imperialistic military adventures nurture the power motive epitomized by the character of Don Juan.

Philosophy as well as literature is influenced by international war. The intensity of European warfare in generation g has a definite impact upon the ideological zeitgeist in generation $g + 1$ (Simonton, 1976g). Roughly twenty years after a major war, the number of philosophers who advocate the sensate positions of empiricism, temporalism, nominalism, singularism, and the ethics of happiness dwindles. Something about being exposed to violent international conflict as a teenager or young adult makes a mature thinker less inclined to propose that sensory input is the sole source of knowledge, that reality suffers unremitting alteration over time, that abstract ideas are mere conventional names, that only individuals (not societies) exist, and that the pleasure principle is the ultimate criterion of moral rightness. Perhaps this philosophical configuration reflects the developmental consequences of wartime propaganda, which attempts to reinforce blind faith in a permanent body politic that is not symbolic but real, and which demands, for its own collective survival, patriotic self-sacrifice and submission to the general will. Curiously, this impact of war upon the ideological zeitgeist of the next generation is almost the precise opposite of the effect of political fragmentation revealed in Chapter 8. It seems that the prevalence of sensate ideas increases a score years after political fragmentation and decreases a score years after international war.

According to fluctuations in casualty figures (though not in frequency of wars), generations that saw the death and maiming of their contemporaries are succeeded by generations of peace. Casualty figures across generations exhibit an autocorrelation of $-.30$: the more casualties in one generation the fewer casualties in the next. Maybe the experience of war creates a cohort of comparative pacifists. Or it may just be a matter of a dearth of healthy bodies to man another military offensive. In either case, as wars have become more sanguine the peaceful times have become more durable and complete.

It would be nice to believe, indeed, that the 50 million or so lost in World War II have made the odds of another all-out war truly small. Perhaps this really could be an era of "limited war" fought more in the pattern of the relatively "harmless" wars that occurred in the eighteenth century: the last war of Frederick the Great of Prussia, the War of the Bavarian Succession (the so-called Potato War of 1778–1779), contained not one bloody encounter. If the horrors of twentieth-century warfare do not now suffice to prevent universal war, and should the unthinkable happen and nuclear war break out on a global scale, the casualty rates in that unfortunate generation would be so beyond counting that peace might reign for generations thereafter—if not forever.

10

THE LAWS OF HISTORIOMETRY

HISTORIOMETRY HAS REVEALED a great deal about eminent creators and leaders. We know that particular developmental experiences, such as birth-order position and the availability of role models, contribute to the appearance of historical figures of a given impact and bent. Presumably these developmental influences are responsible for some of the personality factors, such as intellectual strength, conceptual complexity of thought, achievement and power motivation, style of interpersonal relations (especially dispositions toward dominance and extraversion), and moral caliber, that play a part in the determination of historical events. Another developmental variable, formal education, functions well into adulthood; three separate studies all concur that academic training exhibits a curvilinear relation with creative output.

The potential of a creator or a leader is almost entirely established in adolescence and early adulthood, the rest of the individual's life being dedicated to actualizing this potential genius. Historiometric data indicate that certain prolific persons are responsible for a disproportionate share of the achievements in any given endeavor and that this quantity of productive output is probabilistically connected to quality of impact, or eminence. The principle of cumulative advantage is one basis for the extraordinary individual differences in eminence and influence; this principle also has some relevance to the curvilinear relation between personal age and historical achievement. Though there seems to be a definite productive peak, the constant-probability-of-success model operates for both longitudinal and cross-sectional data, signifying that the odds of a creator's conceiving a quality product are always proportional to the quantity of products, the creator's age notwithstanding.

As for the attributes of the products of genius, the choice of what becomes acclaimed as a masterpiece is not totally capricious; a dramatic or musical masterwork has objective attributes that set it apart from less distinguished creations, and these beneficial attributes may in turn arise from precise biographical events or circumstances, such as life crises or age. In leadership, by contrast, much of what makes for success is out of the individual's hands; the contemporary popularity, the rated historical greatness, and even the concrete political perform-ance of an American president may contain an overwhelming infusion of situational factors, individual propensities only fine-tuning these larger impersonal forces. The interplay of zeitgeist and genius in the course of human affairs is complex, as revealed by studies of political and military leadership and of philosophical, aesthetic, and scientific creativity. Neither the zeitgeist nor the genius is unimportant, though both agents must yield some explanatory ground to chance as well.

The dual agency of situation and individual is also crucial in deter-mining war and revolution. The relevance of population pressure to civil unrest and the relevance of integrative complexity to the political decisions that result in international war both deserve serious consider-ation, while the ideological consequences of political violence—as re-vealed in the law of polarization—must be added to the list of after-effects of outbreaks of strife and battle. It is an important lesson that the repercussions of a given political event may take generations to unfold.

When it comes to discussion of eminent genius, very similar pro-cesses and substantive issues arise in the treatment of creativity and leadership. It often makes sense to jump back and forth between prin-ciples that apply to creators and analogous principles that apply to leaders. The operation of the Matthew effect, the influence of age, the role of intelligence, and the impact of the zeitgeist are just a few exam-ples.

These principles, culled from historical data, have respectable no-mothetic status. Birth-order effects, role-modeling influences, the Matthew effect and the principle of cumulative advantage, Price's and Lotka's law, Planck's principle, the law of polarization, the curvilinear relations between education and accomplishment, between age and achievement, and between melodic originality and thematic success— all of these generalizations are nomothetic findings: they are cross-culturally and transhistorically invariant under the specified conditions. The discoveries of historiometry, to be sure, are far fewer than the laws of the physical and biological sciences, and the discoveries are more probabilistic tendencies than laws. Still, historiometry is a much youn-ger science than any of the so-called hard sciences, and must cope with much more elusive substantive and methodological issues. To be fair, therefore, it is not the absolute level of objectivity and precision that should be judged, but rather the relative increase in objective and precise knowledge. In the language of calculus, it is the value of the first derivative taken at a given point in historical time that is the most just criterion. A contribution must be judged in its proper context.

Naturally, scientists are used to doing this to some extent. Such scientific enterprises as geology, paleontology, and archaeology, for example, are respected within the scientific community as a whole, despite the unreliable nature of the geological, paleontological, or archaeological record. The historical record is far more complete and reliable than these, and the intentions of historiometry are far more immediately directed at the testing of fully nomothetic hypotheses. Where the geologist may concentrate on a particular formation, the paleontologist on a particular lineage, and the archaeologist on a particular site, the historiometrician seeks the general rules of human behavior that underlie the manifestation of, say, creativity and leadership on a large sociocultural scale.

The practical goals of any scientific endeavor are to explain, predict, and control the course of events. Historiometry, too, moves in the quest for explanation, prediction, and control. On many occasions throughout this book I have provided illustrations of the potential explanatory value of certain nomothetic findings. Further, if these laws of history are expressed in precise enough mathematical terms, we can readily use these equations to make predictions, as when I predicted the greatness ratings of various American presidents utilizing a multiple regression equation, or when I predicted creative productivity within individual lives. Thus the young science of historiometry has already made major strides toward adequate explanation and accurate prediction.

Control evades our grasp more thoroughly, however. For instance, as much as I would like to believe that some of the findings on warfare might be used to reduce the likelihood of organized mass slaughter, such practical applications have not yet been attained. But the gap between scientific discovery and technological implementation is often huge. More critically, it may be that the magnitude of human affairs is such that our intervention on behalf of certain desired outcomes, even when predicated on the soundest social-scientific laws, must prove impotent in the end. Astronomers cannot exert their will over the progression of cosmic events, meteorologists must rest satisfied with warning people when to don their raincoats, and geologists can only pray that someday they will be able to confidently order evacuations of cities the day before an earthquake strikes. Still, even if we may not ever be able to control the external world, we may at least gain psychological solace by enlarging the understandability and predictability of the human dimension of that world. The original justification for astronomy was to render the action of the heavenly bodies more predictable and thus less fearsome. To predict a solar eclipse is to deny it the potency to frighten. By the same token, the capacity to anticipate the onset of political violence is the next best thing to the ability to prevent an outbreak.

Human civilization is merely four thousand years old, and at-all-reliable historical records go back only half that far. In the scope of geological, paleontological, and even archaeological time, a millennium is very short. If we assume that millions of years of human civilization stand before us, the urgency of a nomothetic approach to the accumulated historical record must be apparent. With each year that goes by, the richness of the historical data deposited in the archives increases. So millennia from now our descendants will have more means at their disposal for discovering the laws of history. In that far-off time, historiometric equations may be able to predict events with a high confidence built upon a well-confirmed theoretical position: the course of history may even fall partially under the control of the human race. Hegel observed: "What experience and history teach is this—that peoples and governments never have learned anything from history, or acted on principles deduced from it." It is our imperative duty to try with all our might to prove Hegel wrong. "Human history," H. G. Wells warned, "becomes more and more a race between education and catastrophe."

Appendixes
References
Index

Appendix A

Significance Tests and Significant Samples

ALMOST ANY EMPIRICAL study in the behavioral sciences will include statements such as "this correlation was statistically significant." The statistical significance of a measure of association, whether bivariate or multivariate, is normally expressed in terms of probability levels, such as "$p < .05$" or "$p < .01$." These levels of confidence supposedly inform us of the probability that we might have obtained our results just by chance. Thus "$p < .05$" means that the probability of obtaining a statistic of a given magnitude merely by the luck of the draw is less than 5 percent. Such probability statements are derived from some form of "inferential" statistic, such as a chi-square, t, or F test. Inferential statistics permit us to learn whether we can infer relationships or attributes in the larger population of events from our diminutive sample. For example, when a social psychologist conducts a laboratory experiment on how leadership emerges in small groups, the study may include only a half-hundred subjects. The inferential statistics allow the experimenter to state the probability that any effects found in this small sample can be generalized to the larger human population.

Although significance tests play such an important part in experimental and even survey research, I seldom record significance levels in this book. The emphasis here is laid squarely upon "descriptive" rather than inferential statistics. A descriptive statistic is one that describes the characteristics of a given sample. Often, for example, I present correlation coefficients (r's) and standardized partial regression coefficients (β's). Such statistics are extremely informative as gauges of the magnitude of a relationship between two variables within a given sample of analytical units. Inferential statistics, by contrast, do not make any direct assertions about the size of an effect. The probability that results are due to chance is a function of the effect size plus the sample size. Thus a minuscule correlation coefficient can be highly "significant" so long as the sample size is sufficiently large. A sample of just over a thousand cases needs a correlation of only .06 to be significant at the .05 level even though such a coefficient indicates that only about one-third of one percent of the variance in the two variables is shared. Yet some researchers will publish only the probability levels without the corresponding effect sizes. Nonetheless, the fact that I do the exact opposite by declining to report the p values should not be interpreted as implying that the corresponding significance tests have not been calculated or that the cited descriptive statistics fall below conventional levels of statistical significance. On the contrary, virtually every effect discussed in this book is significant at the .05 level and very often at the .01 level or even better. I have merely avoided exhibiting numbers that can be very misleading, particularly insofar as they say absolutely nothing about the magnitude of causal effect.

In truth, my objection to inferential statistics runs much deeper (see Morrison and Henkel, 1970). Significance tests have to make crucial assumptions that I find totally untenable, at least in historiometric studies of genius. In the first place, to test the significance of a correlation coefficient we usually must assume that the distributions of the two variables is governed by a normal bell-shaped curve. This postulate is almost absurd. Many key variables pertaining to creativity and leadership have highly skewed distributions that totally depart from the desired form. True, it would be possible to employ some type of "nonparametric" statistic that does not make the assumption of normality. But such statistics do not lend themselves to the multivariate analyses and quasi-experimental designs that play such a major role in historiometric causal inference. Since neither the correlation coefficient nor multiple regression makes any distributional assumption when considered as descriptors of relationships observed within a sample, there is no reason not to utilize these analytical tools for any set of variables no matter how anomalous their distributions are with respect to the normal curve.

Significance tests assume as well that a given sample has been randomly drawn from an "infinite" population. I believe this assumption is not valid for most psychological research, and certainly not for historiometric investigations. No experimental psychologist randomly draws a sample of subjects from the billions of living human beings, nor even from the proverbial subject pool of college sophomores taking an introductory psychology class. And matters are much worse for historiometric inquiries. To sample subjects according to the eminence criterion is certainly not random. Moreover, the eminence criterion assures us that the sample under scrutiny has the greatest possible intrinsic value in its own right. A sample of the most famous creators or leaders in a particular endeavor is probably more scientifically interesting as a source of nomothetic principles than all the figures that remain in obscurity. For example, even though several hundred composers are responsible for the music heard in the classical repertoire, it is not unreasonable at times to concentrate upon the 10 most famous classical composers. These top 10 creators, after all, account for 39 percent of all pieces performed in the concert hall and recording studio.

Naturally, most historiometric inquiries are less elitist in their sampling provisions. In another study I have sampled almost 700 composers who together account for virtually 100 percent of all classical music heard on concert programs and home stereo systems. In fact, a crucial asset of historiometric studies is just this ability to exhaust the population of greatest intrinsic fascination. My study of 2,012 philosophers excludes no creator from Thales to Nietzsche who has any reasonable claim to have contributed to the history of ideas. Hence, it is ridiculous to ask whether we can generalize from this "sample," to the "larger population." In addition, the size of the sample makes it far too easy for descriptive statistics to be significant. Therefore, rather than inquire whether the results can be extended to some hypothetical population it may be far more productive to ask whether the effects are of sufficient magnitude to be nomothetically noteworthy.

Descriptive statistics thus tell us more about what we really want to know with the fewest possible assumptions, but they are not without hidden presuppositions of their own. In particular, the correlation coefficient, which is the building block of all data analysis, postulates that those individuals who differ most from the average should influence the results more than those who are more close to the mean. The "least squares" principle, which underlies both multiple regression and correlation analysis, places more stress on those individuals who are truly exceptional than on those closer to the average. This stress upon the outstanding cases is well-suited to a search for nomothetic laws about creativity and leadership. It means that in a study of philosophers the most eminent thinkers—those of the stature of Plato, Aristotle, Lucretius, Aquinas, Descartes, and Kant—will influence the correlation statistics far more than will their more obscure contemporaries. Indeed, scores on fame are usually distributed in such a skewed fashion that the least eminent are closer to the mean level of eminence than are the most eminent. Accordingly, the bias of correlation statistics toward the extremes is a bias in the most advantageous direction. The more outstanding the historical figure, the more he or she influences the derivation of the nomothetic laws of history. This enhanced weight is in perfect accord with the aim of finding out why certain individuals have a disproportionate impact on the course of history. We would want our statistics to assign more weight to Hitler or Einstein than to, say, Ernst Röhm or Friedrich Hasenöhrl.

Appendix B

Curvilinear Relationships and Interval Scales

IN CHAPTER 4 I referred repeatedly to the "curvilinear inverted-U" or "inverted backwards-J" relationship between education and achievement. To get an idea of how such statements are justified, let us return to the functional relation found between formal education and achieved eminence as a Cox-sample creator. The formula from which I plotted the lower of the two curves in Figure 1 can be given as $E = 94.81 + 44.34F - 11.96F^2$, where E is ranked eminence and F the level of formal education as previously defined. This equation describes a curve in the Cartesian coordinate system with ranked eminence along the vertical axis and formal education along the horizontal axis in the graph. To be more precise, this equation does not really describe an inverted U, but rather a concave downwards parabolic curve. Parabolic curves are represented by quadratic functions, that is, by equations with both linear (F) and quadratic or squared (F^2) terms.

Given the equation, how do we know where the peak of the curve is? Using calculus we can differentiate the equation with respect to formal education, set this first-derivative equal to zero, and solve for F; the result is 1.85, or some college education just short of a bachelor's degree. All of the optimum points discussed in Chapter 4 were arrived at by applying calculus to the quadratic equation describing the functional relationship between education and creativity or leadership.

I have not said where I got this equation in the first place. The two multiplicative constants that stand before F and F^2 are unstandardized multiple regression coefficients, and the number standing alone to which these two products are added is an "intercept" from a multiple regression analysis. Regression analysis fits the curve to the data points so as to minimize the errors of prediction. Another way of saying the same thing is to note that the equation explains more variance in achieved eminence than any other equation. No matter how we may juggle the three parameters, *no* equation will do a better job of predicting the observed differences in eminent creativity from the given differences in educational level. Actually, it is not the raw errors we are minimizing but rather the squared errors. Since a large number changes more than a small number when it is squared, to reduce the squared errors means that we are more worried about making big blunders than slight slips in our predictions.

The method I have just described for determining curvilinear relationships was exploited repeatedly throughout this book. This application of multiple regression, however, rests on an assumption: Presumably the variables have been measured along an "interval scale," that is, one where the addition of one point at one end of the scale means the same thing as the addition of one point elsewhere on the same scale. In constructing the above equation, for example, I am assuming that going from a high school diploma to a bachelor's degree entails the same quantity of formal education as going from a master's degree to a doctorate. Beyond any doubt such a supposition is only an approximation. I have not even been consistent with the intervals defined in the three studies reviewed in this chapter.

Does this inconsistency mean that a prerequisite for applying regression analysis has been seriously violated? The answer is negative. Looking carefully at Figures 1 and 2, imagine what would happen if we made some intervals narrower and others wider (presumably to better fit what we conceive to be the true increments in formal education). No matter how the intervals are adjusted, the functions will still take the form of a concave downwards curve, yielding a peak level of optimal effect. In point of fact, the rank ordering of the academic levels carries much more weight than do the intervals between the levels. If one were to argue that it takes more total formal education to obtain a B.A. than to obtain an M.A., then the main conclusions of Chapter 4 would be vulnerable. But such an argument would be logically absurd. Since the rank ordering is secure, so is the broad outline of the curves.

To be sure, I have gotten much theoretical mileage out of the specific turn-around point of the curves when large shifts in the intervals can change the maximum or minimum points to some degree. Maybe 1.85 is expressed in too many significant figures given the crudeness of the scale, but we know for sure that the peak in Figure 1 falls somewhere between high school and college graduation, not before or after. Moreover, the diverse intervals notwithstanding, the remaining two studies back up the initial estimate. Thus, something must be happening between the third and fourth years of undergraduate education if the results are invariant across alternative interval definitions.

Too much has sometimes been said about the scarcity of unchallengeable interval scales in the social sciences. Comparison of the crude social scientific measures with the elaborate instrumentation of the physical sciences elicits a lot of blushing. Yet the physical sciences are thousands of years old, whereas the social sciences did not really extricate themselves from philosophy until this century. If we want to make just comparisons we must peer far back into the past. When Galileo, for instance, wanted to study the laws of falling bodies he had no access to a stopwatch. Instead he had to use his pulse, though such a timepiece certainly did not yield equal temporal spaces between beats. Even when Galileo, using his pulse, found that the sweeping of a pendulum marks equal intervals of time, this measurement problem had not been solved. An accurate pendulum clock had to wait Huygens' demonstration that a pendulum is not isochronous unless its course follows the cycloid curve. Simply put, Galileo could not measure time along an invariant interval scale. And yet Galileo was not prevented from discovering the laws of falling bodies. His crude experiments got him close enough to the phenomena under investigation so that his mathematical insights could take over. The mathematical analysis then offered abstract functional forms that could only fit the data in the most approximate way. All of the key topics in the so-called exact sciences began with comparable inexactitude. Historiometry can do the same.

Appendix C

Structural Equation Modeling

I INVESTIGATED 696 COMPOSERS in the Western music tradition in order to identify the determinants of differential eminence, where the individual composer serves as the unit of analysis (Simonton, 1977b). Altogether seven variables were examined as potential antecedents of a composer's greatness: creative longevity, or the length of a composer's career; life span; creative productivity, or the total number of notable themes generated by the composer; creative precociousness, or the age at which the composer began creative productivity (defined as the negative age in order to give it a positive association with other key variables); geographic marginality, or how far the composer was born from the center of music activity in his or her generation; role-model availability, or the number of active composers in the previous generation; and birth year. The basic descriptive statistics for all these variables are depicted *below the diagonal* in Table A.1.

The means tell us that the typical composer in the sample was born in 1796, began creative production at 33, produced 24 major themes, lived to be 63 years old, and had a creative career a decade long. The correlations among all eight variables give some indication of the possible causal determinants of creative eminence. As expected, eminence correlates most highly with creative productivity, that is, the most prominent composers are responsible for the largest numbers of notable melodies in the classical repertoire. Since the fame of these themes is predicated upon their melodic originality, and since melodic originality is founded upon such personal factors as age and biographical stress, we have thus completed the bridge between personal events and sociocultural success. Besides creative productivity, eminence is positively correlated with length of career and with productive precociousness, and is negatively related to such situational factors as birth year, role-model availability, and geographic marginality, though these last three correlations are much smaller than the others. The most famous

Table A.1. Correlations, descriptive statistics, and deviations from model-predicted correlations for 696 classical composers.

VARIABLE	1	2	3	4	5	6	7	8
1. Birth year		.00	.00	.02	.03	.00	.04	.03
2. Role-model availability	.85		.00	.00	.00	.00	.00	.00
3. Geographic marginality	.45	.48		−.03	−.06	.01	−.04	−.03
4. Creative precociousness	.23	.24	.08		.00	.01	.00	.02
5. Creative productivity	.02	−.02	−.07	.32		.01	.00	.00
6. Life span	−.06	−.18	−.14	−.24	−.05		.01	−.03
7. Creative longevity	.09	.03	−.04	.40	.51	.15		−.01
8. Eminence	−.19	−.19	−.14	.26	.71	−.01	.56	
Mean	1796	4.14	2.38	−33	24	63	10	10
Standard Deviation	112	.57	1.08	9	74	14	12	22

SOURCE. Simonton, 1977b.

NOTE. Zero-order correlations are given below the diagonal. Differences between these correlations and those predicted by the model in Figure A.1 are shown above the diagonal. Correlations must be at least .062 to be significant at the .05 level for a one-tailed test.

composers are precocious and creatively durable, are born closer to the geographic center of music activity, have fewer creative role models, and are born long ago rather than more recently. Of the seven potential predictors, only life span bears no linear relation to eminence.

But we must ask whether the six correlates of eminence are direct causes or whether some of them might be indirect causes or even examples of spurious relationships. To clarify the causal interconnections among the eight variables in Table A.1 we must go beyond the correlations. In particular, we must apply the body of techniques known as "path analysis" or "structural equation modeling." In the present case this method entails the employment of multiple regression analysis to estimate the path coefficients or structural parameters that register the causal effects in a complex causal network. The outcome of such an analysis is presented in Figure A.1, which displays the resulting structural equations.

The arrows connecting the eight variables in the study represent the presumed direction of causal influence. All causal relationships are assumed to be "recursive," that is, the causes only flow in one direction without any two-way causality or feedback loops. Thus eminence is said to be a causal consequence of productivity, not the other way around. If no arrow connects two variables, no direct causal relation exists between them. Thus we see that life span exerts no direct effect upon eminence; any effect it might have must take place via creative longevity.

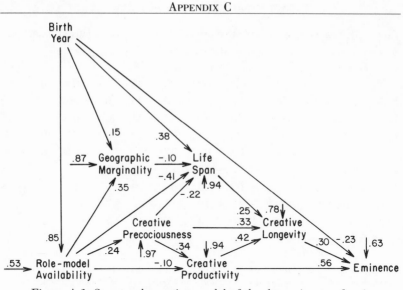

Figure A.1. Structural equation model of the determinants of eminence for 696 classical composers (from Simonton, 1977b). Path coefficients show degree and direction of causal influence.

The decimal fractions alongside each arrow are the causal coefficients that inform us of the relative contribution of each cause to a particular effect. The coefficients are actually standardized multiple regression coefficients or betas. They gauge the impact of one independent variable holding the other direct effects constant. Thus the path coefficient of .56 between productivity and eminence shows us the strength of the influence of productivity after controlling for birth year and creative longevity. These coefficients can be interpreted in much the same way as a correlation coefficient; they tend to range between $+1$ and -1, where a negative value signifies that increases in the causal variable cause decreases in the effect variable. Notice that some of the causal coefficients that impinge upon a given effect variable seem to come out of nowhere. These coefficients record the influence of all unmeasured causes in the network. Needless to say, these omitted causes are prone to have the biggest influence upon any variable in question. If the square of this coefficient is subtracted from one, the difference represents the proportion of variance in that dependent variable that is explained by all the explicit dependent variables put together. In the case of eminence, for instance, 60 percent of the differential fame of the 696 composers $(1 - .63^2 = .60)$ can be explained in terms of productivity, longevity, and birth year.

The causal parameters for the observed variables have the most predictive utility since they tell us how many standard deviations above or below the mean a composer will be on the effect variable if that composer is so many standard deviations above or below the mean on the causal variable. (The standard deviation is the square root of the variance.) Take the coefficient of .42 from productivity to longevity. This value signifies that a composer who is, say, one standard deviation above the mean in the production of melodies (24 + 74 = 98), will be .42 standard deviations above the mean in the length of career, or 15 rather than 10 years (10 + [.42 × 12] = 15). But what about the effect of precociousness upon longevity? At first we might simply conclude that for every standard deviation that a career begins earlier than average, the overall career is about one-third longer than average. If, for example, the career began at 24 rather than 33, we might expect that the career would be around 14 years long (10 + [.33 × 12] = 14). Yet this prediction is wrong since it only includes the direct effect of precociousness upon longevity. Overlooked are two indirect influences, one through life span and the other through creative productivity. Precocious creators tend to be more prolific, but they also tend to die young. Therefore, we must add to the direct effect these two indirect effects. This is accomplished by taking the products of the corresponding path coefficients. The indirect effect of precociousness upon longevity through the intervening variable of productivity is equal to .14 (= .34 × .42), while the indirect effect via life span is −.06 (= −.22 × .30). The total effect of precociousness upon longevity is equal to the sum of the direct and indirect effects, or .41. In other words, when we make all due allowance for the complexity of the causal relation between precociousness and longevity, for every year of delay in the onset of a creator's career that career will be shortened by about 200 days.

Notice that this overall effect coefficient of .41 is remarkably close to the correlation coefficient of .40. This near congruence is no accident. What we have done is to "decompose" the bivariate correlation between two variables, in this case precociousness and longevity, into the sum of separate causal paths, one direct and two indirect. The ability to decompose a relationship into distinct causal components is one of the impressive features of path analysis, particularly when it allows us to avoid erroneous conclusions. As an example, simple inspection of Table A.1 might lead one to surmise that the availability of role models very early in life has very little to do with creative productivity in maturity, yet this inference is entirely fallacious. As we can see in Figure

A.1, role-model availability exerts both a direct and an indirect influence upon productivity, the latter effect occurring via precociousness. The more role models who are around during creative development, the earlier a creator will begin to compose memorable melodies, and yet an ample supply of models may operate to inhibit total productive output of original melodies, perhaps because having many role models may encourage an excessive imitativeness. The positive indirect effect just about cancels out the negative direct effect; adding them yields the virtually nonexistent correlation of −.02. Obviously, the absence of a correlation does not necessarily mean that two variables are not causally related. A zero correlation must always be interpreted in terms of an entire causal network such as seen in Figure A.1. Path analysis makes it possible to decompose a zero correlation into a sum of non-zero direct and indirect causal paths.

To calculate how much of the correlation between two variables is the spurious product of some common cause, simply take the sum of direct and indirect effects and subtract it from the overall correlation. To illustrate, part of the association between longevity and eminence is due to their mutual dependence upon productivity and birth year. If we take the direct effect of longevity upon eminence (there is no indirect effect in this case) and subtract it from the correlation coefficient, we obtain .26 (= .56 − .30). Most of this spurious effect can be ascribed to productivity (.56 × .42 = .24), the remainder to the complex direct and indirect consequences of a composer's birth year. The device of decomposing correlations reveals the rich causal intricacy hidden behind the correlation matrix. This decompositional technique has another advantage: once we know how to decompose a correlation on the basis of a given structural model, and once we have estimated the causal parameters, we can compare the correlations predicted by the model with those we actually observe. When we take the difference between predicted and observed values, we get the results seen *above the diagonal* in Table A.1. Clearly the errors of prediction are rather negligible, the only appreciable discrepancy being that between geographic marginality and creative productivity. There is some residual tendency, not incorporated in Figure A.1, for those composers born far from the musical center to be less prolific, but this disposition is not potent enough to require another arrow in the structural model.

Structural equation modeling is not as simple as this example may make it appear. Nor does the causal model in Figure A.1 represent a finished, polished product. The model is nothing more than a first approximation; but it does serve as an illustration of modeling methods. Such models are capable of capturing the complexities of causal networks in real-world settings, and they make it possible to put forward predictions with superior accuracy and understanding. Eventually it may be possible to summarize all historiometric research on creativity and leadership in terms of structural equations that specify the direct, indirect, and spurious causal connections among all the key variables of theoretical and practical interest.

Appendix D

Assessing the Prominence of Chance

IN THE SECTION on multiple discovery and invention in Chapter 8 I concluded that such multiples may be more a matter of chance than of anything else, the zeitgeist included. On the basis of this inference, I argued that scientific and technological progress may not be inevitable. This interpretation raises the question of how much of history entails the mere haphazard concatenation of events. Machiavelli maintained in *The Prince* "that Fortune is the arbiter of one-half of our actions, but that she still leaves us to direct the other half, or perhaps a little less." Tolstoy, a stalwart defender of the zeitgeist interpretation of history, offered the following mock dialogue in *War and Peace* (1865–1869, p. 646):

> Why did it happen in this and not in some other way?
>
> Because it happened so! "*Chance* created the situation; *genius* utilized it," says history.
>
> The words *chance* and *genius* do not denote any really existing thing and therefore cannot be defined. Those words only denote a certain state of understanding of phenomena.

One of the central aims of historiometry is to provide an objective and quantitative estimate of zeitgeist, genius, and chance as explanatory factors. Historiometric studies have already made some progress in weighing the relative effects of these three factors. In the investigation of military genius discussed in Chapter 8, I noted that tactical victory on the battlefield can be successfully predicted 71 percent of the time using a combination of individual and situational variables. Seventy-one percent is obviously better than a 50 percent success rate based on the flip of a coin, but how much better? As it turns out, about 20 percent of the variance in tactical victory can be predicted, the remaining 80 percent still belonging to chance. Further studies may divulge new variables to insert in the predictive equation that will lower the amount of unexplained variance. In a sense, Tolstoy is correct: a measure of the contribution of chance is tantamount to an assessment of our current state of ignorance.

But taking this partitioning of explained and unexplained variance as a first approximation allows us to subdivide the explained variance into variance that can be ascribed to the three individual predictors (winning streaks, experience, and taking the offensive) and variance that can be attributed to the single situational predictor (divided command). As observed in Chapter 8, 86 percent of the predictive value of the equation is the responsibility of the individual variables, the remaining 14 percent being due to the situational variable. Consequently, victory on the battlefield can tentatively be said to be 80 percent chance, 17 percent genius, and 3 percent zeitgeist. This crude threefold division at least illustrates how historiometry might begin to answer this crucial question.

Another tack can be pursued. Rather than employ prediction equations to slice the explanatory pie into three unequal pieces in an a posteriori way, we can work from the other direction by subjecting a priori theoretical deductions to empirical test. Returning to the problem of scientific multiples, I will formulate a simple model of this phenomenon that will make it possible to specify more clearly how zeitgeist, genius, and chance positions direct us to distinguishable empirical expectations (Simonton, 1979a). We begin with the proposition that for any given invention or discovery there are n individuals capable of producing it, and each has a probability p of success, where $n \leqq 1$ and $0 < p \leqq 1$. We can then utilize the binomial theorem to calculate the proportion of the various numbers of successes, or the grades of multiples.

Take the zeitgeist theory as a starting point. If it is correct, the number of available creators for a given potential contribution should be very large but the probability of success for each creator should be small so that genius is, strictly speaking, irrelevant. Since the maximum grade of a multiple is 9, let us be on the safe side and assume that any given potential contribution has 10 creators working on it, making $n = 10$. In addition, let us assume that each creator has only a 50–50 chance of success, such that $p = .5$. Given these parameter values we obtain the binomial distribution shown in the upper portion of Figure A.2. Here multiples of grade 5 are the most common, accounting for almost one-quarter of all contributions. This modal value is equivalent to the mean of the distribution, which is given by $\mu = np = 10 \times .5 = 5$. Grades higher or lower than 5 will be much less frequent and, most critically, singletons will be quite rare and nulltons virtually unheard of. Indeed, almost 99 percent of all contributions to science and technology will be made by two or more independent creators. Under this scheme, scientific progress must be not only inevitable but preeminently redundant as well. This prediction that multiples will far outnumber singletons and that multiples of certain higher grades will actually outnumber multiples of lower grades is not dependent upon the specific parameter values selected for illustration. As long as np exceeds unity by some noticeable amount, the same general picture will

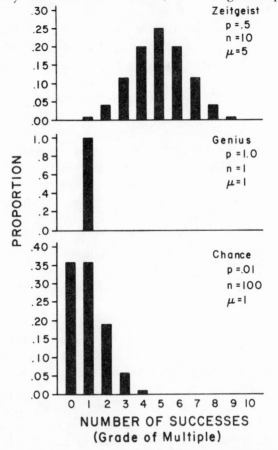

Figure A.2. Predicted probability distributions obtained by interpreting the three alternative theories of the causes of multiple discoveries in terms of the binomial distribution with different values for the number of attempts (n) and the probability of success (p) (from Simonton, 1980a).

result. Indeed, if we retain $n = 10$ but oblige the probability of success to be much higher, such as $p = .9$, high-grade multiples will be very common, low-grade multiples quite rare, and scientific progress indeed inevitable.

Now turn to the opposite extreme. A genius theory would, in its purest form, argue that for any given potential contribution there is one and only one creator capable of making that contribution. Further, that lone genius has a 100 percent probability of success. Granting this ideal case, $p = 1.0$ and $n = 1$, yielding the degenerate binomial distribution in the middle part of Figure A.2. Now the mean and modal grade is one (that is, $np = 1$) with a variance of zero, meaning that there are no multiples and no nulltons, but only singletons. No multiples occur because there is only one genius who is capable of producing a given contribution, and there are no nulltons because each genius has perfect odds of success. Naturally, few advocates of genius would put forward such an extreme case. The value of n might be permitted to be 2 or 3, while p might be allowed to be somewhat less than unity. Nonetheless, even when we relax these prescriptions, a genius interpretation must imply that singletons are vastly more probable than either multiples or, by inference, nulltons.

Chance theory assigns very different values for the two key parameters of the binomial distribution. Assume that the number of trials is very large but the probability of success per trial is very small. For the purposes of argument, make $n = 100$ and $p = .01$: for a given discovery or invention there are 100 scientists or inventors at work, but each of these has only 1 chance out of 100 of succeeding. The mean of the resulting binomial distribution is again one $(np = 1)$, but its shape is rather different, as can be spotted immediately from the lower portion of the figure. Under these parameters, fewer than one-third of the trials will generate multiples, the remaining two-thirds-plus being distributed evenly between singletons and nulltons. Note, too, that as the grade of the multiples increases, the probability of contributions of that grade shrinks. There should be fewer doublets than singletons, fewer triplets than doublets, and so on. Recall that this distributional shape is precisely the same as has been empirically observed for every sample of multiples ever collected. In point of fact, when p is very small and n very large, the binomial distribution approaches the Poisson distribution as a limiting case. The Poisson distribution has been proven to fit the data almost perfectly, the departures from the predicted values being no greater than could be expected on the basis of random sampling error (Simonton, 1978b, 1979a). Additionally, the mean of the

Poisson distribution has been empirically determined to be fairly close to unity. Accordingly, the probability of distribution shown for the chance model in Figure A.2 can be said to be typical of the actual observed distribution. The chance explanation of multiples appears to be substantiated by the historiometric data. The value of the parameters, especially the small size of p, should also make it self-evident why the Poisson process tends to be most applicable to rare events.

It is possible to modify our conception of the model so as to make it more compatible with both zeitgeist and genius theories while preserving the overall dominance of chance (Simonton, 1979a). There is no theoretical or empirical reason not to presume that the true parameters of the binomial model are $p = .1$ and $n = 10$. These values will still generate a Poisson-like distribution with a mean of unity, thereby endorsing the chief tenets of a chance interpretation. Yet to say that there are nearly a dozen creators who are proficient enough to arrive at any given discovery or invention seems to support the contention of the zeitgeist viewpoint that the advance of science is by no means dependent upon any single individual, genius or not. Furthermore, though there are many more nulltons than a purely zeitgeist interpretation implies, the fact that the mean of the distribution is one signifies that every nullton is balanced by a multiple such that the average number of times an idea is conceived is one. At the same time, it hardly contradicts a genius standpoint to hold that only 10 scientists are potentially capable of creating a given scientific idea. All in all, it is possible to reinterpret this simple binomial probability model so as to accommodate all three perspectives, albeit the genius and the zeitgeist positions must do most of the compromising.

This model, of course, for all its predictive and explanatory adequacies, is highly oversimplified. It overlooks the fact that some scientific ideas are necessary prerequisites for others. It is inconceivable to imagine Newtonian physics without Kepler's laws, Galileo's mechanics, and Cartesian analytical geometry; Kepler, Galileo, and Descartes were three of the giants on whose shoulders Newton stood to survey the cosmos. But to say that a given idea is necessary is not the same as to claim that an idea is a sufficient cause of another. And if ideas are only necessary but not sufficient, then just the order of scientific progress is determined, not its specific timing. Galileo's discovery of Jupiter's moons took place only one year after the invention of the telescope, the necessary prerequisite. But Leeuwenhoek's discovery of bacteria did not occur until two centuries after the invention of the microscope.

The existence of numerous *simultaneous* independent discoveries and inventions might seem to prove that scientific progress is not so indeterminant. Yet it is possible to design a chance model that predicts the occurrence of simultaneous contributions without forfeiting the fundamental postulate that such occurrences are mere coincidences. All we need to do is to introduce a little "contagion" mechanism into the probability model. Assume that once a particular discovery has been published other creators will have no interest in replicating what has already been accomplished and will accordingly move on to something else. Of course it takes time for scientific knowledge to diffuse, and the delay is even greater when the information must cross linguistic and cultural boundaries, but this complication can be built in as a further refinement of the model. Given these assumptions, it would follow that simultaneous discovery would indeed be common, even in comparison to nonsimultaneous but nonetheless independent multiples. Once one scientist makes a discovery, another scientist may not be precluded from making the same discovery almost immediately after, but as time goes on and knowledge of the first discovery spreads about, more and more independent investigators are forestalled in their own quests of the same goal. Since the diffusion time is longer across linguistic and cultural frontiers, furthermore, a multiple that contains contributions separated widely in time is most likely to involve contributors of different nationalities.

The main point is this: a chance model that allows for unstable probabilities due to a contagion process can easily yield simultaneous multiples without any presumption that the zeitgeist tells scientists when to engage on what specific project. And should we make this model more realistic by adding a certain ordering to some of the potential contributions (that is, by assuming that the occurrence of one prerequisite discovery raises the probability of its dependent from zero to nonzero), the predictive precision of the model should become all the more impressive without relinquishing in any way the predominant role of chance.

This discussion has not proven this chance interpretation to be correct. But it does challenge advocates of the zeitgeist interpretation of scientific advance to come up with critical tests that will show that there is something more to zeitgeist than the weak temporal ordering of certain events and the time lag in the diffusion of knowledge.

Appendix E

Generational Time-Series Analysis

IN THIS BOOK I have repeatedly exploited a technique known as generational time-series analysis. Generational analyses start by defining the unit of analysis. The first step is to determine the cross-sectional unit across space: are we dealing with generations from the history of a single nation or from an entire civilization. The choice depends on the nomothetic hypotheses to be tested. For instance, generalizations about the generational fluctuations in literary genius can probably be best approached via national units, for literary traditions tend to be highly nationalistic in nature. The next step is to delimit the time unit. For almost all of the generational analyses reported here, this unit consists of 20 years.

A key feature of the generational analysis in this book is that geniuses are allotted to the 20-year periods in which they celebrate their fortieth birthday, on the theory that this age represents the best all-purpose estimate of the peak productive age of a creator. Take Beethoven to illustrate this procedure. Born in 1770, he was 40 years old in 1810, which places him squarely in generation 1800–1819. Let us denote this period generation g. Then we can properly inquire about what was happening to Beethoven in the previous generation, $g - 1$. Obviously in that period Beethoven was 20 years younger, a youth subject to the developmental influences of the age. He would be susceptible to role-modeling effects, vulnerable to the course of political events, and influenced by the philosophical fireworks of his time. The creative potential he acquired in his late teens and early twenties will become the creative output of Beethoven's compositional career. To be sure, it is not very precise to say that Beethoven is 40 in generation g and 20 in generation $g - 1$. In truth, his age ranges from 30 to 49 in the former period and from 10 to 29 in the latter. But these age ranges make it possible to speak of the years between 30 and 49 as Beethoven's peak productive period. Likewise, we can view the years between 10 and 29 as his developmental period.

Admittedly, I have selected Beethoven because he fits the methodological scheme with minimal hardship. Since his fortieth birthday falls right in the middle of generation 1800–1819, his peak productive phase—in fact what is known as his impressive Second Period—coincides almost perfectly with the schematic historical periodization. Shakespeare fits the schema less well. Born in 1564, he reached his age-40 acme in generation 1600–1619. And in fact such dramatic masterworks as *Hamlet, Othello, King Lear, Macbeth,* and *The Tempest,* along with his great sonnets, all date from this interval. Still, *The Taming of the Shrew, Romeo and Juliet, A Midsummer Night's Dream, The Merchant of Venice,* and *Julius Caesar* all belong more correctly in generation 1580–1599. An even more telling example is Raphael, who was born in 1483 and therefore would be assigned to the generation 1520–1539. But this assignment is absurd: *all* Raphael's major paintings date from before 1520, and in fact he died in 1520. He did not live to be 40, and he lived just a few months into the generation in which the methodology assumes he was most active.

In responding to these difficulties I must stress three points. First, generational analysis is *not* engaged in tabulating creative products but rather in assigning creative persons to the consecutive 20-year intervals. Second, the reason for doing so is simply to devise a way of assessing the developmental impact of the sociocultural or political surroundings on the emerging genius. Third, this developmental causal inference is not based on a mere handful of particular cases but rather on hundreds and even thousands of creative subjects. Given these realities of the technique, it does not matter that in some instances the peak productive phase falls into two generations. For every creator who turned 40 near the beginning of the 20-year-period there is another creator whose fortieth birthday falls near the end; thus the average age of creators in any given generation across a large sample will remain around 40. And since the sample size is so large, such embarrassments as Raphael present no problem. Only 11 percent of Cox's 301 geniuses lived less than half a century, so the distortion produced by early deaths is negligible. It is not even necessary to postulate that Raphael would have continued to produce masterpieces had he lived longer. It is less important that creators are alive in the productive period generation than that they grow up in a generation containing their developmental phase, something which has to be true for them to become famous at all.

The best justification for this schematic approach to history is what historiometricians accomplished with it thus far. As I have noted, gen-

erational time series lend themselves to such quasi-experimental designs as cross-lagged correlation analysis and to such multivariate techniques as multiple regression time-series analysis, methods that enlarge
our capacity for causal inference regarding developmental influences.
Let us look at one example of each of these applications, beginning
with cross-lagged correction technique. Figure A.3 illustrates the basis
for my assertion that the political milieu affects the creative development of philosophers (Simonton, 1976g). In this particular case, the
ethics of happiness is seen to be a time-lagged response to the occurrence of civil disturbances a generation earlier. There are three main
components of this diagram. First, there are two autocorrelations that
indicate the extent to which the level of a variable at generation g is
correlated with the level in generation $g + 1$. The autocorrelation for
civil disturbances is rather small (.17), indicating that such events are
more or less randomly distributed across time, with only a slight tendency for popular revolt and rebellion to cluster into contiguous generations across the 122 generations of European history. The ups and
downs in hedonistic and utilitarian moralities are far more stable, however, as judged from the higher autocorrelation of .75 for the philosophical variable. Many members of generation $g + 1$ will in fact be

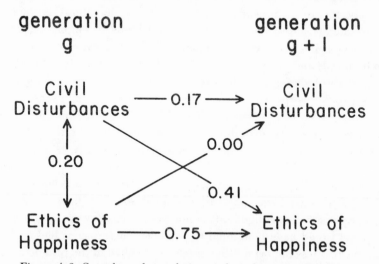

Figure A.3. Cross-lagged correlation analysis for generational data
on the causal relation between civil disturbances and the appearance
of philosophers who advocate hedonistic or utilitarian moral systems. The numbers within the arrows are Pearson product-moment
correlation coefficients.

disciples of eminent hedonists or utilitarians in generation g. The next component is synchronous correlation between the political milieu and the philosophical zeitgeist assessed both at the same point in time. This correlation is a modestly positive .20, indicating that civil disturbances have some contemporaneous association with the ethics of happiness. The true import of this synchronous correlation can be understood only when it is compared to the two cross-lagged correlations. One such correlation is that between the number of happiness-oriented ethical thinkers in generation g and the frequency of civil disturbances in generation $g + 1$. That correlation is, to the second decimal place, zero. Clearly, an upsurge in such ethical ideas cannot be held accountable for producing a generation of rebels, though it might be that the effect operates almost simultaneously in a manner consistent with the synchronous correlation. What makes it possible to discount the latter possibility is that the other cross-lagged correlation, from the index of civil unrest in generation g to the happiness-ethics indicator in generation $g + 1$, is a respectable .41, more than twice as large as the synchronous correlation. This correlation gives credence to the conclusion that exposure to civil disturbances as a teenager or young adult increases the probability that a mature thinker will advocate moral theories based on the pleasure principle.

I hasten to add that the diagram simplifies matters appreciably. Nonetheless, it should serve as an introduction to generational analysis. Logic demands that we establish temporal priority for the hypothesized causal variable, and this demonstration is achieved in the cross-lagged correlation analysis shown in Figure A.3.

It is also important to control for possible sources of spurious relationships—generated by extraneous third variables or common causes. To appreciate how this control is attained, turn to Table A.2. This table is taken from my study of the factors responsible for generational fluctuations in the number of discursive creators (Simonton, 1975c). The dependent variable is the number of scientists, philosophers, literary figures, and composers who are active in generation g, where each creator is weighted according to eminence. Since there are thousands of creators in the sample, I can confidently assert that the average age of each creator in each of the 127 generations is 40, the methodological acme of a career. Several independent variables are in the equation, including the amount of discursive creativity at generations $g - 1$ and $g - 2$; measures of political fragmentation, imperial instability, and political instability at generation $g - 1$; and the intensity of war and cultural

persecution at generation g. In addition, some distinctly methodological controls have been introduced: a time variable to control for linear
trends and four generational intercept dummy variables to handle potential dating bias. For all the substantive and methodological variables
the following statistics have been computed: the unstandardized partial
regression coefficient, b; the standard error of that same coefficient SE;
a t-test value; and the probability of attaining that particular t by mere
chance, p. By conventional criteria, p should be less than .05, that is,
the chances should be smaller than 1 out of 20 that the results emerged
by the luck of the draw. Hence, the first five variables in the table are
the only ones that provide statistically significant predictors of the dependent variable. And all except the last of these exhibit positive regression coefficients (since these are unstandardized, the relative sizes
mean nothing). Thus we can conclude that the weighted count of discursive creators at generation g is a positive function of the weighted
count of discursive creators in generations $g - 1$ and $g - 2$, a positive
function of the amount of political fragmentation and imperial instability in generation $g - 1$, and a negative function of the intensity of political instability in generation $g - 1$.

Table A.2. Time-series analysis: Weighted discursive creativity at
generation g.

INDEPENDENT VARIABLES	b	SE	t	p
Discursive creativity ($g - 1$)	.36335	.0852	4.266	.00004
Discursive creativity ($g - 2$)	.36533	.0834	4.379	.00003
Political fragmentation ($g - 1$)	.01370	.0056	2.423	.01701
Imperial instability ($g - 1$)	.34403	.1192	2.887	.00467
Political instability ($g - 1$)	−.02247	.0109	−2.067	.04104
War (g)	.00068	.0034	.205	.83790
Persecution (g)	.05524	.0327	1.688	.24193
Time	.00226	.0019	1.167	.24576
Second generation	−.20855	.1773	−1.176	.24193
Third generation	.00581	.1780	.033	.97401
Fourth generation	.05711	.1767	.323	.74716
Fifth generation	−.19033	.1757	−1.083	.28114
Intercept (first generation)	.6164	.226	2.729	

SOURCE. Adapted from Simonton, 1975c.

NOTE. For each variable, the table shows the unstandardized multiple regression coefficient (b), the standard error of that coefficient (SE), the t
value for the significance test, and the probability p of obtaining the given
effect just by chance. There are 111 degrees of freedom for the significance
tests. Squared multiple correlation (R^2) is .72.

Two facts make this historical generalization all the more secure. First, a cross-lagged analysis was previously executed to make sure that the generational lags were indeed the appropriate ones, thus taking full advantage of the criterion of temporal priority. Second, the effect of each predictor variable in the time-series equation is estimated while controlling for all other variables simultaneously. Therefore, it is possible to say that holding all other factors constant, the number of distinguished scientists, philosophers, writers, and composers is diminished by the amount of political instability in the previous generation. In addition, the equation depicted in Table A.2 accounts for 72 percent of the variance in the generational changes in discursive creativity. Most of this explanatory power is due to the effects of role-model availability.

Like Figure A.2, Table A.2 is a simplified example—but the two together illustrate the advantages of generational time-series analysis, one of the most valuable for unearthing the laws of history.

References

Adams, B. N. 1972. Birth order: A critical review. *Sociometry* 35:411–439.

Adorno, T. W., E. Frenkel-Brunswik, D. J. Levinson, and R. N. Sanford, eds. 1950. *The authoritarian personality.* New York: Harper.

Albert, R. S. 1971. Cognitive development and parental loss among the gifted, the exceptionally gifted and the creative. *Psychological Reports* 29:19–26.

———— 1975. Toward a behavioral definition of genius. *American Psychologist* 30:140–151.

———— 1980. Family positions and the attainment of eminence: A study of special family positions and special family experiences. *Gifted Child Quarterly* 24:87–95.

Allison, P. D. 1980. Estimation and testing for a Markov model of reinforcement. *Sociological Methods and Research* 8:434–453.

Allison, P. D., and J. A. Stewart. 1974. Productivity differences among scientists: Evidence for accumulative advantage. *American Sociological Review* 39:596–606.

Armajani, Y. 1970. *Middle East past and present.* Englewood Cliffs, N.J.: Prentice-Hall.

Aronson, E. 1958. The need for achievement as measured by graphic expression. In *Motives in fantasy, action, and society*, ed. J. W. Atkinson. Princeton: Van Nostrand.

Ashton, S. V., and C. Oppenheim. 1978. A method of predicting Nobel prizewinners in chemistry. *Social Studies of Science* 8:341–348.

Barnett, H. G. 1953. *Innovation.* New York: McGraw-Hill.

Baron, R. A., and V. M. Ransberger. 1978. Ambient temperature and the occurrence of collective violence: The "long, hot summer" revisited. *Journal of Personality and Social Psychology* 36:351–360.

Barron, F. X. 1963. *Creativity and psychological health.* Princeton: Van Nostrand.

Barron, F. X., and D. M. Harrington. 1981. Creativity, intelligence, and personality. *Annual Review of Psychology* 32:439–476.

Beard, G. 1874. *Legal responsibility in old age.* New York: Russell.

Becker, G. 1978. *The mad genius controversy.* Beverly Hills, Calif.: Sage Publications.

Bednar, R. L., and C. A. Parker. 1965. The creative development and growth of exceptional college students. *Journal of Educational Research* 59:133–136.

Bell, E. T. 1937. *Men of Mathematics.* New York: Simon and Schuster.

Bennett, W. 1980. Providing for posterity. *Harvard Magazine* 82(3):13–16.

Berlyne, D. E. 1971. *Aesthetics and psychobiology.* New York: Appleton-Century-Crofts.

Blackburn, R. T., C. E. Behymer, and D. E. Hall. 1978. Correlates of faculty publication. *Sociology of Education* 51:132–141.

Blondel, J. 1980. *World leaders.* Beverly Hills, Calif.: Sage Publications.

Bloom, H.S., and H. D. Price. 1975. Voter response to short-run economic conditions: The asymmetric effect of prosperity and recession. *American Political Science Review* 69:1240–1254.

Bradburn, N. M., and D. E. Berlew. 1961. Need for achievement and English economic growth. *Economic Development and Cultural Change* 10:8–20.

Bramwell, B. S. 1948. Galton's "Hereditary Genius" and the three following generations since 1869. *Eugenics Review* 39:146–153.

Bueno de Mesquita, B. 1978. Systemic polarization and the occurrence and duration of war. *Journal of Conflict Resolution* 22:241–267.

Campbell, D. T. 1960. Blind variation and selective retention in creative thought as in other knowledge processes. *Psychological Review* 67:380–400.

Carlsmith, J. M., and C. A. Anderson. 1979. Ambient temperature and the occurrence of collective violence: A new analysis. *Journal of Personality and Social Psychology* 37:337–344.

Cattell, J. McK. 1903. A statistical study of eminent men. *Popular Science Monthly* 62:359–377.

Cattell, R. B. 1963. The personality and motivation of the researcher from measurements of contemporaries and from biography. In *Scientific creativity*, ed. C. W. Taylor and F. Barron. New York: Wiley.

Cell, C. P. 1974. Charismatic heads of state: The social context. *Behavior Science Research* 9:255–305.

Clark, K. E. 1957. *America's psychologists.* Washington, D.C.: American Psychological Association.

Cole, S. 1979. Age and scientific performance. *American Journal of Sociology* 84:958–977.

Cole, J. R., and S. Cole. 1973. *Social stratification in science.* Chicago: University of Chicago Press.

Constant, E. W., II. 1978. On the diversity of co-evolution of technological multiples: Steam turbines and Pelton water wheels. *Social Studies of Science* 8:183–210.

Cortés, J. B. 1960. The achievement motive in the Spanish economy between the 13th and 18th centuries. *Economic Development and Cultural Change* 9:144–163.

Cox, C. 1926. *The early mental traits of three hundred geniuses.* Stanford, Calif.: Stanford University Press.

Crane, D. 1965. Scientists at major and minor universities: A study of productivity and recognition. *American Sociological Review* 30:699–714.

Cronbach, L. J. 1960. *Essentials of psychological testing.* 2d ed. New York: Harper and Row.

Cropper, W. H. 1970. *The quantum physicists.* New York: Oxford University Press.

Davis, H. T. 1941. *The analysis of economic time series.* Bloomington, Ind.: Principia Press.

Davis, R. A. 1954. Note on age and productive scholarship of a university faculty. *Journal of Applied Psychology* 38:318–319.

DeCharms, R., and G. H. Moeller. 1962. Values expressed in American children's readers: 1800–1950. *Journal of Abnormal and Social Psychology* 64:136–142.

Dennis, W. 1954a. Bibliographies of eminent scientists. *Scientific Monthly* 79:180–183.

———— 1954b. Predicting scientific productivity in later decades from records of earlier decades. *Journal of Gerontology* 9:465–467.

———— 1955. Variations in productivity among creative workers. *Scientific Monthly* 80:277–278.

———— 1956. Age and productivity among scientists. *Science* 123:724–725.

———— 1966. Creative productivity between the ages of 20 and 80 years. *Journal of Gerontology* 21:1–8.

Dewey, E. R. 1970. *Cycles.* Pittsburgh: Foundation for the Study of Cycles.

Dressler, W. W., and M. C. Robbins. 1975. Art styles, social stratification, and cognition: An analysis of Greek vase painting. *American Ethnologist* 2:427–434.

Eisenman, R. 1970. Creativity change in student nurses: A cross-sectional and longitudinal study. *Developmental Psychology* 3:320–325.

Eisenstadt, J. M. 1978. Parental loss and genius. *American Psychologist* 33:211–223.

Eisenstadt, S. N., ed. 1968. *Max Weber on charisma and institution building.* Chicago: University of Chicago Press.

Ellis, H. 1904. *A study of British genius.* London: Hurst and Blachett.

Etheredge, L. S. 1978. Personality effects on American foreign policy, 1898–1968: A test of interpersonal generalization theory. *American Political Science Review* 78:434–451.

Farnsworth, P. R. 1969. *The social psychology of music.* 2d ed. Ames: Iowa State University Press.

Finison, L. J. 1976. The application of McClelland's national development model to recent data. *Journal of Social Psychology* 98:55–59.

Fogel, R. W., and S. L. Engerman. 1974. *Time on the cross.* Boston: Little, Brown.

Galton, F. 1869. *Hereditary genius.* London: Macmillan.

———— 1874. *English men of science.* London: Macmillan.

Goertzel, V., and M. G. Goertzel. 1962. *Cradles of eminence.* Boston: Little, Brown.

Goertzel, M. G., V. Goertzel, and T. G. Goertzel. 1978. *Three hundred eminent personalities.* San Francisco: Jossey-Bass.

Goldstein, E. 1979. Effect of same-sex and cross-sex role models on the subsequent academic productivity of scholars. *American Psychologist* 34:407–410.

Gray, C. E. 1958. An analysis of Graeco-Roman development: The epicyclical evolution of Graeco-Roman civilization. *American Anthropologist* 60:13–31.

———— 1961. An epicyclical model for Western civilization. *American Anthropologist* 63:1014–1037.

———— 1966. A measurement of creativity in Western civilization. *American Anthropologist* 68:1384–1417.

Grossman, J. C., and R. Eisenman. 1971. Experimental manipulation of authoritarianism and its effect on creativity. *Journal of Consulting and Clinical Psychology* 36:238–244.

Grush, J. E. 1980. Impact of candidate expenditures, regionality, and prior outcomes on the 1976 Democratic presidential primaries. *Journal of Personality and Social Psychology* 38:337–347.

Haddon, F. A., and H. Lytton. 1968. Teaching approach and divergent thinking abilities. *British Journal of Education Psychology* 38:171–180.

215

Haefele, J. W. 1962. *Creativity and innovation.* New York: Reinhold.

Hall, G. S. 1922. *Senescence.* New York: Appleton.

Harmon, L. R. 1961. The high school backgrounds of science doctorates. *Science* 133:679–689.

Harrington, D. M., and S. M. Anderson. 1981. Creativity, masculinity, femininity, and three models of psychological androgeny. *Journal of Personality and Social Psychology* 41:744–757.

Helmreich, R. L., J. T. Spence, W. E. Beane, G. W. Lucker, and K. A. Matthews. 1980. Making it in academic psychology: Demographic and personality correlates of attainment. *Journal of Personality and Social Psychology* 39:896–908.

Heyduk, R. G. 1975. Rated preference for musical compositions as it relates to complexity and exposure frequency. *Perception and Psychophysics* 17:84–91.

Hoffman, B. 1972. *Albert Einstein: Creator and rebel.* New York: Plume.

Hollingworth, L. S. 1926. *Gifted children.* New York: Macmillan.

Holmes, T. S., and R. H. Rahe. 1967. The social readjustment rating scale. *Journal of Psychosomatic Research* 11:213–218.

Hoyt, D. P. 1965. The relationship between college grades and adult achievement. *American College Testing Program, Research Report No. 7,* Iowa City.

Hudson, L. 1958. Undergraduate academic record of Fellows of the Royal Society. *Nature* 182:1326.

——— 1966. *Contrary imaginations.* Baltimore: Penguin.

Hull, D. L., P. D. Tessner, and A. M. Diamond. 1978. Planck's principle: Do younger scientists accept new scientific ideas with greater alacrity than older scientists? *Science* 202:717–723.

Hutchins, R., ed. 1952. *Great books of the Western world.* 54 vols. Chicago: Encyclopaedia Britannica.

Jorgenson, D. O. 1975. Economic threat and authoritarianism in television programs: 1950–1974. *Psychological Reports* 37: 1153–1154.

Kenski, H. C. 1977. The impact of economic conditions on presidential popularity. *Journal of Politics* 39:764–773.

Kernell, S. 1978. Explaining presidential popularity: How ad hoc theorizing, misplaced emphasis, and insufficient care in measuring one's variables refuted common sense and led conventional wisdom down the path of anomalies. *American Political Science Review* 72:506–522.

Knight, F. 1973. *Beethoven and the age of revolution.* New York: International Publishers.

Koestler, A. 1964. *The act of creation.* New York: Macmillan.

Kroeber, A. L. 1944. *Configurations of culture growth*. Berkeley: University of California Press.

Kuhn, T. S. 1970. *The structure of scientific revolutions*. 2d ed. Chicago: University of Chicago Press.

Kynerd, T. 1971. An analysis of presidential greatness and "president rating." *Southern Quarterly* 9:309–329.

La Rue, J. 1970. *Guidelines for style analysis*. New York: Norton.

Leach, P. J. 1967. A critical study of the literature concerning rigidity. *British Journal of Social and Clinical Psychology* 6:11–22.

Lehman, H. C. 1953. *Age and achievement*. Princeton: Princeton University Press.

———— 1966. The psychologist's most creative years. *American Psychologist* 21:363–369.

Lotka, A. J. 1926. The frequency distribution of scientific productivity. *Journal of the Washington Academy of Sciences* 16:317–323.

Lyons, J. 1968. Chronological age, professional age, and eminence in psychology. *American Psychologist* 23:371–374.

MacKinnon, D. W. 1960. The highly effective individual. *Teachers College Record* 61:367–378.

Maranell, G. M. 1970. The evaluation of presidents: An extension of the Schlesinger polls. *Journal of American History* 57:104–113.

Martindale, C. 1972. Father absence, psychopathology, and poetic eminence. *Psychological Reports* 31:843–847.

———— 1975. *Romantic progression*. Washington, D.C.: Hemisphere.

Maslow, A. 1962. *Toward a psychology of being*. New York: Van Nostrand.

Matossian, M. K., and W. D. Schafer. 1977. Family, fertility, and political violence, 1700–1900. *Journal of Social History* 11:137–178.

Mazur, A., and E. Rosa. 1977. An empirical test of McClelland's "Achieving Society" theory. *Social Forces* 55:769–774.

McClelland, D. C. 1961. *The achieving society*. New York: Van Nostrand.

McNemar, O. 1964. Lost: Our intelligence? Why? *American Psychologist* 19:871–882.

Merton, R. K. 1961. Singletons and multiples in scientific discovery: A chapter in the sociology of science. *Proceedings of the American Philosophical Society* 105:470–486.

———— 1968. The Matthew effect in science. *Science* 159:56–63.

Meyer, L. B. 1956. *Emotion and meaning in music*. Chicago: University of Chicago.

Moles, A. 1968. *Information theory and esthetic perception*. Trans. J. E.

Cohen. Urbana: University of Illinois Press. (Originally published, 1958.)

Morrison, D. E., and R. E. Henkel, eds. 1970. *The significance test controversy.* Chicago: Aldine.

Mueller, J. E. 1973. *War, presidents and public opinion.* New York: Wiley.

Myers, C. R. 1970. Journal citations and scientific eminence in contemporary psychology. *American Psychologist* 25:1041–1048.

Naroll, R., E. C. Benjamin, F. K. Fohl, M. J. Fried, R. E. Hildreth, and J. M. Schaefer. 1971. Creativity: A cross-historical pilot survey. *Journal of Cross-Cultural Psychology* 2:181–188.

Ogburn, W. K., and D. Thomas. 1922. Are inventions inevitable? *Political Science Quarterly* 37:83–93.

Over, R. 1982. The durability of scientific reputation. *Journal of the History of the Behavioral Sciences* 18:53–61.

Padgett, V., and D. O. Jorgenson. 1982. Superstition and economic threat: Germany 1918–1940. *Personality and Social Psychology Bulletin* 8:736–741.

Paisley, W. J. 1964. Identifying the unknown communicator in painting, literature and music: The significance of minor encoding habits. *Journal of Communication* 14:219–237.

Porter, C. A., and P. Suedfeld. 1981. Integrative complexity in the correspondence of literary figures: Effects of personal and societal stress. *Journal of Personality and Social Psychology* 40:321–330.

Price, D. 1963. *Little science, big science.* New York: Columbia University Press.

———— 1976. A general theory of bibliometric and other cumulative advantage processes. *Journal of the American Society for Information Science* 27:292–306.

Rainoff, T. J. 1929. Wave-like fluctuations of creative productivity in the development of West-European physics in the eighteenth and nineteenth centuries. *Isis* 12:287–319.

Raskin, E. A. 1936. Comparison of scientific and literary ability: A biographical study of eminent scientists and men of letters of the nineteenth century. *Journal of Abnormal and Social Psychology* 31:20–35.

Rejai, M. 1979. *Leaders of revolution.* Beverly Hills, Calif.: Sage Publications.

Richards, J. M., Jr., J. L. Holland, and S. W. Lutz. 1967. Prediction of student accomplishment in college. *Journal of Educational Psychology* 58:343–355.

Roe, A. 1952. *The making of a scientist.* New York: Dodd, Mead.

———— 1972. Maintenance of creative output through the years. In *Climate for creativity,* ed. C. W. Taylor. New York: Pergamon.

Rokeach, M. 1960. *The open and closed mind.* New York: Basic Books.

Russett, B. M., ed. 1972. *Peace, war, and numbers.* Beverly Hills, Calif.: Sage Publications.

Sales, S. 1972. Economic threat as a determinant of conversion rates in authoritarian and non-authoritarian churches. *Journal of Personality and Social Psychology* 23:420–428.

Schaefer, C. E., and A. Anastasi. 1968. A biographical inventory for identifying creativity in adolescent boys. *Journal of Applied Psychology* 58:42–48.

Schlipp, P. A., ed. 1951. *Albert Einstein.* New York: Harper.

Schmookler, J. 1966. *Invention and economic growth.* Cambridge, Mass.: Harvard University Press.

Sheldon, J. C. 1980. A cybernetic theory of physical science professions: The causes of periodic normal and revolutionary science between 1000 and 1870 A.D. *Scientometrics* 2:147–167.

Sigelman, L. 1979. Presidential popularity and presidential elections. *Public Opinion Quarterly* 43:532–534.

Simon, H. A. 1955. On a class of skew distribution functions. *Biometrica* 42:425–440.

Simonton, D. K. 1974. The social psychology of creativity: An archival data analysis. Ph.D. dissertation, Harvard University.

———— 1975a. Age and literary creativity: A cross-cultural and transhistorical survey. *Journal of Cross-Cultural Psychology* 6:259–277.

———— 1975b. Interdisciplinary creativity over historical time: A correlational analysis of generational fluctuations. *Social Behavior and Personality* 3:181–188.

———— 1975c. Sociocultural context of individual creativity: A transhistorical time-series analysis. *Journal of Personality and Social Psychology* 32:1119–1133.

———— 1976a. Biographical determinants of achieved eminence: A multivariate approach to the Cox data. *Journal of Personality and Social Psychology* 33:218–226.

———— 1976b. The causal relation between war and scientific discovery: An exploratory cross-national analysis. *Journal of Cross-Cultural Psychology* 7:133–144.

———— 1976c. Does Sorokin's data support his theory?: A study of generational fluctuations in philosophical beliefs. *Journal for the Scientific Study of Religion* 15:187–198.

———— 1976d. Ideological diversity and creativity: A re-evaluation of a hypothesis. *Social Behavior and Personality* 4:203–207.

———— 1976e. Interdisciplinary and military determinants of scientific productivity: A cross-lagged correlation analysis. *Journal of Vocational Behavior* 9:53–62.

———— 1976f. Philosophical eminence, beliefs, and zeitgeist: An individual-generational analysis. *Journal of Personality and Social Psychology* 34:630–640.

———— 1976g. The sociopolitical context of philosophical beliefs: A transhistorical causal analysis. *Social Forces* 54:513–528.

———— 1977a. Creative productivity, age, and stress: A biographical time-series analysis of 10 classical composers. *Journal of Personality and Social Psychology* 35:791–804.

———— 1977b. Eminence, creativity, and geographic marginality: A recursive structural equation model. *Journal of Personality and Social Psychology* 35:805–816.

———— 1977c. Women's fashions and war: A quantitative comment. *Social Behavior and Personality* 5:285–288.

———— 1978a. The eminent genius in history: The critical role of creative development. *Gifted Child Quarterly* 22:187–195.

———— 1978b. Independent discovery in science and technology: A closer look at the Poisson distribution. *Social Studies in Science* 8:521–532.

———— 1978c. Intergenerational stimulation, reaction, and polarization: A causal analysis of intellectual history. *Social Behavior and Personality* 6:247–252.

———— 1979a. Multiple discovery and invention: Zeitgeist, genius, or chance? *Journal of Personality and Social Psychology* 37: 1603–1616.

———— 1979b. Was Napoleon a military genius? Score: Carlyle 1, Tolstoy 1. *Psychological Reports* 44:21–22.

———— 1980a. Land battles, generals, and armies: Individual and situational determinants of victory and casualties. *Journal of Personality and Social Psychology* 38:110–119.

———— 1980b. Techno-scientific activity and war: A yearly time-series analysis, 1500–1903 A.D. *Scientometrics* 2:251–255.

———— 1980c. Thematic fame and melodic originality: A multivariate computer-content analysis. *Journal of Personality* 48:206–219.

———— 1980d. Thematic fame, melodic originality, and musical zeitgeist: A biographical and transhistorical content analysis. *Journal of Personality and Social Psychology* 39:972–983.

———— 1981a. *Formal education, eminence, and dogmatism: The curvi-*

linear relationship. Davis, Calif.: University of California. ERIC Document Reproduction Service no. ED 201 276, abstracted in *Resources in Education* 16:89.

———— 1981b. The library laboratory: Archival data in personality and social psychology. In *Review of Personality and Social Psychology,* vol. 2, ed. L. Wheeler. Beverly Hills, Calif.: Sage Publications.

———— 1981c. Presidential greatness and performance: Can we predict leadership in the White House? *Journal of Personality* 49:306–323.

———— 1983a. Creative productivity and age: A mathematical model based on a two-step cognitive process. *Developmental Review* 3: in press.

———— 1983b. Dramatic greatness and content: A quantitative study of 81 Athenian and Shakespearean plays. *Empirical Studies of the Arts* 1: 109–123.

———— 1983c. Esthetics, biography, and history in musical creativity. In *Motivation and creativity: Documentary report on the Ann Arbor symposium on the application of psychology to the teaching and learning of music (Session III).* Reston, Va.: Music Educators National Conference.

———— 1983d. Intergenerational transfer of individual differences in hereditary monarchs: Genes, role-modeling, cohort, or sociocultural effects? *Journal of Personality and Social Psychology* 44:354–364.

———— 1983e. Quality, quantity, and age: The careers of 10 distinguished psychologists. *International Journal of Aging and Human Development,* in press.

———— 1984a. Leader age and national condition: A longitudinal analysis of 25 European monarchs. Department of Psychology, University of California, Davis. Typescript.

———— 1984b. Leaders as eponyms: Individual and situational determinants of monarchal eminence. *Journal of Personality,* in press.

Singer, J. D. 1981. Accounting for international war: The state of the discipline. *Journal of Peace Research* 18:1–18.

Sorokin, P. A. 1925. Monarchs and rulers: A comparative statistical study. I. *Social Forces* 4:22–35.

———— 1926. Monarchs and rulers: A comparative statistical study. II. *Social Forces* 6:28–40.

———— 1937–1941. *Social and cultural dynamics.* 4 vols. New York: American Book.

———— 1969. *Society, culture, and personality.* New York: Cooper Square. (Originally published, 1947.)

Stein, M. I. 1969. Creativity. In *Handbook of personality theory and research,* ed. E. F. Borgatta and W. W. Lambert. Chicago: Rand McNally.

Stewart, L. H. 1977. Birth order and political leadership. In *The psychological examination of political leaders,* ed. M. G. Hermann. New York: Free Press.

Stimson, J. A. 1976. Public support for American presidents: A cyclical model. *Public Opinion Quarterly* 40:1–21.

Stogdill, R. M. 1948. Personal factors associated with leadership: A survey of the literature. *Journal of Personality* 25:35–71.

Suedfeld, P., and A. D. Rank. 1976. Revolutionary leaders: Long-term success as a function of changes in conceptual complexity. *Journal of Personality and Social Psychology* 34:169–178.

Suedfeld, P., and P. Tetlock. 1977. Integrative complexity of communications in international crises. *Journal of Conflict Resolution* 21:169–184.

Suedfeld, P., P. Tetlock, and C. Ramirez. 1977. War, peace, and integrative complexity. *Journal of Conflict Resolution* 21:427–442.

Taagepera, R. 1979. People, skills, and resources: An interaction model for world population growth. *Technological Forecasting and Social Change* 13:13–30.

Tetlock, P. E. 1979. Identifying victims of groupthink from public statements of decision makers. *Journal of Personality and Social Psychology* 37:1314–1324.

——— 1981a. Personality and isolationism: Content analysis of Senatorial speeches. *Journal of Personality and Social Psychology* 41:737–743.

——— 1981b. Pre- and postelection shifts in presidential rhetoric: Impression management or cognitive adjustment. *Journal of Personality and Social Psychology* 41:207–212.

Thorndike, E. L. 1936. The relations between intellect and morality in rulers. *American Journal of Sociology* 42:321–334.

Tolstoy, L. 1865–1869. *War and peace.* Trans. L. Maude and A. Maude. Chicago: Encyclopaedia Britannica, 1952.

Toynbee, A. J. 1946. *A study of history.* Abridged by D. C. Somervell. 2 vols. New York: Oxford University Press.

Tyndall, J. 1897. *Fragments of science.* Vol. 2. New York: Appleton.

Uhes, M. J., and J. P. Shaver. 1970. Dogmatism and divergent-convergent abilities. *Journal of Psychology* 75:3–11.

Walberg, H. J., S. P. Rasher, and J. Parkerson. 1980. Childhood and eminence. *Journal of Creative Behavior* 13:225–231.

Wallach, M. A., and N. Kogan. 1965. *Modes of thinking in young children.* New York: Holt, Rinehart and Winston.

Wendt, H., and P. C. Light. 1976. Measuring "greatness" in American presidents: Model case for international research on political leadership? *European Journal of Social Psychology* 6:105–109.

White, R. K. 1931. The versatility of genius. *Journal of Social Psychology* 2:460–489.

Winter, D. G. 1973. *The power motive.* New York: Free Press.

Woods, F. A. 1906. *Mental and moral heredity in royalty.* New York: Holt.

———— 1911. Historiometry as an exact science. *Science* 33:568–574.

———— 1913. *The influence of monarchs.* New York: Macmillan.

Zuckerman, H. 1977. *Scientific elite.* New York: Free Press.

Zusne, L. 1976. Age and achievement in psychology: The harmonic mean as a model. *American Psychologist* 31:805–807.

Index

Achievement, as motivation, 49–50
Acton, Lord, 59
Adams, B. N., 27
Adams, J. C., 161
Adams, John, 102
Adams, John Quincy, 63, 68
Adorno, T. W. E., 66
Aeschylus, 119
Aesthetics, 113–120; of classical music, 115–119; of drama, 119–120
Age, 93–112; age curve, 94–95; quality vs. quantity, 95–100; composers and, 97–98, 100; scientists and, 98–100; interdisciplinary contrasts in, 100–102; writers and, 101; poets and, 101–102; mathematicians and, 101–102; leadership and, 102–105; monarchs and, 104–105; productivity and, 111–112
Albert, R. S., 2, 27, 28, 84, 85, 86, 88
Alexander the Great, 91, 143, 145, 153
Allison, P. D., 87, 88, 106
American Men of Science, 82, 84
Analytical unit, 8–9
Anastasi, A., 74
Anderson, C. A., 169
Anderson, Carl, 88
Anderson, S. M., 29
Aquinas, Thomas, 156
Aristophanes, 119
Aristotle, 2, 134, 145
Armajani, Y., 144
Aronson, E., 50
Ashton, S. V., 82
Auden, W. H., 83
Autocorrelations, 35–36, 39

Bach, Carl Philipp Emanuel, 31
Bach, Johann Christian, 31
Bach, Johann Sebastian, 31, 78, 85, 160
Bach, Wilhelm Friedmann, 31
Barnett, H. G., 74, 170
Baron, R. A., 169
Barron, F. X., 45
Beard, G., 22, 94, 108, 109
Becker, G., 55
Bednar, R. L., 70, 73
Beethoven, Ludwig von, 2, 28, 46, 56, 59, 93, 118, 134, 159, 160, 206–207
Behymer, C. E., 108
Bell, Alexander Graham, 161
Bell, E. T., 45
Ben Gurion, David, 121
Bennett, W., 83
Berlew, D. E., 50
Berlyne, D. E., 113, 115, 117
Bernoulli, Jacques, 26
Bernoulli, Jean, 26
Binet, Alfred, 45, 78
Birth order, 26–28
Bismarck, Otto von, 144
Bivariate correlations, 13
Blackburn, R. T., 108
Blake, William, 101; *Songs of Innocence*, 101
Blondel, J., 30, 102
Bloom, H. S., 122
Bohr, Niels, 38
Bonaparte, Napoleon, 8–9, 28, 43, 91, 151–152, 153
Bradburn, N. M., 50
Brahms, Johannes, 3
Bramwell, B. S., 31
Bryant, William Cullen, 21
Buddha, 103

Personality, 42–62; intelligence,
43–49; motivations, 49–53; intel-
lectual complexity, 53–55; emo-
tional instability, 55–57; social
style, 57–61; morality, 59–61
Peter the Great, 105
Phidias, 134
Philosophers, and zeitgeist, 155–158
Philosophic beliefs, 39–41
Piaget, Jean, 85
Picasso, Pablo, 78, 84
Planck, Max, 37–38, 77
Plato, 2, 25, 134
Poets: productivity of, 83, 85; age
and, 101–102; enthusiasm and,
109
Poincaré, Henri, 45, 81, 84
Political fragmentation, 143–146
Political violence: civil disturbances,
167–173; international war,
173–180
Politicians: IQ and, 46, 47; power
needs of, 51–53; dominance/extro-
version and, 58–59; education and,
66, 67–68; age and, 102, 103,
104; charisma of, 121–133; elec-
tion success of, 123–124
Polk, James, 128
Polygnotus of Thasos, 134
Porter, C. A., 118, 173, 176
Power, as motivation, 51–53
Precociousness, 83–84, 91
Presidents: IQ and, 46, 47; power
needs of, 51–53; dominance/extro-
version and, 58–59; education and,
67–68; age and, 104; charisma of,
121–133; popularity of, 122–123;
election success of, 123–124; performance of, 124–132
Price, D., 80, 87, 136, 164
Price, H. D., 122
Productive longevity, 85–86, 91
Productivity: creative inequality and,
78–81; of musicians, 79, 82, 85,
88–89; of writers, 80; of mathematicians, 81; of scientists, 81–82,
84, 85; quantity and quality of,
81–83; of poets, 83, 85; precociousness and, 83–84; cumulative
advantage and, 86–88; life span
and, 88–90; of military leaders,
91–92; age and, 111–112

Productivity rate, 84–85, 91
Psychometric theory, 18

Quantitative analyses: unit definition
and sampling, 8–10; scales, variables, and variance, 10–12; covariation and the correlation
coefficient, 12–14; causal inference, 14–17

Rabelais, François, 49
Rahe, R. H., 11, 119
Rainoff, T. J., 137
Ramirez, C., 175
Rank, A. D., 53–54
Ransberger, V. M., 169
Raphael, 207
Rasher, S. P., 27, 28, 35, 43, 49
Raskin, E. A., 85
Rationalism, 39
Ratio scales, 11
Realism, 40
Regression analysis, 15, 191–192,
195
Rejai, M., 102
Reliability coefficients, 20–21
Rembrandt van Rijn, 78
Revolution, see Civil disturbances
Revolutionaries, 53–55
Richards, J. M., Jr., 74
Riemann, Bernard, 81, 88
Robbins, M. C., 143
Roe, A., 28, 57, 76, 107
Rokeach, M., 66
Role modeling, 34–37
Roosevelt, Franklin D., 52, 59,
63–64, 67, 121, 126, 127, 128,
143
Roosevelt, Theodore, 51, 52, 59,
63
Rosa, E., 51
Rossini, Gioacchino: *The Barber of
Seville*, 93
Russell, Bertrand, 84
Russet, B. M.: *Peace, War, and Num-
bers*, 173

Sales, S., 142
Samples, significant, 187–188
Sampling, 9–10
Scales, 10–12, 192–193
Schaefer, C. E., 74

DATE DUE